D0291097

Advance Praise for *The Art of Empowered Parenting*

"*The Art of Empowered Parenting* provides many insights which will be helpful to parents and the professionals with whom they work. Fisher and his colleagues have pulled together many theoretical perspectives to provide readers with an easy-to-read, common sense–based book. I found the chapters on temperament and attachment of particular personal and professional interest. This book will help parents avoid the power struggles that diminish their capacity to engage in effective parenting, and it will help them see that many of the conflicts they experience are the result of parent-child psychological intersections."

—Gregory C. Keck, PhD, Attachment & Bonding Center of Ohio, and co-author of *Adopting the Hurt Child* and *Parenting the Hurt Child*

"Written by seasoned professionals with years of practical experience, this book refreshingly addresses issues of parenting often not discussed, including approaches to power and emotion and temperament and attachment. The authors also help parents see the wisdom of looking at themselves to understand their children. As a pediatrician, I feel that this book strongly addresses what can help parents the most."

—David Thompson, MD, FAAP

"No parenting book has ever packed so much usable information into one book. The authors don't just give you tips, they help you to build strategies to last for a lifetime of successful parenting. Advice and help can be found in this book for every family. It truly lives up to its title."

—Jean Scott Martin, Attorney at Law, former Guardian ad Litem

THE ART
of
EMPOWERED PARENTING

THE MANUAL YOU WISH YOUR KIDS CAME WITH

Erik Fisher, PhD, Steven W. Sharp,
and Diane Fivaz Wichman

OVATION
Books

THE ART OF EMPOWERED PARENTING: THE MANUAL YOU WISH
YOUR KIDS CAME WITH
PUBLISHED BY OVATION BOOKS
PO Box 80107
Austin, Texas 78758

For more information about our books, please write to us, call
512.478.2028, or visit our website at www.ovationbooks.net.

Printed and bound in China. All rights reserved. No part of this
book may be reproduced in any form or by any electronic or
mechanical means including information storage and retrieval
systems without permission in writing from the copyright holder,
except by a reviewer, who may quote brief passages in review.

ISBN-13: 978-0-9790275-4-3
ISBN-10: 0-9790275-4-3

Copyright© 2007 by Erik Fisher, PhD, Steven W. Sharp, and
Diane Fivaz Wichman

Library of Congress Cataloging-in-Publication Data

Fisher, Erik A., 1966-
The art of empowered parenting / Erik Fisher, Steven W. Sharp,
and Diane Fivaz Wichman.
    p. cm.
Includes bibliographical references.
ISBN 978-0-9790275-4-3 (pbk. : alk. paper)
1. Parenting. 2. Parent and child. I. Sharp, Steven W. II. Wichman, Diane Fivaz, 1958- III. Title. HQ755.8.F563 2007
649'.1--dc22
                              2007000855

❧ TABLE OF CONTENTS ❧

∽ PREFACE ∾

Greetings! We're glad you've decided to take this journey with us. Thank you for taking the time to read our labor of love. Literally, years of work went into writing and rewriting *The Art of Empowered Parenting*. This book is meant to be one you will use throughout your children's lives, and then hopefully pass it down to them. It covers many aspects of child development and the issues you may run into as parents, but most importantly it addresses how you can look at yourself and grow as a parent and a person. In relation to other parenting books this one is quite voluminous. We felt that so many topics, tips and strategies were important, and we wanted to include as many as possible.

The Art of Empowered Parenting was written by a practicing psychologist and a parent trainer, with the assistance of a freelance writer. Both professionally and personally we enjoy children immensely and have over forty years of combined experience working with children and families. We have experienced much success in our work helping these children and families from a different, more empowering perspective than many other approaches. Rather than focus on what children do wrong, we help those who guide them to see how all the members in the family may contribute to the difficulties at hand. We look at each person in the family as being integral to successful performance of the family as a whole. No one person is more important than another, and all should be encouraged to find their strengths and strengthen their weaknesses. You as a parent are seen as a guide and a supportive agent to your children's growth, and they are in your life to help you grow. We believe that the belief that the parent is more important than the child can contribute to many of the difficulties we see.

You will notice that the book is mostly written from the perspective of "we." This means we are writing about our collective experiences. Some passages in the book are written from the perspective of "I." These are written from Dr. Fisher's experiences as a psychologist and some personal experiences. We hope that this explanation clarifies those passages that could be confusing to you, the reader.

You will notice that there are many examples in the book. These examples are comprised from combinations of our experiences and do not represent any one person or family. Genders and details have been changed to protect confidentiality; however, there were also many cases we have seen that had so many similarities, and in these cases, some details may have been merged and/or omitted. We did, however, work very hard to maintain the realism in our examples so that they would be applicable to you, the reader. You will also notice that in situations where we refer to gender, the masculine and feminine pronouns (he, she, his, her…) will be alternated in the chapters of the book, and sometimes throughout each chapter. Finally, the book contains research from various sources. We purposely did not reference the sources in the text because we felt that doing so might be confusing to readers and sometimes impact the flow of reading. Since this is a self-help book and not an academic text, we did not want to bog you down. However, all our sources can be found in the Reference List in the back for your review.

You are likely reading this book for one of two reasons. Either you are having some difficulties in your family and are looking for solutions, or you are working on bettering yourself and your family and want some additional strategies for success. This book will meet either of those needs. Many parenting books offer tips to help you deal with your children's behavior. *The Art of Empowered Parenting* provides you not only with tips and tricks but also explains why what you may be doing is not working, and why what does work continues to work. We also discuss the interaction between temperament/personality and the quality of your child's attachment. Collectively, you will find that you will not only be able to apply the information in the book to any number of family situations, but also to any area of life. The intent is not just to give you some ideas about what to do in specific situations, but also to provide you with the tools to extend your strategies to any number of situations as you more fully understand both your own and your child's motivations. That is why we truly feel that you will see it as *The Manual You Wish Your Kids Came With*. This part of the book title actually came from a colleague who read the book and said that there was so much information in the book, it was like a manual.

We have included a poem provided by one of the parents we have worked with. It perfectly captures the message that we are trying to provide. Thank you, in advance, for your interest to better your life and the lives of your children, and we wish you the best on your journey. Always remember that your children are a gift to you; likely the greatest gift you will ever receive.

✑ HELP ME GROW ✑

Please, be consistent with me.
Then I can trust your words and actions.
Comfort me
When I'm scared, hurt or sad.
Then I'll know that I'm okay,
Even when I'm not feeling strong or happy.

Take responsibility for all your feelings and actions.
Then I also won't blame others,
And I'll take responsibility for my life.

Communicate what you feel hurt or frightened about
When you feel anger with what I have done.
Then I'll feel I'm a good person,
And I'll learn how to constructively deal with my feelings.

Tell me clearly and specifically what you want.
Then I can hear you,
And I'll also know how to communicate my needs
In a positive way.

Express to me that I'm okay
Even when my words or behavior may not be.
Then I can learn from my mistakes,
And have high self-esteem.

Balance your life between work and play.
Then I can believe that I can grow up be responsible,
And still have fun.

Remember what you wanted when you were my age.
Then you'll better understand my needs and interest.

Understand and accept me.
I may be different from you,
And I'm okay

Trust me as an individual.
Then I'll know that I can be my unique self.

Hug me and tell me that you care about me.
Then I'll feel lovable and I'll express caring to others.

Author Unknown

ꙮ ACKNOWLEDGMENTS ꙮ

Erik Fisher

To my parents, Gorman and Cathie, thank you for your love and guidance and for helping me to find my direction without a forced hand. From you both I learned compassion and ambition, dedication, and hard work. To Mom, you were my cheerleader when I couldn't be my own. To Dad, you modeled parenting and wisdom when you acknowledged your mistakes and made the effort to do it better. Thank you for also for letting me guide you both when you saw my wisdom. To Gorman, you were my dad when Dad was working, and even in your absence, your "presence" still taught me. Melanie and Aleta, you taught me through my observing how you lived your lives and parented your children. I feel proud to be your brother. To Christine, thank you for being my best friend, wife, and co-parent. It is our partnership and love that I look forward to passing on to Grace. You have inspired me to want to be a better person and partner. To Emily, you have taught us the meaning of selflessness and what true love for your child is. And to Grace, you have taught me how to love with all my heart and soul. I look forward to the rest of our journey together.

Steven Wayne Sharp

It is only fitting that I dedicate this book to my parents, Sara Ann Campbell and Robert Wayne Sharp. Like every other family that I know, we had our hard times and we all made our share of mistakes mixed in with many good memories and special times. Money and fancy things were scarce in my family, but love never was. In fact, I feel like a wealthy man, although not for what my parents gave me—for what they taught me. They have both been excellent models for what it means to be honest, hard-working, and caring people who are loved and respected by those around them and especially by me. Thanks for everything, Mom and Dad.

Diane Fivaz Wichman

To my parents, Bill and Marilyn, thank you for establishing the foundation from which none of this would have been possible—for providing me with the values and morals that not only have endured in my life but in those of my children and their children. To Dad, thank you for always bringing humor and laughter to the table and for your unselfish giving to your family and others. To Mom, thank you for being the rock of the family as well as for being my mentor and my friend. To my children, Jake and Erin, her husband, Brent, and their daughter, Ella, I thank you for being my teachers and the beacons of light that will forever shine in my heart and soul. Last but certainly not least, I want to thank my husband, John. You are my love, my friend, my soul mate and my sanity. Your calmness and gentle ways have given me a sense of peace, and your understanding goes far beyond any expectations imaginable. Live, love and laugh always!

❧ Chapter 1 ❧
The Journey Begins

The day Grace was born was filled with excitement, anticipation, fear, and many questions. Not only were there all the possible issues with the delivery (though we were assured that everything should run smoothly) but more important were the many questions about how our lives would be forever changed. How would we adapt to the forecasted lack of sleep, middle-of-the-night feedings and diaper changes, changes in freedoms and schedules? Would Grace connect to us and love us? What kind of parents would we be, and would we, as parents, be able to work together as a team as well as we had as husband and wife? How would we react if she spit up all over our freshly changed clothes, threw tantrums in public, colored on the wall, pulled the dog's tail, told lies, called us names, stole, took our car, ran away... How would our marriage fare through the years? These questions had mounted in the previous years and more urgently in recent months, and they were about to be answered.

When we brought Grace home, she and I spent the first night together while my wife slept. I, as a new father, soaked up this experience. We talked back and forth, soul to soul, in silence. I wanted to set the stage for the rest of her life, to try very hard to listen to her, and I wanted her to feel my presence. I let her know that I would do the best I could, but I was prepared to make mistakes and learn from them. I told her that she would be one of my greatest teachers, and I looked forward to the opportunity to learn. I talked about us having a partnership of trust. I had to be open to what she had to teach me if she was going to be open to what I felt was important for her to learn. I let her know that I wanted her to be whatever she wanted, not what I wanted for her. I knew that from day one I had to be clear about my main goals, knowing that I would learn along the way, and that there might be some room to change, with growth.

I knew that the biggest issue with my approach to life was getting out of the way. Many times I tried to push my wants or needs onto others, not acknowledging what they needed. I did not want to repeat this pattern as a parent. My concern was that my insistence on being right, or good, or strong, could prevent me from doing what might be in Grace's best interest. The desire to take charge has been almost automatic throughout my life when I feel my frustration rising. It was my hope that I would have the wisdom to see it.

I think we all have those words of advice inside our heads, almost a silent conversation that occurs many times in a day. Sometimes the words are kind and supportive, sometimes not. These silent voices often have a strong influence on the way we parent our children.

When I feel criticized or frustrated, and potential failure rises, it is as if voice inside says, "Don't let them tell you what to do…don't admit to that mistake…they don't know what they're doing." That voice has a lot to say, and it speaks even while other options rise from an even deeper place inside. I recognize that that voice is not from the present, but from my past. It is not a parent's voice, it is a hurt child's voice inside me. It is up to me to take care of the child inside and out.

That first night with Grace I realized it was not up to her to feed my ego, or to be quiet when I wanted her to be, or to feel hungry when I was ready to feed her, or to tell me how great a parent I am. It was up to her to be herself, and I was in charge of my own ego, and my actions and reactions. I had waited a long time to be a dad and I wanted to do it to the best of my ability and not rationalize, justify, or make excuses. I knew that I would never be totally ready for this wonderful job, but Grace was there, and I would learn along the way.

That night I found a sense of peace that remains between me and Grace, and I continue to find ways to grow every day.

My co-authors and I hope that you consider this thought, that there may be more times than you realize when your own personal issues may interfere with your true intentions to parent your children.

PARENTING TYPES

Countless times in our work with parents we hear phrases like, "If it was good enough for me..." or "My parents did it this way so..." from parents who feel defensive, helpless, resentful, or angry. Often they feel guilty and shameful as well, and need to justify and rationalize their actions. Many times parents with these attitudes are in denial about the major issues with their children but they feel that they have to be "in control." We often tell them, "If we consistently followed in the paths of those that came before us, we would still be in the Stone Age." We want to be able to honestly tell our kids, "I want you to do it better than I did. I want you to be able to learn from my mistakes."

Parents do not have to "control" their children be successful parents. Many kids appear to be out of control so we think that their parents just need to take control. Permissive and unstructured parenting is not solved by more control, and we will address this issue further in the book.

Consider the phrase, "Spare the Rod, Spoil the Child." There are two ways to read this. The most common interpretation is if you spare the rod, you will spoil your child. I prefer to consider the interpretation, spare the rod, and spoil your child. This does not mean give them everything they want, but that you do give them everything they need.

If you planted a tree, how would you help it grow? You would give it everything it needed—water, plant food, sunlight—to successfully grow into a healthy adult. If the environment does not fit the tree's needs, it will not grow. Additionally, their growth can be influenced by harsh storms as well as by drought, excessive rain, and multiple insults to the tree.

Kids are not too different from trees—they need nourishment of all kinds, and shelter from life's storms. Most importantly, children need love in order to build their confidence and self-image, to build relationships, and to grow into healthy adults.

In the psychology literature, researchers tried to identify different types of parenting styles. We would not be doing a parenting book justice if we did not refer to these. We will briefly discuss these parenting types, and allow you to see where they may fit into some of the issues we will address. The four types are authoritarian, authoritative, permissive, and uninvolved.

AUTHORITARIAN PARENTS

Authoritarian parents tend to be highly controlling and demand respect regardless of how they are treating their children. They rely on punishment and think that fear is the best way to teach their children. They demand obedience and submission, and do not value give-and-take. They discourage expressions of disagreement with their decisions. Researchers reported that the children of authoritarian parents tend to lack social competence, have lower self-esteem, and rarely take the initiative in activities. They show less intellectual curiosity, are not spontaneous, and usually defer to those they perceive as stronger than themselves.

AUTHORITATIVE PARENTS

Authoritative parents are loving, supportive, and communicate well with their children. At the same time, they maintain their authority and promote mature behavior from their children. They respect independence and the power to make decisions in their children, while holding firm in areas that they feel are important to the boundaries and limits that they want their children to learn. Children with authoritative parents are typically the best adjusted children, particularly in terms of social competence. Both authoritarian and authoritative parents have high expectations of their children and use control but there's a difference in their styles. The authoritarian parent blindly expects his child to accept their decisions and do not allow the children freedom of expression. On the other hand, authoritative parents give their children more freedom so that they can develop competence, confidence, and independence.

PERMISSIVE PARENTS

Permissive parents are warm and accepting, but mainly concerned about not stifling their child's creativity. They may be seen as coddling parents that place few limits on their children. They make few demands for mature behavior. The researchers found that the children of permissive parents generally have difficulty controlling their impulses, are immature, and reluctant to accept responsibility.

UNINVOLVED PARENTS

Uninvolved parents demand very little from their children and respond minimally to their children's needs. In extreme cases, neglect and rejection may be the result of their inaction.

HOW MIGHT EACH RESPOND IF...?

Consider this example of the responses different parenting types may make.

John is playing with his younger brother and pushes him when his brother takes his toy. An authoritarian parent might say, "Get to your room right now young man, and if I hear one word out of you, I will give you something to cry about." An authoritative parent might use this as a teaching opportunity, and say, "I know you may feel upset that your brother took your toy, but do you think that it was a good idea to hit your brother? I think you might want to apologize, to each other. What to you think?" A permissive parent might believe that John should be allowed to express his impulses freely, and would not use the opportunity to help him solve the problem. He might make excuses for John's behavior and might expect that John and his brother would figure out how to handle the situation themselves. An uninvolved parent might overlook the incident entirely, and ignore that it happened.

As you consider these examples see where you might fit in. Most parents display a variety of these behaviors in different situations, which can send very confusing messages to their children.

READY, SET, PARENT

How many parents truly feel ready for kids? Even as their children grow, how ready are they to handle not only the unexpected events, but also the day-to-day issues? How many times have you questioned if you are doing the "right thing," or wondered if you are messing up your child for life? What if you are so damaged that your child is doomed? We had a friend who told us about a parent who was keeping a Trauma Journal, writing down all of the events in her child's life that might eventually be brought up in therapy; therefore, the child wouldn't have to work as hard at remembering. While this is done with a little tongue-in-cheek, it seems that this could prove valuable. It potentially says to your child, "I made some mistakes with you that I want to acknowledge and take responsibility for. For that, I am sorry and want to give you the opportunity to explore the impact my behaviors have upon whom you became." Chances are that with an approach like that, your child will likely not need to use it.

Let's put some of your fears to rest. The shelves of the bookstore or libraries in the parenting section are filled with hundreds, or even thousands, of books written by authors who range from professionals to parents. Furthermore, if you look around your block you will see many different ways that parents raise their kids, some seemingly better than others. We personally don't believe in any one right way to do things with your kids. Instead we believe in developing a philosophy or a model from which to approach parenting. In other words, *there is no single right way of parenting.*

Over the years, many times parents had asked me if I was a parent when I was giving them advice about their kids. Before Grace I replied, "No, I am not a parent but the most important thing is that I remember what it was like to be a kid." I still think this way. I'm sure my clients wanted to know what my parenting credentials were, and maybe they hoped to hear that I had several children and had been through struggles, problems, and failures similar to their own. I did not feel shy about sharing my truth and letting the results speak for themselves.

Just as maintaining trust is an essential aspect in my relationships with my clients, it is also true that maintaining trust is the basic foundation for successful parenting. Parents must realize that most problems with children arise because the children don't feel they can trust their parents. When trust becomes compromised, children feel that they have to look out for themselves. After all, they feel, their parents aren't looking out for them since they don't seem to understand their needs. This issue can arise shortly after birth and may become accentuated in teenage years. Once trust is damaged it is very difficult to repair, at any age. Therefore, the best way to help change your child's behavior is to look at yourself, own your faults, flaws, and mistakes. If your child was not doing well in a class at school, would you let him avoid reading, studying and perhaps getting extra help in that class, or would you want him to work harder? Why should your task be any different?

In the movie *Parenthood* with Steve Martin, Keanu Reeves, and others, Keanu Reeves makes a profound statement. He talks about needing a license to fish, hunt, drive a car, and do many other tasks in our world, but the most important task in life, parenting, doesn't require a license. We recognize the insight in this observation; however, needing a license to have kids is not going to happen. In our process of teaching parents, we often talk about the training and learning that people need to go through to do their jobs, whether as a film developer, teacher, or doctor, and accentuate that no training is required to become a parent. Therefore, it is up to each of us to assume the responsibility to parent our children to the best of our ability, to be willing to learn, ask questions, and see our weaknesses. Once again, that requires our willingness to monitor ourselves and be aware of how we may or may not be doing the best we can for our kids. Sometimes, this monitoring can even lead to the very hard realization that maybe we are not ready to have another child.

I once worked with a woman, whom we'll call Sue, whose parental rights were terminated. A court ruled that Sue was unable to safely parent her child, and the child was taken from her. If you have any experience with the foster care system you may know that it is not uncommon for parents who have a child removed to have another, psychologically replacing the one that was taken. In a discussion with Sue soon after the court's ruling, she stated that having another child should not and would not happen. She recognized that she had exposed her child to many of the same undesirable experiences and patterns she had experienced during her own childhood. No matter how much she hadn't wanted to repeat the things that had been done to her, she repeated them anyway. Sue also knew that she probably lacked the strength to do the therapeutic work to heal these issues. Sue misses her child very much, to this day, but she knows that having another child would not fix the problem. This realization is one of the most courageous decisions I have ever seen a parent make. Even though she is no longer considered to be a parent, she is still parenting.

JUST THE FACTS MA'AM

It can be debated that parenting today is perhaps more difficult than at any other time in history. Considering financial issues, working parents, television, video games, computers, drugs, sex, the media, divorce, step-parents, educational considerations, etc., modern parents have many issues with which to contend. Whether you are an experienced parent, a newcomer, a step-parent, or are deciding if you want to take the plunge into parenting, there are so many issues to consider that it can feel overwhelming. What happens when you allow yourself to get bogged down in life's demands? How does that then translate to how you treat others? If you perceive your children to be the source of your stress, how do you treat them? Even if you feel that you are keeping your feelings of frustration to yourself, do your kids still sense it? Consider these questions as you read on through the book.

Let's take a minute to look at some of those issues that we face and which add up to stress.

The demands to meet the financial needs of a family have always been difficult, but with our consumer culture, our kids seem to want more, more, more. Debt is a huge problem in our culture, with a 33 percent increase in bankruptcies filed in the early twenty-first century, and there seems to be a shrinking middle class. Still, parents today want to provide all they can for their kids. Because of our consumer culture, many parents feel the need to spend more and more money on stuff to make their kids happy, especially if both parents are working, leaving less time to spend together.

Does making sure our kids have all they want make up for the lack of time we have with them, and/or does it contribute to a sense of entitlement? More often than not it can feed a sense of entitlement; however, entitlement can also come from not having everything I want, while seeing other people who seem to have it all. It is always an issue of personal power… more on that later.

Many parents feel it is impossible to survive on a single income, especially if they want their kids to have what others have. In many cases, having two working parents is necessary to have just the essentials. Sixty-six percent of the children in America live in a household with two working parents. Fifty-nine percent will live in a single-parent household at some time. All of this makes it even more difficult to give children everything they need and want. Furthermore, this country has an approximately 60 percent divorce rate which can make the spending game even more complex when parents feel the need to keep up with each other.

Kids seem to be clamoring for electronics. Thirty-eight percent of all American homes have video game consoles, 67 percent have PCs, 17 percent have mobile audio devices (such as an I-Pod) and 67 percent have a mobile phone. These numbers will only continue to rise over time, almost by the day, as more parents feel the pressure and more kids have the wants. We are continually amazed at the things kids in today's culture feel they are entitled to have. Between video consoles to cell phones to clothes, the list goes on. Many parents often blame their kids' selfishness for all of their wants. But as parents, we have to take accountability and see that we have helped to feed this culture, and we continually do. If we surrender our freedoms and work more for our kids' wants, or are spending on frivolous items for ourselves, we still need to see where our responsibility lies. If we choose to feel helpless to stem this tide, our kids will pay the price.

Beyond providing for our kids, we are faced with the challenges of protecting them, especially from the influences of drugs and sex.

At the beginning of the 21st century, young people's drug use overall, from the ages of 12–17, was up 120 percent over a five year period. Heroin use was up 875 percent and marijuana use was up 125 percent since 1991. Use of methamphetamine had also drastically increased, and the proliferation in making the drug has made it easier for kids get it.

In the first years of the twenty first century some encouraging signs when comparing statistics suggested that drug use was declining. Continued declines will depend on how much effort we as parents, and we as a society, make toward helping our children understand better ways of living. Overall usage of drugs with teens appears to be around 10 to 15 percent. The drug business has not changed over the years. Dealers are looking to get children and teens to use drugs because they know that they will build their customer base, much like the cigarette industry was accused of doing. As a child begins to use drugs like alcohol and marijuana, odds become greater that the child will move on to harder and even more dangerous drugs. A parent's ability to know of a child's drug use and experimentation depends heavily upon the parent's ability to communicate with the child.

Statistics on teen sexual activity aren't looking much better than the figures related to drugs. We live in a society that sells sex, and sex sells products ranging from hamburgers to cars and nearly everything in between. Kids are bombarded by sexually-charged images long before they have the skills to understand what to make of this sexual content. Eighty-three percent of the episodes of the top twenty television programs had scenes that involved sexual content, and 42 percent of the top CDs did as well. The internet is also a major source of sexual content and in many cases is uninvited when spam emails are sent to kids and teens. Nationally, about 25 percent of fifteen-year-old females and 30 percent of fifteen-year-old males have had sex, while 66 percent and 68 percent of eighteen-year-old females and males have. Nearly one million females under the age of twenty become pregnant each year, and 25 percent of sexually active teens acquire some type of STD each year.

This book will not be statistically-based, but we feel that it's important to consider the numbers as they relate to the issues our kids may face. Too often we see parents ignore the fact that their children could become involved in many of these behaviors. This parental denial, or lack of willingness on the part of parents to look at their kids as human beings, can result in unfavorable outcomes. Avoiding looking at the truths in life never helped anyone to grow, and it doesn't help our kids learn to face life head on.

Life seems to be very complex these days. Look back to your childhood and ask yourself, was life easier when it was simpler? Was there this much stress to succeed and keep up with everyone else when you didn't have to have so much stuff and have so many things you could and/or should do? Why do we, as a culture, have to have so much stuff? And why do we have to keep our kids up with all of their activities? Is it our kids who are really asking for it? Are they echoing what they are seeing around them in society? Is it possible to remove yourself and your family from some of these pressures? Society often changes one person at a time. If you are waiting for the rest of the world to change its approach to parenting before you do to see how it works, you may be for a waiting a long time. We hope that this book will help you find some insight to see your way through these stormy seas and find the confidence to do what you feel is in the best interest of all.

SETTING THE STAGE

What, exactly, will we talk about to help you become a better parent? The first issue will be the manner in which you look at the concept of power as a parent. One approach is similar to the "my way or the highway," or authoritarian approach. This approach is more control-based. While many parents would profess that they don't do this and often frown on parents who commonly treat their children this way, most unavoidably resort to this style every now and again. Whether it is saying, "Go to bed or else," or forcing your child to clean his room or face serious physical punishment, this "my way or the highway" attitude comes out in many different ways. Physical punishment is often associated with this style of parenting but emotional manipulation may occur just as much, if not more often. Emotional manipulation—variations on "If you love me, you'll do as I say"—comes in the forms of bribing ("I'll take you out for pizza if you'll clean your room"), using guilt and fear ("After all I do for you, you should be ashamed of yourself for behaving this way"), idle and real threats ("You do that once more and I'm going to bust your butt"), playing favorites and comparing ("Why can't you make straight A's in school like your brother Tommy does?"), and other techniques that will be discussed. Too often we don't pay attention to our control-based behaviors and manipulations when they happen, and then wonder why our kids are doing these things.

Opposite to the "my way or the highway" approach to parental power is one in which there is a sharing of power. This approach is often met with fear and skepticism; if parents share power with their children, their children will run over and/or will not learn to respect them or others. Many people trapped in the fears of losing control and power believe that this model means that parents and kids are buddies and friends. This comes with the fear that children will parent themselves, and parents will let them do as they wish. Surely we have all seen children running rough-shod through restaurants and malls, yelling at their parents and treating everyone as if they are less than human. This type of parenting is still a "my way or the highway" approach, but the child is in charge, often because of the lack of structure and guidance. Since they don't have structure they don't know how to get it, but they may respond very favorably to it when they respect someone who is trying to teach them.

In the equity-based approach we will address, sharing power means being willing to understand that a child comes to this world with a sense of power, and that it is a parent's job to help him grow into it. As parents, we are guiding agents helping children foster their strengths and grow from their weaknesses. As a model to them, a parent must be willing to do the same. Parents are both teachers and students, just as the children are. A parent with an equity-based relationship with his children realizes that comparing his child to others only makes the child want to be better than someone else, often at any cost. Instead, equity-based parenting allows a child to use others as role models. Instead of arrogance, a child learns self-confidence and pride. Yes, this can be done, but it requires a hard look at ourselves as parents, and at the world around us. The world can be a wonderful training ground for us all to learn from. Don't keep your child from living in this world. Let it become his canvas.

As I have spent time with my parents as an adult, I continue to notice similarities and dissimilarities between us. I have physical and verbal mannerisms similar to both my mom and dad. Some I like and others...well, you know. It is part of the give and take of who we are. We can accept it and honor these similarities or detest them in ourselves and others for the rest of our lives. I often tell people in my practice that you can't grow up in France without learning to speak French.

Many of our traits seem to be inborn, from the obvious such as eye and hair color, to the more subtle traits such as sleep patterns, gestures, and verbal patterns. Research with twins has taught us much about what is hard wired in us and what may be due to environment, and still there are no consistent findings about how much of our attitudes and affinities are predetermined.

Temperament, or how we approach the world, is one of those issues. Some of us are easier going than others; others take some time to warm up to changes in life. While we can moderate some of these patterns with some hard work, sometimes we have to accept that we may have to modify our first response with one that is more acceptable. Similarly, a child may be hard-wired to respond to the world in certain ways that we may or may not appreciate or enjoy. It is most important to realize that you may approach the world in a similar manner, which is why the two of you clash.

We will discuss this and related issues that can help you see ways to modify your own temperament as well as your child's. All too often parents are unaware of how their approach and interactions with the world affect their child's approach and interaction with the world. Often, both a parent and child are both a bit difficult and moody, and/or willful and stubborn. Or, a parent may be easy-going and adaptable with a child who seems very rigid. In either case, they may clash from the beginning when the parent wants the child to take a bottle *now* and the child refuses it, or when the other parent cannot understand why everything has to be such a big deal to the child. Their relationship begins to suffer almost from the start. What are the consequences of these interactions? Often it becomes a gradual drifting apart of the parent and child. Both of them feel unloved and confused, and anger and hatred can grow as the years progress. Often one parent can feel put in the middle, and this can strain even the best of marriages.

In today's society parents and children find themselves in many different types of situations. The once typical family, where the mother and father lived in the same household with the children, is now considered statistically out of the norm. This book was not written with only this typical family in mind. The approach we take addresses a variety of family settings, including multi-generational settings. We understand that today's families require an approach that provides structure and is adaptable to any setting. We will discuss various family issues that parents may want to consider, as well as the many mixings of parents with children. In all of these situations, the parent wants to consider his role and the effects on the child.

When relationships become strained between a parent and child, disruptions in the attachment between the parent and the child almost always occur. Even when few or no problems between the parent and child are apparent, attachment can be an issue. Attachment is the process by which a parent and child feel connected. The parent/child bond begins at birth (or even before according to some) and continues through the lifetime of both parent and child. In my practice I have noticed that a person may appear to have had a very comfortable childhood. His parents had remained married; often, the mother stayed home with the kids, the child had all of his physical needs met, the child played with his friends, did well in school… It was a picture-perfect childhood. However, this person, now an adult client in therapy, finds that he has an empty place inside, and feels that he is wandering through life without a connection to anything. He may have "failed" marriages, job changes, little or no relationship with his children, depression, anxiety, and other issues. In these cases it appears that the family he grew up in went through the motions without a deep connection or attachment. The parents may have loved their children but there was something missing. My patients describe it as an emotional investment or energy that was not present...something that can be felt but not touched. What was lacking was the emotional connection, critical to attachment. We will spend a considerable amount of time on this issue of attachment because we see how crucial it is to a healthy individual and healthy family. We hope you will take the time to closely examine this issue.

In a nutshell, we hope to help you look at your family's interaction and understand the way you use your power, as a parent. This in turn will help you understand how power relates to your family's temperament characteristics, and the strength and type of attachments that exist. This sounds simple doesn't it? Well maybe not. However, as we take this apart, piece by piece, it will become easier and there will be plenty of examples to help you along the way. We will have an entire chapter devoted to looking at how parents' conscious and unconscious attitudes affect their parenting style. We hope you will take a close look at these issues to see if you find yourself or others playing these roles.

After we cover the basics, we will dive into the tips and tricks of parenting from a more empowered approach. As you may be realizing already, parenting begins before the birth of your child and lasts a lifetime. If you already are a parent it is never too late to learn more, and if you are a parent-to-be you are in good hands in reading this book. In essence, understand yourself, from your childhood to the present and it will open doors for you and your children. If you think you already know what you need to know, you may not hear those doors closing.

Beyond these primary issues mentioned above that form the basis for *The Art of Empowered Parenting*, we want to offer a context for a number of ways to apply them. Understanding behavior and why you and your kids are doing what you are doing is probably the biggest issue to address. Additionally, we want to give you strategies that will contribute to more empowered behaviors for all, including learning time management and imposing consequences that have more meaning than those that often evoke more anger and defiance.

In today's society, communication is a key issue in successful families, especially with kids and parents on the go. It is not necessarily the quantity of communication, but the quality that can make the most difference. How many families do you see where the parents are lecturing their kids regularly, only to have the kids do whatever they wish or just tune their parents out? There are many subtle patterns in the communication game that can contribute to difficulties. We will address those issues and give you strategies to help you all grow closer, considering not only what is said, but more often what is not.

Many parents complain that they have a major problem in getting their children to cooperate. This is often a two-way street. By leading by example, communicating, and understanding your power as it relates to your child's power, you can productively encourage children to cooperate and behave as a productive member of the family. Later, we will help you get to the meat of the issue and provide strategies for success.

All too often, kids and families need help from professionals, but parents do not know when to get that help and where to find it. Sometimes parents' fears of failure and/or guilt and shame prevent them from seeking help. We want to help parents know when they should consider getting some extra help or support, and we will discuss this in detail.

Because we are spending so much time helping parents to look at themselves, we wanted to take some time to talk about finding balance in your lives as a parent. How many parents, especially mothers, feel guilty about spending time away from their children? The pressure of others in society, especially extended families, often promote the idea that parents are supposed to surrender their lives to their children. You should consider that if you want to raise your children to live a life of opportunity, then it is unproductive to model a life of sacrifice and obligation. It is possible to take care of yourself and your children, and find balance in this. We firmly believe that finding a balanced life helps your children in the long-run. Keep this in mind as you read through the book.

Finally, what would a parenting book be without having the chapter that gives you many tips and strategies to help children and families succeed for a lifetime? With all you learn throughout the book you will be able to fully understand the suggestions we make in the final chapter.

While we address many serious issues involved in parenting, we do hope that a new awareness, as well as developing better skills to handle your children's issues, will help you to enjoy every day with them. Parenting should be fun and your children should be among the greatest joys in your life. You both teach them, and learn from them. Please don't forget that.

And now, on with the Show...

∽ Chapter 2 ∾
CONTROL-BASED PARENTING

John and Elizabeth were frustrated parents. Their fourteen-year-old daughter, Hillary, was constantly in trouble at school and at home. The school principal sometimes called two or three times a week, and many times one or the other parent had to pick Hillary up from school and leave work for the rest of the day to do this. She was failing almost every class and didn't seem to care. At home, Hillary often defied their requests. She would not clean up after herself; she started fights with her siblings, and on a few occasions she snuck out of the house at night. John and Elizabeth were concerned about her getting involved in drug and alcohol use, and she had many male friends with whom they feared she might be sexually involved.

John and Elizabeth arrived at a point where they felt as though they wanted to throw their hands in the air and give up. They had removed everything from Hillary's room except the bed and the dresser. They took her bedroom door off its hinges so that she could not hide anything, and they put locks on the doors to the other kids' bedrooms to keep her out of them. Hillary was not allowed to go out with friends after school or on the weekends, and the school provided daily reports on her performance. Hillary's parents could not understand why, after all these restrictions and limits were put in place, she did not see the wisdom in cooperating and improving her behavior. As they put more limitations on her, she behaved more rebelliously and her feelings of anger worsened. John and Elizabeth equated their approach to parenting as similar to breaking a wild horse; if someone rides a wild horse long enough, it would succumb to the control of the person in charge. They felt that if they gave Hillary anything without her earning it, it would set a dangerous precedent. They felt sorry for her, on one hand, but they also felt sorry for themselves. They felt like prisoners in their own home. When they took her out with the family, Hillary often tried to humiliate them with verbal and behavioral outbursts.

John and Elizabeth didn't realize the degree to which they expressed their frustration and anger not only to Hillary but also to other family members and friends. They sometimes spoke of Hillary's behavior in her presence or within earshot of her, and they did this with the hope that it would pressure her to behave. Since Hillary's bedroom door had been taken off its hinges, she heard much more that was going on around the house than John or Elizabeth realized, and she felt that she had no privacy.

Nobody seemed to recognize how humiliating this felt to Hillary. When Hillary told them to stop talking about her, John or Elizabeth sometimes responded, "I'm the parent, and I will do what I want, when I want. You don't tell me what to do, young lady. Just watch your own behavior." When the family had severe conflicts, John and Elizabeth sometimes told Hillary that they were sick and tired of her behavior, and if she didn't like living by their rules she could just get out. But when Hillary tried to leave, they told her that if she ran away they would have her arrested and thrown in jail. Hillary's brother and sister were led to feel that Hillary was a bad kid, and they avoided her.

Although Hillary wasn't allowed to use any of her siblings' clothes or other belongings, they occasionally used her things. When she commented about this or expressed anger, her parents often reminded her of all the times she had taken their things without asking. John and Elizabeth made the other kids return the things they'd taken from Hillary, but there were never any consequences for their actions. When Hillary complained about these double standards, her parents often told her to mind her own affairs and reminded her that she was not the boss. Hillary and her parents expressed much frustration and impatience with each other, and the two sides acted and spoke out of feelings of anger, resentment, confusion, and many other emotions. Both sides stuck firmly to their respective positions, and no one wanted to budge. The family's problems worsened with each passing day.

As parents, we may feel inclined to ask, "What is Hillary's problem? If she would just listen and follow directions, she wouldn't have these problems." Right? And there's the other old standby often expressed about children with behavioral problems: "That kid just needs a good whipping." We have even heard a police officer say, "Give me a few days with him at my house, and we'll see how he is behaving then." If solving behavioral problems was as easy as establishing who the boss is, why don't we have a perfectly cooperative society where everyone follows directions and works together without incident?

THE KING HAS SPOKEN

The issues regarding Hillary and her behaviors have to do with perceptions of power experienced by her and others. By that, we are referring to how she sees her ability to navigate or "control" her world relative to others. Furthermore, she will take matters into her own hands if she feels that she cannot trust others to look out for her wants and needs. The issues Hillary is having are all too common in our culture. The duration and severity may vary, but the behaviors stay the same.

One model, called the hierarchical model of power, addresses these issues and behaviors. It involves the way we look at power through more control-based methods, and influences our emotions, attitudes, and behaviors. This model is based on the idea that hierarchies are developed in our world, and the individuals in those hierarchies are supposed to command a certain position of status power. You can readily see this in the military and in business organizations. While hierarchies may be a little more informal in families, most people experience their first hierarchy in the form of their own family. For children, the family hierarchy is usually based upon age. However, depending upon the rules established by those "in power," gender, intelligence, and/or physical ability, and many other factors, could form the basis for how much status each family member has. In other words, the individuals in charge of the hierarchy establish the rules of that hierarchy.

In our society, many of us are members of more than one hierarchy. They may pertain to family, race, economics, grade in school, level of education, job position, athletic ability, and the list goes on. People will often orient themselves toward the hierarchies that fit their view of the world. This means that if people want to be in more of a leadership role, they will affiliate themselves more with those hierarchies in which they have higher levels of status, or they will remain in hierarchies where they can rise to higher levels. On the other hand, if people feel the need to be cared for, they will likely remain in, or switch to, hierarchies that allow them to feel cared for and secure.

As an example, consider teenagers and their peer groups. Some teens will stick with a group in which they feel empowered to direct the actions and behaviors of the other members, while others will be content to follow behind what others are doing. In both of these situations, the teens may have migrated away from the family for different reasons. The more dominant teens want to feel a sense of having more power and control, and often feel that their parents will not give them what they want. Still other teens (often followers) may want to belong to something and feel happy to fit in somewhere. These more insecure teens often migrate away from their families because they may feel less significant than their siblings, or may feel criticized by their parents/families. Their families may not feel safe to them, and their peer group is more than willing to accept them. These situations, wherein young people feel unaccepted by their families, sometimes lead kids to join gangs, cults, or fringe groups in order to feel a sense of belonging and acceptance.

The hierarchical model involves a series of circles from small to large, in which the level of status power increases with the size of the circle. In Figure 1, each circle becomes larger from person to person. In a hierarchy, the members often try to change the order or position of their circle, and/or increase their circle size. The larger circles (those people with more status power) are considered to have more ability to make choices, control others, make rules, etc. The individuals further down in the hierarchy are supposed to answer to those above. Our years of experience show that, when asked, a child will usually indicate that she wants to be the biggest circle. The problem lies in the fact that two people cannot occupy the same space or position of power at the same time, and a parent often feels that she is supposed to command the highest position of status, at all times. This struggle for power often begins even before a child can speak.

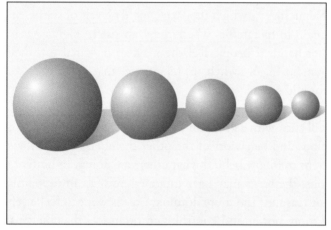

Figure 1: Hierarchical Model

What happens when someone, especially a child, starts to challenge someone at a higher level of status for her position? Those at higher levels of power don't like it. When entering into a hierarchy, individuals are supposed to accept their position and "like it." But, how do they get more power or move up the hierarchy? The "acceptable" choices are to 1) sit around and wait until a higher-ranking member is demoted or leaves the hierarchy, 2) do what they are supposed to do to be promoted by those of higher status, or 3) do nothing and accept their lot in life. Otherwise, they may learn to manipulate those around them by undermining and/or usurping the power of those above, and/or create unrest in the hierarchy and a change in how status and power are defined. A revolution occurs when a group made up of those lower in status band together to overthrow those at the top of the hierarchy.

How many people want to be in the lowest position in the hierarchy? Not many. While some circumstances lead some people to feel encouraged to remain in the lowest position in a hierarchy (we will examine this later), generally if we don't like our position, we aren't likely to sit around and wait for it to change; we want to do something about it. Think about sibling rivalries, name-calling, competing for attention, tattle-tailing, comparing abilities, bedtimes, gifts given and received, and similar things. Kids are in a constant battle for power, and unfortunately, their parents often are too.

Another issue arises when a person realizes that she can rise only to a certain level of status. In a family, as kids get older, they realize they will never rise to a higher level of status than their parents. As they move into their teen years, kids seek power outside the family in an effort to attain a level of power they cannot attain within the family. As teens spend more time with their peers, they try to figure out where they fit into these hierarchies.

Perhaps the most important issue to address in this discussion concerns where people get their power? Look at the issues. 1) I do not get what I need in lower levels unless someone recognizes me (someone feeds me when I cry). 2) I am not promoted unless someone else promotes me (Mom or Dad lets me know when my bedtime or curfew changes, when I can baby-sit my siblings, when I get to drive the car, etc.) 3) I cannot manipulate others unless they play into my manipulations.

In other words, people in a hierarchical model get their power when other people bestow them with power. We live in a society that tells us to believe in ourselves but the hidden message says, "Yes, believe in yourself as long as your belief in yourself does not challenge those in power above you." What happens when our children want a later bedtime because they feel confident that they can get up the next day and go to school without a problem? We can either agree with them or tell them "no." The problem arises when we say "no." Many reasons may lead us to tell our children no; however, when we do, our children may see it as a challenge to their belief in themselves. A parent cannot help the child's perceptions in some of these circumstances, but, we should be aware of how being told "no" can feel to a child. This is part of what feeds children's "need" to challenge us for more power, to disempower us. And in reality, would we want children to do what everyone told them to do?

DO AS I SAY

Lack of trust is a huge issue that feeds power struggles. What happens when people at lower levels of power do not trust those at higher levels? They may try to combine their efforts to undermine or usurp the power of those "in charge." We call this a revolution. If we think about it, we will likely realize that this is what kids are trying to do in their own way when they challenge us. Revolutions promote change and are a consequence of hierarchical systems. Many times, change can be good, but not always. Revolutions occur when trust and communication has eroded between those at different levels of power.

Parental hypocrisy is a major factor in the erosion of trust as kids grow older. A parent may say, "Don't hit your sister" but then slap or spank the children when they don't listen. Parents tell their children not to smoke and ground them when they are caught, but often the parents themselves smoke a pack a day. Many times we want our kids to do the things we tell them to do, while we do as we please. The "do as I say" philosophy—where a child sees her parents doing things the child wants to do, but has been told not to—gives rise to many issues that continue into adulthood. As these children grow up, they relish the thought of being able to do what they want when they want to do it. With time they gain a position of higher status, and as adults they reject the idea that anyone would tell them what to do, especially a kid. When they have children, they continue to act on this philosophy and in so doing, the parent acts as a hypocrite by parenting in a way that goes against what she knows to be fair. It is common to hear parents say, "That was how my parents raised me, and I turned out all right." Or "If it was good enough for me, it's good enough for my kids." These comments are examples of rationalization and justification; defensive tactics people use to protect themselves from feeling "negative" emotions.

Hypocrisy is based in resentment, and it amounts to an abuse of power. A parent's resentment about what happened to her as a child is the parent's issue, not the child's. Some parents may feel that because they have lived with or without certain things, they deserve to get what they want later in life. However, wanting something is not the same as needing it, and it's more important to consider how we affect others than to preoccupy ourselves with getting what we want. Let's consider the example of Darrin.

Darrin grew up in a family without money. Most of his clothes were hand-me-downs and didn't fit well. Sometimes his family went hungry for days at a time. Darrin started working when he was twelve and paid his way through school. He became a businessman and earned a moderate income. His wife also worked and they had two kids. They lived in a nice neighborhood and Darrin belonged to a golf club. He bought a new car every two years, and a new wardrobe every year. He bought the latest electronics and had a movie collection to rival MGM's, and he watched his movies on his state of the art media system and plasma TV. But Darrin and his wife were in debt. They had a second mortgage on their house, credit cards at their limits, and were only able to pay the minimum balances on their credit lines. Darrin's kids wanted the latest toys and video games, expensive clothes, trips, and all of the things their friends had.

When Darrin's kids asked for things, Darrin would say, "I grew up with next to nothing, and I learned to live with it. When you're working and making money, then you can spend it how you want to. You will have to work for what you want and learn to afford it and manage your money like I did." The kids often heard their parents arguing over money. They knew their parents were financially strapped, but felt that they deserved their piece of the pie; they felt that their father deprived them while managing to get everything he wanted.

Do you see a problem here? This situation is all too common in our culture. Darrin held an underlying belief that his things would give him more power, and when he had the power, no one was going to tell him what to do. He was so blinded by his need for power and status, he didn't realize his abuses and excesses and the neglect of those around him. Where did Darrin get his power? From the things he bought and the seeming status he earned from being the father and bread-winner. It was never enough.

What lessons do you think his kids learned from his example? Often, parents become so blinded by their own issues that they do not even realize they are sending out the "Do as I say, not as I do" message. Darrin was telling his kids to work hard and spend responsibly. He may have worked hard, but he was rationalizing and justifying his irresponsible spending habits. The longer this continued, the more mistrust and neglect his children felt.

Their feelings led them to feel that they had to fight for what they wanted, and to them it felt like a battle for survival. The kids came to believe that if they screamed loudly enough, they might get what they wanted. They acted increasingly belligerent with their parents as time passed, and the parents felt that they had selfish and ungrateful kids. As a result, more and more limits were put in place and their freedoms were curtailed. This pattern seemed to feed the downward spiral in their family. It's worth noting that when Darrin was a child, his father had a gambling problem, and that's why the family often went hungry. Although Darrin does not go to the race tracks or casinos he is gambling with his family's future every time he spends money they do not have, without regard for his family's needs. If his "gambles" result in a bankruptcy, it will make it very difficult to keep his family fed. When will the pattern end?

FAKE IT 'TIL YOU MAKE IT

One of the more common issues that therapists address with their clients is the impostor syndrome. This seems to be a direct consequence of the hierarchical issues that we grow up with in our culture. An impostor, in this context, is someone who feels that she has risen to a level of status above her earned or deserved status. In other words, a person feels that she has no business doing what she is doing, and it is just a matter of time until others figure that out. The imposter does not believe in her personal power. Impostors can take on many roles, and they do not have to command the highest levels of power. They are often parents, but can also be teachers, bosses, athletes, celebrities, politicians, or practically anyone in a position of responsibility. Many people may not realize that they are surrounded by people who feel like impostors. The major task of the impostor is to keep up the act, not only to fool others but to fool themselves. They cannot let others know that they feel as they do; they fear they would lose their power and control.

We could probably agree that in order to command a position of power, a person should be trained for that position. Yet, when we become parents we are thrust into the highest positions of power in the hierarchy with little or no formal training. This often results in the feeling of being an imposter, not really a parent at all.

Impostors often react from a sense of fear, and they do not want to be questioned about their qualifications so they may become defensive and redirect discussions when challenged. How often do we see others (or ourselves) doing this with our children? Even more, how often do we see children doing this? Yes, children can feel like impostors, too. In fact, the impostor syndrome often starts in childhood and can last a lifetime. Most of us can think back to times when, as children, we found ourselves in a school play, on an athletic team, or playing solo in the band, and it led us to feel uncomfortable. Because, as children, we want to prove our worth and value to others to get power, we feel that we have to impress them. When we are rewarded with the acknowledgement we seek, the pattern is reinforced time and again. We feel that we have to do more and more to continue to be fed the recognition and attention we thirst for.

The stress on the impostor can feel unbearable at times. While some are able to deal with it or deny it, others live in constant fear that they will be figured out. It would be difficult to overstate how many people are consciously and/or subconsciously sabotaging aspects of their lives because they feel unworthy of their success, rewards, and/or status. If they truly felt worthy of what they gained, why would they destroy their growth and success? Who are they doing all their work for? Do they believe they do it for themselves, or for the world that is supposed to recognize their power? Finally, how often do parents portray this pattern of the impostor to their children?

The Good, The Bad, and The Ugly?

The hierarchical model of power is based on a number of rules. One rule states that hierarchical structures are supposed to make life ordered and, therefore, more simple. We often believe, as parents, that if we can provide fewer choices for our kids we will make life easier for them, because fewer choices mean less confusion—the fewer the better.

Four primary dichotomies (literally meaning the state of cutting things into two) exist in a hierarchical model: Good or Bad, Right or Wrong, Strong or Weak, and Win or Lose. Consider how often parents tell their children they were a good boy or bad girl, or that they did something right or wrong. This happens all the time. Some children's first word is "bad" or "no." Some children's first phrase is "bad Daddy or bad Mommy." Sadly, in many situations the child had a point in making such a comment, but the parent may not want to hear that. Consider the image of the world we create when a child believes she is either and only good or bad, or has done something either right or wrong. Any other choice than the one "right" choice is therefore wrong. Any behavior other than the good ones are "bad," and children begin to see themselves as bad when they are punished.

How about strong or weak? Parents don't tell a child she is behaving strongly or weakly in the same way they might use good or bad, or right or wrong, but they insinuate strength or weakness indirectly. We may tell a girl that she should "suck it up," "stop crying," or tell a boy that "big boys don't cry." Some parents call their children cry babies, scaredy cats, wimps, or chicken. We once had a parent call his four year-old child a chicken-s#!% in our presence while his child was sitting in the room. What is the impact of a comment like this? It might not be evident at the time it is delivered, but parents may often see a child taking her aggression out on others to see who she can get to feel like a chicken-s#!%. What did that comment teach that child about strong and weak?

Our kids see images in the home, on TV and in society of people we call strong, and they see how we, as adults, are supposed to behave and feel. By the age of three, most children can correctly identify emotions that society sees as strong or good and those seen as weak or bad. Many parents find it baffling to realize that their toddler has already adopted these beliefs—parents may say that they don't teach their children these things, but how did the child form these beliefs? Small children learn from the world around them. We live in a culture that tries to express strength and hide weakness, at any cost. The need to show strength helps us ascend the hierarchy to become a "bigger circle." But at what cost? Does proving our strength to others help us believe in ourselves? No. Look at the way you and others around you use arrogance, flippancy, defiance and sarcasm. Look at how people at home, in public and in the media threaten others and get their way. Pay attention to how many times your children see words and weapons used to intimidate and eliminate others on TV and in movies. Look at how politicians use their influence and power to manipulate and cover lies. These are only a few examples of how our children learn strong and weak, yet how many times have they been exposed to them?

Win versus lose could be called the ultimate dichotomy. People, almost unconsciously use win versus lose to measure their ultimate success or failure in life. In life, we seem to add up the goods and bads, rights and wrongs, strengths and weaknesses to see if we are winning or losing "the game." However, in that process we want to forget, minimize, or deny the bads, wrongs and weaknesses, because we do not want to be seen as or think about ourselves as a "loser." In our mind and by much of society's standards, nobody loves a loser, and losers have no power.

Think about this example. A child is shooting baskets and she misses. How do you respond? She then makes a shot. How do you respond? Most parents will clap or say "good job" and make a big deal when their children make a basket and ignore or even criticize them when they miss. Otherwise, the parent may say encouraging things like "keep trying" when they miss, but the voice tone is different. Kids learn, very early, that they get more attention and acknowledgement when they "do good," "look strong," "do the right thing," and look like winners. Attention and acknowledgment are often translated into and misunderstood as love. His/her thought may be, "The more attention that I get, the more I must be loved, and when I feel loved, I feel like a winner." Kids also learn to make others look bad so that they can look better. They often think, "If I look better than you, then I am a winner and you are a loser." Many adults can remember doing things, when they were pre-schoolers, to undermine other kids so they could feel better about themselves.

Many parents think that their children don't see things in that way. They believe that if they never taught the child to manipulate or undermine, then the child doesn't know how to do it. Do not underestimate your children and their ability to understand things, whether said or unsaid. While they would have a hard time putting these dichotomies into words, children know that they do not want to be seen as bad, wrong, or weak.

People tend to see life from a certain dichotomy, and often their behavior will demonstrate this. This is often very subtle when you may first look at it but becomes more obvious when you examine a child's behaviors. This does not mean children will always respond from their more predominant dichotomy, as we will discuss shortly, but a dominant perspective can be seen. We may notice that boys orient themselves more toward a strong/weak perspective, wanting to be seen as strong. You might notice this through many of the things they do, in how they play, and in how they respond to situations. Girls, on the other hand, often orient themselves toward a good/bad perspective, wanting to be good. They seek approval and acceptance and don't want to upset the proverbial apple cart.

Some kids need to be "right" all the time. These children may not care so much about being perceived as good or strong. Often they are seen as "know it alls," and that is where they feel that they get their power. In turn, they use that power to demonstrate their strength over others. Furthermore, these people, even as adults, have a very difficult time admitting when they made a mistake or did not have the correct answer for something.

The reason that children view the world through these varying perspectives is most likely due to a combination of genetic, hormonal, and environmental influences. Children's behavior is also influenced by temperament and parental/societal issues, as we will discuss in later chapters.

In some instances, girls and boys do not view the world from their more expected dichotomies. Some boys want to be seen as good more than strong, which can result in difficulties with peers because they do not assert themselves and may be picked on for it. However, these boys may be rewarded by adults for their behavior. We also know that some girls want to be seen as strong at any cost. These girls, like Hillary in the discussion above, will challenge both adults and children, and because they are girls, many adults are not sure how to handle them. In Hillary's situation, and most others like hers, her actions were likely due to a combination of temperament and environmental influences. As we said, this is a very subtle issue but when recognized, it can change the way you approach your child.

∽ GIRL POWER ∽

Why is it that girls in today's society are seemingly getting into more trouble than in previous generations? On a more societal level, we see girls wanting to be seen as stronger. This is because of the shift in thinking since the days of "women's liberation" which enables females to express their power in ways other than looking good to gain approval. We see the emphasis regarding girls being seen as equals to boys as a positive thing; however, as they have started to emulate the same competitive and aggressive behaviors as boys, society has not understood why or what to do about it. Simply stated, girls' more assertive/aggressive behavior is due to the manner in which we reward "strong" behavior in our culture, and girls are seeing that they can get some of the pie, whether it be in academics, sports, bullying, politics or the world of business through these behaviors.

What makes the problem more challenging for girls and women is that those who assert themselves aggressively are often considered to be wrong or bad by those who do not understand. They are also called unkind names by others who feel threatened or confused by their behaviors. This judgment puts more pressure on girls to have to walk the line of looking good and not "too" strong very closely, when there are no rules about how to do this correctly. The standards and expectations placed upon them are unfair relative to their ability and rights to pursue the same successes that many boys and men have enjoyed in the past.

The idea that "boys will be boys", which has justified many behaviors and actions over time is a double standard to the idea that girls should be held to higher standards when they are exploring their power in a society that has reinforced efforts to look strong and powerful at the expense of others as a sign of success. Rather than point fingers at girls and saying that their behavior may need to change, the answer lies in helping society see how it encouraged and promoted this behavior. It is not just that we want to change the manner in which girls approach power, but also boys. There is a great deal of value in a life of balance among the three dichotomies, and we all can win.

Let's return to Hillary. In her family, it is clear that she was seen as bad and wrong. However, she did not want to lose so she attempted to appear strong at all costs. Remember, if you are bad and wrong and weak, you are guaranteed to "lose." The other issue is that if someone looks strong, she may have a better chance of winning, and controlling the situation thereafter. "If I win, then I define what good and right are because I make the laws and rules." If Hillary could be the strongest one in the family, then she could make the rules.

The next issue relates to the fact that kids want to be good at things, even Hillary. In Hillary's family, it started to become clear that Hillary was not going to command the "good" role because she heard how often she behaved "badly." When she was young, her parents felt that she wanted to be seen as good, but that changed quickly when she did not get what she wanted. Furthermore, if she was behaving badly, that was not the "right" behavior, so she was seen as "wrong." However, the more she behaved badly, the better she became at it. What started as accidental became purposeful. Hillary was "good at being bad." She began to feel arrogant (and powerful) because she felt that she could upset everyone. It doesn't mean that she felt good about what she did. That ability to manipulate people gave her a sense of power. This is similar to throwing a stone into a lake just to see a big splash. Did that get her what she wanted? No. She really wanted to feel loved, but because she felt "bad and wrong" inside, she did not feel worthy of love.

Once again, many parents do not believe that their children may think this way but this phenomenon of children "being good at being bad" is common. As we look at our kids' behavior (and our own), we should consider the dichotomies we see the child using, and the ones we use. Most parents want to interpret their kids' behaviors as good/bad or right/wrong. When they do this and the children thereby feel bad or wrong, it sets up a situation in which they revert to the strong/weak dichotomy by using emotions like anger, defiance, arrogance, flippancy (the "I don't care" emotion), hatred and rage, in an effort to appear strong and to win. Most parents are unwilling to let their children "be stronger" than they are, so they feel they have no choice but to respond to their child's uprising. This is often when conflicts between parents and children escalate. Both the parent and the child are each trying to be stronger, to win. For a more in-depth discussion of this escalation of conflict we would refer you to Chapter 14 in The Art of Managing Everyday Conflict.

An important part of parenting involves trying to see when you and your children are approaching an issue from different dichotomies. When people are reacting from two different dichotomies they will never find resolution, whether it is parent and child, husband and wife, peer to peer, or employee to manager. We should try to be aware of the dichotomies that enter into our conflicts and monitor our reactions.

ALL THE WORLD'S A STAGE

If you look closely at this hierarchical model and the way it works, you will see that people play different roles. Each of those roles serves a different purpose, and all of us have likely played these roles multiple times. They are the Victim, the Persecutor, the Rescuer, and the Instigator. In the world we live in, and especially in our families, it is crucial to understand these roles and the interplay between them. Let's first begin with our discussion of the Victim.

The **victim** feels that something bad happened to him. This bad thing can range from name-calling or an angry facial expression to physical and/or emotional abuse. The victim often feels unable to respond to protect himself for fear of retaliation, and depending on the frequency and duration, over time may feel that the abuse will never end. When a victim feels attacked, he may feel powerless, effectively giving him power to the "attacker" or persecutor as they will be called. Victims feel like the smallest circle in the hierarchy, but they do not necessarily have the lowest status. (For example, sometimes the middle child in the family complains that the other kids are picking on him.)

While most people want to avoid being seen as a victim, there are many fringe benefits to this role. (Note: Before we discuss these benefits, it is important to note that many children and adults in our culture are truly victimized. This discussion does not take away from those circumstances and by no means do we imply that all victims are seeking benefits from others.)

A victim feels that something unjust was done to her. If something unjust was done, then she did not deserve what happened. Therefore, she is not responsible and therefore does not have to feel blame, shame, guilt, failure, etc. She is off the hook.

The person playing the victim role will often cling to this role in order to reap the rewards of having little or no responsibility in the matter. In order to play the victim, one has to be seen as good and right, but weak. A would-be victim should not do "wrong or bad," or no one would feel sorry for him. For example, you see your children arguing and scuffling, and you confront them. Almost immediately, both children point at the other and say, "She/He started it!" Why? A main reason is that both know there will be consequences for the instigator who could also be seen as the persecutor. And if you perceive one as the instigator, that child cannot thereafter play the victim role. We will discuss the instigator further in a moment.

The **persecutor** is the person who caused the victim pain. She is usually bigger or higher in status, but not always. Persecutors are often called bullies. Underneath every bully are feelings of fear and cowardice, no matter how old or big a bully is. A bully's desire is to prove her power over her victim and to create fear in others so she doesn't have to feel her own fear. If a bully can do that, she "takes" the other person's power. However, because that sense of power is not lasting, a bully has to continue to persecute or bully others to maintain it. By rule, bullies are more powerful than victims or can gain access to more power than the victims (think of the older brother or sister who picks on the younger brother or sister). At the time the persecutor is "messing with someone else's power" she is seen to have more power than the victim.

Persecutors do not believe in themselves on their own merit, they only believe in their ability to intimidate and negatively affect other people's power. Persecutors are seen as being bad and wrong, but strong. Remember the philosophy discussed earlier, "If I am strong and I win, then I make the rules and define was is good and right."

In the face of more strength, "cowardly" persecutors will often hide and "play nice" with others, but strike at their "victims" when someone with more power turns his back. This is common in abusive families when a parent is abusive to the children or a spouse, but then behaves nice when the police show up at the door. When the police leave, often the abuser turns on the children/spouse again. This pattern is learned in childhood and continues through adulthood. Some children behave perfectly with adults but persecute other children when the adults' backs are turned, using their power to diminish the power of others. The Eddie Haskell character from the old TV show "Leave it to Beaver" comes to mind as a classic "cowardly" persecutor.

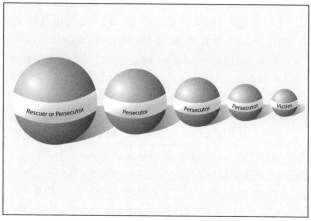

Figure 2: VPRI

The **rescuer** takes care of and protects the victim, and this is where they get their power. Former victims will often play to rescuers, especially if the rewards are big. For example, a child who was picked on by others may grow up to become a police officer. By rule, the rescuer is the largest circle in the hierarchy or the most powerful person present at the time, because she has the power to crush the persecutor and save the victim. Review Figure 2 to see which roles each person in a hierarchy can play.

The rescuer has to be seen as being good, strong, and right; if she were bad or wrong, she would likely be seen as someone's persecutor. Therefore, many rescuers use their status as parent, teacher, politician, etc. to deny their faults and flaws and/or to justify their actions. Because we depend on others to define our power, the rescuer may try to hide any ulterior motives that may be considered to be bad or wrong by others. If they are skilled at this, they can often influence others to believe that they are good and right. Think about the politician who is taking money from lobbyists or priest who is molesting children, or the parent who is abusing their children. These individuals may be able to convince anyone that they have done nothing wrong and may do anything to hide the truth, or they would be seen as persecutors. The benefits of being the rescuer are that people look up to them, and they often get their power from this admiration; such attention can be intoxicating.

The final major role is the **instigator.** The instigator is not a separate role, but instead is played by one or more people playing the role of the victim, persecutor, or rescuer. The instigator is the person who starts the conflict, either directly or indirectly. This may be the younger sibling who pokes fun at the older child until the older child retaliates. Or, it may be the big brother who punches the younger brother in the arm or teases, or the parent who favors one child over the other to the point that conflict is caused between siblings, allowing the parent to punish the "least preferred" child. Each person plays roles for different reasons, but the conflict is instigated to gain power in some way.

In many situations, people learn to play victim, persecutor, and/or rescuer on an almost habitual basis. These people become chronic victims, chronic persecutors, and/or chronic rescuers.

The game of the chronic victim is "How much do you Love Me?" The game of the chronic persecutor is "How Much Do You Fear Me?" The game of the chronic rescuer is "How Much Do You Worship Me?" When we discuss the game of the chronic rescuer, many people will have a reaction to the word "worship" because they feel this word is reserved for religious circumstances. If the word "worship" is put in terms of the dichotomies, a person having the desire to be worshipped would be seen as bad and wrong, but strong. In order to be a rescuer, one is supposed to be good, strong, and right. However, if we look at the hierarchical model of power, those who want to be the biggest circle, including some parents, often have what is sometimes called "God Complexes." Not every rescuer takes care of people for this purpose but in chronic rescuers, the use of the term is likely accurate. The games of the victim, persecutor, and rescuer are important to understand and observe because the more an individual is able to play the game, the more the pattern becomes ingrained. For a more in-depth discussion, you may want to review Chapter 5 in *The Art of Managing Everyday Conflict*.

It is important to address the **chronic victim**, because this condition exists throughout our society and it is fostered and groomed in the family. When children learn to play the victim, they learn to get power from other people. Because of this, they learn that they do not have to rise to higher levels of status; instead, they just wait for someone to take care of them. Furthermore, they never have to take responsibility for things they do, so they are never wrong. A huge sense of entitlement can come with this condition, and these children—and the adults they become—expect to get what they want when they want it, because they expect to be taken care of. When things do go wrong for the chronic victim, someone else is always to blame.

When victims are rescued, they surrender their power to the rescuer. They then expect the rescuer to take care of them. However, eventually the rescuer will make a demand on the victim; maybe ask for help, maybe impose a condition of worth, and/or the victim may feel that she was set up for failure by the rescuer. At this time, the victim's perceptions often turn the rescuer into their persecutor. What does the victim then have to do? Find another rescuer. When this happens, the pattern starts all over again, with the victim ultimately moving from rescuer to rescuer to rescuer. In the family, the chronic victim may move from parent to parent or even to older siblings, often moving back and forth between them. A victim can become very skilled at instigating conflicts and splitting up family members so that someone comes to the rescue. Victims may also work very hard to divert attention away from others so that they can remain the center of attention. It is not unheard of for a parent to also play a chronic victim (or that of the "martyr," more on that shortly), and this often results in their kids adopting the same roles, because this becomes the only way that children can get attention.

On the other side of this, when the parent plays a chronic victim, her children may take on a "**parentified child**" role and behave in a manner geared more toward taking care of others than themselves. Parentified children can often behave extremely responsibly, may be admired and praised by adults, and can rise to positions of status and success in school and at work. However, they often put themselves last and may develop emotional and physical problems later in life, because the only way they (subconsciously) feel they can let down their guard or rest is if they are sick or have a problem that seems out of their control. However, consciously, when they cannot fulfill their role, they feel stressed and believe that they have let everyone down, causing more stress.

Several other roles that are sometimes played are offshoots of victim, persecutor, and rescuer. To begin this discussion, we have to look at a situation where there is no rescuer. When this happens, a persecutor has free reign to exploit the chosen victim. The victim has a couple of options. Her or she can take the abuse and play helpless, hoping that the abuser will stop or that at some point a rescuer will come along (this is called **learned helplessness**). In contrast, the victim can fight back and try to defend himself. If a rescuer appears, the victim can justify his actions in the name of self-defense. A parent who confronts fighting kids will find that both want to be seen as the "**justified persecutor**." As such, each child claims that the other started it, and that fighting back was the only option. It is then often up to the rescuer to play judge, jury, and executioner. The parent may then hear things like, "You always take her side." At this point the child is playing the victim and the parent has become their persecutor. With this example you can understand how these situations can unravel so quickly.

When the rescuer feels taken advantage of, abused, unappreciated, or manipulated, she plays the role of the martyr. In other words, the martyr is a victimized rescuer. The goal of the **martyr** is to elicit guilt from the people she is supposed to rescue and thereby receive appreciation or admiration from them. Martyrs often play the role of a **chronic rescuer**. If you look back on the martyr's life, you may find that as a child, she played the chronic victim. Becoming a martyr allows a rescuer to continue to be a chronic victim but with the status power of rescuer.

Who has the most power in the victim/persecutor/rescuer interplay? Take a moment to think about this. Most people would assume the rescuer is the most powerful, because of her status power. But consider these questions. Who decides who the victim is? Remember that a persecutor can pick who he wants to pick on, but the people picked on decide how they will respond. Who decides when to surrender power? Who decides who their persecutor is? Who decides who their rescuer is? Who decides when their rescuer becomes their persecutor? And finally, who decides how long to play the victim and when to become the justified persecutor? The victim. Therefore, the victim is, paradoxically, the most powerful role a person can play. Ironically, by surrendering my power, I get power.

If you reflect on the actions of your children, as well as your own, you will probably see examples of this. When a child is screaming bloody murder, only the child can make the decision to behave differently. You may be able to do something to influence her, but it is still her choice to change.

When a family comes in for therapy with a "problem child," the child usually feels like the victim of everyone else, and the parents feel helpless to change this child. The child then often seems shocked to hear about everyone else's feelings of helplessness and victimization. In other words, most people in the family feel like the victim, which keeps the problems going.

Let's look at Hillary again. In the example at beginning of the chapter, it is clear that Hillary feels victimized by her parents and siblings. Because of this, and her belief that her siblings were the ones always being rescued by her parents, she had no rescuer. This gave her two choices. One was to respond from a learned helplessness model and give up. The other was to become the justified persecutor and fight back. As long as she can play the victim, her behavior toward others is always justified, and therefore she is blameless (in her mind) for her actions. Her actions were always someone else's fault. To her, things will remain this way for as long as she chooses to see her family and the world in this light.

On the other hand, Hillary's parents and siblings feel persecuted by her, and her parents feel that their job is to protect and rescue the other kids from Hillary's behaviors. Hillary's parents often reminded her of all they had to put up with from her, and all they had done for her—playing martyrs. As you can see, this pattern feeds itself and no one wants to take responsibility for changing; everyone else should "go first." Many times, the parents and children are all waiting to see change in each other before they will change. Parents sometimes need to be reminded that they are the models for behavior change, and often the parent needs to take the first steps. If the child chooses not to follow, then restrictions are put in place. Those who play the hierarchical games will suffer the hierarchical consequences. By the time the family finally realizes that they need help, trust has been destroyed on many fronts.

Throughout the book, we will provide scenarios and strategies for dealing with similar situations.

NEVER LET THEM SEE YOU SWEAT

To this point in this chapter, much of this is common sense—nothing new, just a different spin. So, knowing what you already know, why do these issues continue to occur? Many people feel family issues have no rhyme or reason. However, one underlying common denominator cannot be removed from the equation—emotion. In a hierarchical model of power, emotions are categorized through the various dichotomies. For example, sadness would be seen as bad, wrong, and weak Anger would feel bad, wrong, and strong. Love could be seen as good, strong, and right, but when we feel love for someone whom we believe is exploiting us, it can feel bad, wrong, and weak. Fear is often seen as bad, wrong, and weak, but if it helps us out of a jam or saves our life, we might see it as good, right, but likely still feeling weak. Do you get the picture? For a more complete discussion of emotions and how we use them in hierarchical models, I will refer you to Chapters 8 & 9 in *The Art of Managing Everyday Conflict.*

Most people want to try to remove emotion from interactions, especially parents. This is next to impossible to do. Most of being human is experiencing emotions. We can, however, decrease the "negative influence" of emotions, but that only happens after you consider all you are feeling and put it into perspective. One way to attempt this is to use logic in a conflict. Logic is seen to be good, strong, and right. Conflict often begins when two people's logic does not agree and both want to hold on to their perspectives and power. Alternately, logic is sometimes a safe place from which to approach a conflict. If I am thinking, then I am not feeling. If I am not feeling, then I do not hurt. If I do not hurt, then you cannot hurt me. If you cannot hurt me, then I cannot lose. If I cannot lose, then I must win. i.e., logic is king.

In order for a conflict to occur, someone has to at least feel threatened, but often they feel more than that. The conflict escalates as each person's power feels more impacted by the other person's actions or reactions. In other words, each is allowing the other person to affect and determine her perceptions of power. Many parents feel powerless, fearful, threatened, helpless, confused, misunderstood, and other emotions when their children do not respond as they wish. However, parents also feel some fear and apprehension about letting their children see these emotions—apparent weakness—due to the fear that their children will try to take control. So, the conflict builds when parents try to protect their power, and nobody wins.

AND THE WINNER IS...

In the hierarchically-based ways of approaching problems and issues, there's hardly ever a winner. Ironically, most parents feel that their kids are winning the battles and most kids feel that their parents are winning. Still, and paradoxically, something keeps this hierarchical model running strong—fear. Fear is what keeps this model surviving and thriving in our world, and it keeps winning more and more every day, generating anger, hatred, dependence, mistrust, and conflict.

Fear occurs at every level of the hierarchy. The people at the lowest level fear that they will need others to take care of them, and/or that those same people or others with more power will hurt them. The next people in the hierarchy fear the people above them for the same reasons but also fear that the people below them may try to undermine or usurp their power. And so it goes, all the way up to the people at the top. What do they have to fear? Both that the people below them may try to undermine or usurp their power, and that somewhere out there is someone or something that could crush, punish, or control them.

Alternatively, the heads of the hierarchies (or the big circle as we call it) could fail, leading to a collapse of the hierarchy wherein all people in positions of lesser power would also fail. The person at the top often feels a sense of responsibility for each person in the hierarchy, and if any of them fail, the most powerful may feel it is his/her fault. For this reason, there is often an incredible burden on parents (as the big circles) in our "power-oriented culture," and the stress can feel overwhelming. This underlying stress often drives us to push our kids too hard and create unrealistic expectations.

SUMMARY

Although we have covered only one model of power in this chapter, we covered a lot of ground. The intent was to provide you with an overall understanding of the issues without delving too deeply into the finer points. The most important point is to recognize that the way in which we look at the world, from this perspective of power, often leads to more problems than solutions. Our world and many of our families are based on this control-based model, and we cannot seem to see any other options. As you look at all of the difficulties that arise when people parent by this model, you can see many reasons to consider other options. However, in life, and in parenting our children, change is very difficult. It takes time and introspection to understand how these changes affect all involved.

As we have taken our journey through the hierarchical model, we have discussed how and where we get power and the problems with this, the roles we play and why, and how emotion plays into our perceptions of power. While there are many disadvantages to the manner in which we use hierarchies, there are also advantages we cannot discount. Order and structure are helpful, and people with certain skills should be in positions of management, or power. Using power with moderation and balance often leads to harmony; abusing power means moderation and balance—and therefore harmony—are lost. The main issue we wanted to address was the manner in which people tend to use and abuse their power in this model and the problems to which it often leads. We hope you are beginning to examine yourself and your family so that you can put what you are learning into action.

⌒ Chapter 3 ⌒
EQUITY-BASED PARENTING

Amber, 10, and Jon, 8, were brother and sister. Neither of them had perfect grades in school, but they were known to behave responsibly and their parents seldom had to ask them to do their homework or complete their chores. They completed task lists on time in order to receive the rewards and privileges they enjoyed. They did not fight with each other, they shared their toys, and they did not compete for attention, grades, or friends.

Amber was outgoing with her peers, played soccer in a competitive league, and was learning to play the trumpet in band. Jon was a little shyer, tried soccer for a season, was enjoying learning golf, and played tennis. Both had friends and were generally seen as likable by their peers, and they did not have many conflicts with other children. In fact, both were known to try to help other kids seek resolutions to conflicts.

Neither Amber nor Jon was shy about showing affection or their emotions, and their parents, Janet and Dan, modeled that at home and in public while teaching them to honor the boundaries of others. Mistakes were seen as an opportunity to learn, and Janet and Dan made sure not to shame, humiliate, or guilt their children into compliance. Neither parent could remember the last time anyone in the family raised his voice. They did acknowledge times of feeling anger, but also recognized the underlying feelings that prompted the protective emotions.

As husband and wife, they respected each other and knew that while they would not always agree on things, they would seek to honor each opinion and try to find compromise when necessary. Physical punishment was not an option, but they did not believe in permissiveness. Respect for all (irrespective of status), consistency, structure, immediacy in learning from mistakes, and follow-through on actions were their parental mantras. They wanted their children to learn from example rather than from the "do as I say and not as I do" hypocrisy their parents had instilled in them. When they made a mistake, they allowed their children to point it out and were willing to live by the same consequences they expected their children to live by.

Janet and Dan were committed to attending their children's functions and if both could not go, at least one made it regardless of inconvenience. They believed that their children were not property, but gifts to be unwrapped, revealing a little more every day. If they weren't willing to be present for Amber and Jon's daily happenings, why bring them into this world? They also helped guide their children's attitudes and beliefs, without controlling their choices. Jon's decision to stop playing soccer after one season was accepted, and when he chose golf instead, because his Dad played, they helped him find a good teacher. Jon's parents did not want their children to feel that they had to be the best. Simply stated, they wanted them to be the best they could be.

Dan and Janet felt that their largest difficulties involved helping Amber and Jon to understand the reactions of others. The kids were often confused about others' actions. Why did people make fun of others and put them down? Why did other parents yell and scream at their kids and jerk them by the arm?

No question was a stupid question, and Dan and Janet made an effort to finish every discussion when time was available, often turning the questions around to see what Amber and Jon thought about certain things. As a result, the kids sometimes asked teachers and other adults questions that were so "to the point" that the adults would not know how to respond. Some adults accused Amber and Jon of not respecting them, but it was always in a situation when the adult was abusing their power and the kids called them on it.

Some adults called Amber and Jon too sensitive because they sometimes cried if they felt hurt, but Amber and Jon believed it was okay to cry to honor their sadness. They did not carry grudges, and they did not feel afraid to assert their wants and needs and/or the wants and needs of others.

Janet and Dan had a date night every other Saturday, and every night they took the time to talk about each other's day before they went to sleep. Each had individual hobbies but made sure to do things together, as a couple and as a family. Balance in every aspect of their life was important for the entire family. They divided the household tasks, and Janet and Dan participated in the task list with the kids..

It took many hours and many learning experiences for all to foster Amber and Jon's growth. Janet and Dan had consulted books and a few therapists to learn how to be better people and better parents, and to discover their own issues; they took the opportunity to use these issues as stepping stones for growth. They knew that they were not perfect parents, nor were Jon and Amber perfect children. They all just tried to do the best they could with what they knew at the time.

EQUITY FOR ALL

If you are wondering what world these people grew up in, you are not alone. Do you feel that such a life is possible to achieve, or did you hear that internal voice saying, "Yeah right"? Were you feeling skeptical, doubtful? Maybe you felt a sense of failure, inadequacy, irritation, and/or anger. Since you've read the chapter on hierarchical parenting, you now may understand how this example may have affected your sense of power. To many, these are dream kids in a dream family, and therefore unreal and impossible. It is easier to dismiss your hopes and dreams, and believe that such a dream family is impossible, rather than hold on to your dreams and face feelings of failure, shame, and guilt. But remember, our feelings are there for a reason (to teach us), just as our children are.

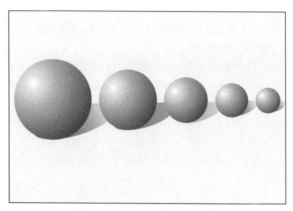

Figure 1: Hierarchical Model

We are generally taught from an early age that someone has to be in charge, and that whoever is in charge must have more power than others. Because we are surrounded by so many examples of hierarchies in our society, we may not know that any other type of social structure exists. Many of us didn't like growing up in hierarchical households and we may have sworn that we would never be like our parents, knowing we wanted something different and better. But we don't know how to create and perpetuate a positive change, and the current—the hierarchical system we know—seems too strong to resist. Most parents want their kids to be individuals, but only insofar as this allows them to fit in with society. Still, somewhere inside us, as parents and as people, we often feel that there is a different and better way. That is probably a major reason that you're reading this book.

So just what is this equity parenting stuff and how does it apply to each of us?

You may remember that in the hierarchical model, power and status decrease from the individual at the top of the system to the one at the bottom. In the equity system, as its name implies, each individual has the same amount of power. It is at this point that most parents say, "Stop the boat. I'm getting off." But, if these skeptics stick around they're usually glad they did.

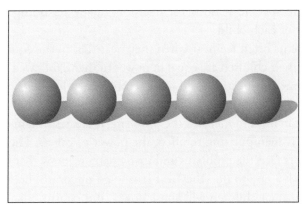

Figure 3: Equity Model

We need to be clear what we mean when we say "equity model." Some parents mistakenly believe that this term means that everyone in the family has equal rights, privileges, responsibilities, and power. However, having an equity-based system really means that each member of the family is allowed to have and feel his or her own sense of power. It does not mean, that the children should be granted equal rights and privilege irrespective of their emotional and developmental level of maturity. In simpler terms, parents serve as guides to their children, making accurate assessments—and good decisions based upon those assessments—of their emotional development, physical needs, and maturity level.

No outsider can answer all a parent's questions with a blanket "yes" or "no" answer. Is it all right to leave a twelve-year-old alone for a few hours at night while Mom and Dad go to a movie? Is a thirteen-year-old capable of watching his two-year-old sister while Mom goes to the doctor? It depends upon the individual child(ren) involved. Even within an equity-based household, it is necessary to set boundaries for each of the children, based upon their individual level of development. A seven-year-old may feel that it is unfair that she has to go to bed earlier than her older brother does, and in situations such as this, where a child perceives unfairness or disparity in the treatment that he receives as compared to that of a sibling, we need to carefully explain that there are specific reasons for decisions made regarding the best interest of each child.

Parents often feel fear when they hear that in the equity-based system their children are equal in power to them, followed by rationalization, justification, and some semblance of logical explanation about why that is not going to happen in their house. But consider the hierarchical model and the problems it creates in families—everyone is manipulating to affect the power of others. Hierarchical behaviors feed the problems and many parents know that but don't know what else to do. They fear letting go of control because they fear that their children will abuse power. But control is an illusion. We do not have control of our children; they choose to comply.

The idea of equity is simple—equal power. But, how do we get there? Equity comes from the combination of different strengths, weaknesses, handicaps, gifts, wisdom, experience, knowledge, and understanding. Everyone, of every age, every level of intelligence, handicapped, healthy, or anything in between, has some gift to share with the world. Our life is a process in seeking out and enhancing our strengths and improving and learning from our weaknesses to grow into our personal power. Our child's life is no different, and it is our job as parents to see them along their path.

Living a life of equity involves seeking our potential and being in a constant state of growth; rest periods and times of evaluation are necessary and acceptable. A parent's job is to be a guiding and supportive agent to his children through their growth process instead of trying to be a dictatorial boss who reigns over them.

The ideas behind creating an equity environment in the home involve many things. We learn to believe in ourselves since others do not wish to undermine or usurp our power. We do not see feedback as criticism, feedback is about learning. We do not strive to be better than others, we strive to be the best that we can be. We may see the accomplishments of others as measuring sticks for our growth, but we respect what they have done. We know that when we accomplished something, we did it with honesty, honor, and integrity. Winning is an outcome, not the end-all goal. If we learned something from an experience or activity, then we have won. If we made improvement, we won. If we had fun in the process, we won. Losing is a perception, not a reality.

Many disagree with the equity model because they believe that removing the competitiveness of hierarchical system promotes lack of ambition and apathy. But imagine your child being self-motivated, structured, and organized. You don't have to yell or scream. They ask you for help with their homework when they need it, and it gets done without you having to ask them to do it. They take responsibility for their actions and don't have to hide what they did, because they do not fear what you will do. This does not sound like apathy. If you don't believe this can happen, then stop and look at yourself and your beliefs. Yes, our children are human and may have difficulties with some of these issues. Also remember that for years your kids have been raised in a hierarchical model and will still live in a world that is largely control-based. You may then say, "Why bother? If everyone else is trying to mess with each other's power, then aren't I setting my child up for failure?" No you aren't. A person with an equity base should not be naïvely taught that everyone else is going to honor their power and respect them. We must teach them that others may try to manipulate their power.

Until every person in this world lives an equity life, hierarchies will exist. The goal is to live an equity life in a hierarchical world. We know and understand that others will try to affect our power and we don't let them. Still, because we are oriented to respect ourselves, we respect others. We do not feel the need to manipulate the power of others, but we do assert our needs. We seek to treat others with dignity and honor, despite how they treat us. Our behavior is modeling what we would want from others. A conflict is not about winning, it is about mutual resolution and understanding.

What to do if a child tries to manipulate others? This will happen—it is the process of learning to live a more equity-based life. Life often has natural consequences for those who try to undermine certain tenets of it. When people overstep their bounds, playing hierarchical games, they suffer the hierarchical consequences. Kids step outside the bounds of the law and go to court, and sometimes to boot camp. Until they can see the wisdom of living a more eq-uity-based life, they will have to learn these difficult lessons.

Parents who continually bail their children out of messes may falsely believe that they are doing so out of love for the child. Bail-ing someone out of a jam is not always about love, it is often about avoiding fear, guilt, shame, helplessness. Likewise, some parents dole out harsh and extreme punishment under the misguided belief that their "tough love" approach is about love; but these parents are often acting out of anger, hatred, resentment, fear, betrayal, mis-trust, and other less empowering emotions.

An equity approach does not involve needlessly continuing to bring up people's mistakes. The "I told you so" approach is off lim-its; it only leads to shame, humiliation, and resentment. If children keep making similar mistakes, a discussion of past experiences can help illustrate how they can learn from them and what was missed. We will cover more of this throughout the book. Regardless of how you address it, if a child continues to make the same mistakes he is not learning something from the experiences. Emotional reactions to these discussions—anger, sadness, guilt, shame, etc.—will occur. This is part of learning. The question is, is the child valuing what his emotions are trying to teach him?

EQUITY AND EMOTIONS

Take a moment to think about what happens when your child approaches you with a problem. You probably have an emotional reaction—fear, frustration, confusion, anger, helplessness, under-standing, acceptance, or something else. Many people try to push them to the background and use logic to address the problem, but emotions typically come out in the reaction to the child or to the source of the problem. Let's look at an example.

Joan is having a hard time doing her math homework and asks her mother to help her. Joan's mother was never very good at math and when she realizes that her daughter is depending on her, she recognizes her own weakness which can produce shame, guilt, em-barrassment, and a feeling of failure. To protect herself, she makes an excuse, tells Joan she's too busy and suggests Joan ask her father.

Let's say, instead, that Joan's mother decides to try to give her a hand but as she looks at the math problems it brings back memories of her old school days and poor math grades. While she can help Joan with a few of the problems, soon it becomes too hard. At that time, she might say, "They're giving way too much homework these days. Don't your teachers give you time to do this in class? I don't know how they expect parents to have the time to help their kids with all of this work."

In both variations of this example, a hierarchical/victim mentality is at work. First, Joan's mother played the victim to all of her work and to the inconvenience that Joan put upon her. In the second example, Joan and the parents were victims to the teachers who gave too much work. What lesson did Joan learn? Was her mother honest about her emotions? No. Did her mother feel her own power? No. Clearly, her mother felt threatened by the task, but blamed it on other things because she did not want to feel inadequate and stupid. Furthermore, her mother did not want to look stupid in front of her daughter, fearing Joan's impression of her would be degraded.

Let's look at another option. Let's say that Joan's mother is a little more enlightened and feels comfortable with her strengths and weaknesses. She accepts challenges as they come and tries to model this with her children. Joan is having a tough time with her math and asks her mother for help. Her mother is in the middle of doing something and she tells Joan, "Try a few more problems while I finish this, and I will be right there." After she finishes her task, she sits down with Joan and says, "Let's see what we can do here. I am not sure if you knew this, but when I was your age, I had a hard time with math. I know it can feel very frustrating. It's not one of my stronger skills, but I'll do my best, and hopefully we can both learn something together. If there is anything we cannot figure out together, we can ask your father." After she reviews the lesson, she asks Joan to explain what she understands. They then try to work through some problems together. What they can't do, they ask Joan's father to help them with.

Throughout the above example, Joan's mother degraded no one, made no excuses, and followed through on her word. She explained that she might not be able to help Joan, but was willing to try her best. She also empowered Joan by asking her to explain what she understood first, implying that her daughter has the ability to teach her something. Finally, she was willing to sit down with Joan's father and learn along with her daughter. Granted, time constraints in many families may prohibit both parents helping at the same time, but there are those moments when this can happen.

When people live a more equity-based life, and they have grown to understand emotions, they are more conscious and able to avoid reacting to others. Children may be taught in society that name-calling, sarcasm, anger, and hatred are protective emotions and behaviors. As parents we can give them a way to understand these emotions and actions when encountered, rather than react with their own impulses. With our help, our children can learn about the balance of emotions. The more we can truly communicate what we are feeling, the more our children (and we) have the opportunity to learn the purpose emotions serve.

Let's take a moment to look at the value of a few emotions. In the hierarchical model of power, almost all emotions are seen to serve little value or purpose; in fact, they are seen as obstacles to getting what we want—more power. However, a more informed perspective holds that these emotions would not exist if there was not a higher purpose for them... greater understanding of ourselves and others. As we understand each emotion more fully, we understand more. The following provides a list of emotions and a more enlightened perspective.

- *Love* lets us know when we feel an affiliation toward ourselves, another person, or a thing.

- *Anger* protects us when we feel threatened.

- *Rage* protects us when we feel in fear for our lives or our integrity feels threatened.

- *Fear* keeps us from doing harmful things and/or prompts us to act to keep from being harmed.

- *Failure* let's us know when it is time to learn. This is a very important concept to keep in mind. In our culture, we often surround feelings of failure with shame, guilt, insecurity, rejection, and we try to hide it. If instead we explored what we could learn when we feel failure, we would be less likely to keep making the same mistakes.

- *Sadness* lets us know when we feel emotional pain.

- *Happiness* lets us know when life is running smoothly.

- *Guilt* lets us know when we need to fix or rectify an action.

- *Shame* lets us know when we have done something to ourselves that needs to be fixed or rectified. Even when we do something to harm someone else, shame lets us know that we have not acted to our greatest potential, therefore harming ourselves.

- *Frustration* lets us know when we need to look for other options. It feels like banging our head against a wall. When we feel this, we often call on anger to knock the wall down. While knocking the wall down is an option, it is unlikely to be the best one.

- *Confusion* lets us know when we need more information.

- *Loneliness* lets us know when we need comfort.

- *Misunderstanding* lets us know when we need to give others more information about ourselves or our feelings.

- *Pride* lets us know when we feel good about ourselves.

- *Arrogance* protects us with a shield of false pride when we feel vulnerable or threatened.

- *Sarcasm* can be used with varying intensity. It uses humor to protect us from feeling a threat and in a non-aggressive way tells people to back off. Hierarchically, sarcasm can be used as a weapon. It is protective and can seek to destroy the other person's confidence. Many fights between kids, teens and adults start when one person does not have a comeback for another's sarcastic comment, they may resort to physical aggression to hide their perceived loss of power.

We will revisit this concept of emotions throughout the book, but we hope that through reviewing this short list, you can see the value of not only helping your children to understand these emotions, but also see the wisdom in further exploring your understanding of these and other emotions.

GIFTING POWER

One of the secrets of an equity model relies upon a willingness to share power through sharing experiences, wisdom, time, strengths, and even weaknesses. In a hierarchical model, the sharing of power means it will be taken, never to return. If we want it back, we have to fight for it. However, in an equity-based model, we learn to believe in our power and we understand that no one can take it. Furthermore, there is plenty to go around. People who share are much more likely to have people share with them. We see this every day in our own lives. What would we like to model to our children? Do we want them to see us as selfish and mistrustful? How does our behavior and what we say teach our children about power and how to use it? Too many times we see parents punish their children for not sharing, but those same parents do the same thing.

Giving a gift means giving without expectation of getting anything in return. This is equity. Sometimes we share our gifts with others although we might not get anything back at that time—or ever. But somewhere, sometime, someone shares something with us. Think of a person who stops on the roadside and helps someone change a flat tire. The person who helps change the tire never sees the person with the flat again, but sometime when they need help with something, someone will appear. This type of gifting is not about keeping score.

A gift does not always have to be a positive thing. Some therapists offer the gift of baring their own weaknesses and mistakes to their clients. This action alone, when used strategically, often prompts people to grow more than any other approach to teaching. Instead of seeing a therapist as having all the answers and making no mistakes, a client can see that his therapist has faults, flaws, and handicaps. In this line of work, a therapist who believes in equity-based models does not try to separate himself from the people he is guiding; such a therapist shows the client that his path is not so different from the client's path. As a parent, don't you have the same goal? If your child feels that you don't make mistakes, or never feel fear or insecurity, then how can he think that you will understand when he makes a mistake or feels insecure? It creates distance between you and your child if you believe that you have to be the model of perfection. When faced with someone they see as perfect, children are likely to feel that they have to hide their weaknesses, not because they realize that you hide yours but because they may believe you do not have any.

Sometimes a parent will share a weakness with his child only to have the child use this against him. This is an abuse of power; it might happen because the child has learned to abuse power or manipulate other people's power from the parent. If this happens in your family you can ask the child about sharing vulnerability, then talk about trust, betrayal, and the power of using shared information wisely if they want to have healthy relationships. Be willing to accept feedback if they feel that you betrayed them in turn. Accepting your responsibility and the fact that they taught you is what equity is all about. If you want your child to think that you don't make mistakes, it might be time to examine your goals more clearly. The benefits of sharing far outweigh the consequences.

THE GOLDEN RULES

A few gems of wisdom are given to us as rules to live by, to set the course of our lives. Some of these phrases are practical (don't look a gift horse in the mouth) and some leave people scratching their heads (a bird in the hand is worth two in the bush). And a few phrases capture the essence of the equity and hierarchical models.

The golden rule of the equity model is, "Do unto others as you would have them do unto you." We have heard this simple rule throughout our lives, but how often do we live this way and model this for our children? For example, Doug hits Barry, and Barry's parents tell Barry to hit him back. This simple rule is probably the most difficult to live by because of our emotions, the emotions of others, and the way we use them. Mistrust, betrayal, hurt, anger, vengeance, hatred, and rage often prompt us to do to others what they did to us.

Another gem similar to this is, "Don't get mad; get even." Does this imply equity? Is getting even the same as equality? Do we want our children to use this as their explanation and ultimately their excuse? Probably not. Retaliation is often not about evening the score, but one-upping. Consider the following story. Will was at school and someone called him a name and made a comment about his family. He retaliated in an effort to "get even" (his words) by punching the other child in the mouth three times. As a consequence, he was suspended and had to write an essay discussing the situation. He wrote an interesting comment that would not have likely come out in any discussion. He stated, "I punched the kid three times, once for my Mom, once for my Dad, and once for me." Imagine how this perspective might function in a world in which slights and name-calling might turn into punches, and then into worse, as our children grow up. This is not so different from the world we live in.

Some parents feel that if they don't teach their child to seek revenge for injustices, the child will be a patsy and get pushed around. But when children live an equity-based life, they seek resolution, not retaliation. They seek to talk about their issues and concerns, and if that doesn't work, they seek help and support from others. Ideally, children would seek to resolve the issue with others first, then seek help from a teacher, bus driver, and/or you. And then, if no one was there to protect them, they might have to take steps to protect themselves. The difference is that they get involved in an altercation only as a last resort. If the child has learned the value of the equity system, then by virtue of understanding emotions and why people use them, they know that others may be trying to intimidate them and manipulate their sense of power. Children who feel confident do not have issues with bullies, because bullies are looking for people further down the hierarchy. Furthermore, children who live an equity-based life are more likely to be liked by their peers and therefore will have peer support.

The second golden rule of the hierarchical model is,, "He who has the gold makes the rules." Is this true? Let's take a look at what many people in our society are seeking: more money, more things, more strength, more guns, more bullets, etc. It is easy to become detoured by what is truly inconsequential. Many parents often think that they will get back to the equity model—later. There is always a reason, an excuse, or a better time to try to change the way we live our lives or how we raise our kids. How many times do people justify what they do by what someone else does or has? How many times have you done this? Think about how you may inadvertently pass this rule on to your child.

ALL FOR ONE AND ONE FOR ALL

In an equity model, people get their power from within. However, while we learn to believe in ourselves, we also realize that we benefit from others and the things they can offer us. Each individual does not wish to stand above others; instead we wish to feel our own power within the context of others, to help others because we mutually benefit. As we teach others and help them grow, they will likely teach us and help us grow. The team is accentuating the individual, and the individual accentuates the team.

The hierarchical model is all about the individual. The attitude is completely self-centered. I have to look good, often at the expense of others. I want others to notice me because I get power from that. I will reach the top by whatever means necessary. I may work in a team, but only because it will help me reach my goals—either I will take the credit at the end or the team will carry me along and I won't have to do much. Because of the underlying fear that someone else will want to "take my power" I cannot truly benefit because I may hold back to protect myself.

THE DRIVING FORCE

We hope that the value of the equity model is clear and under-standable, and that it decreases conflict and increases self-empow-erment, independence, and self-reliance. It is nearly impossible to live in its true form, but it is a model to aspire to on a daily basis. In our discussion of the hierarchical model we talked about how the underlying emotion was fear. At each level of the hierarchy, fear motivated the behaviors of others. Consider what emotion may be the driving force behind an equity model. What do we associate with love? Often, people use words like "understanding," "compas-sion," "trust," "generosity," "caring," "forgiveness"…in other words, feelings of the more empowering variety. These same forces are at work in an equity-based system. By offering support and guidance to others, we foster relationships and bonds that we cannot create with the competitiveness, vengeance, retaliation, or domination of those around us that a hierarchical system encourages.

Love is at the core of the equity model. We learn to love our-selves, and others. We learn to believe in ourselves, and in others. And we learn to respect ourselves, and others. We talk about two types of respect: fear-based and love-based. If I am told to respect my elders (hierarchical) I learn to give them lip service and may show them respect as long as they are in my presence, but once they turn their back, I will say and do as I please. Therefore, I am not learning to respect them; I'm learning to respect their status. I may fear angering them, but I do not respect them as people. As long as I think they can do something to me I may listen to them, but when I gain power I will do what I want, which may even include harming them. In contrast, in a love-based respect, we honor others no matter what level of status. We do not wish harm to them even if they have harmed us. We wish for them to learn from their lessons. Younger, older, white, black, brown or red, male or female, we re-spect them for being a living being on this planet. Each person is of value and deserves to be treated with respect, honor and dignity.

This sense of love-based respect comes from a person who has learned to love and respect himself. If you search deep inside yourself, you will find that this is what you are seeking to teach your child. It is a process of exploration to be undertaken together. As you are learning a new way of parenting and helping your children along this path, you are learning together. Equity-based parenting is a constantly unfolding process toward living an equity-based life.

This all sounds so wonderful, but the bottom line is that we still live in a largely hierarchically-based world. Remember the goal stated earlier in the chapter is that we learn to live an equity-based life in a hierarchical world. When you communicate with your child about how the world works, you can help him understand that people may do things simply to mess with his power so they can feel better about themselves. Your children will behave hierarchically at times in the process of discovering how they want to use their power. It is how you respond to them that will reinforce or discourage these behaviors.

As we continue our journey through this book, we will continue to allude to the difference between hierarchical and equity-based parenting styles to help you understand the differences. In that sense, our discussion has only begun. Enjoy the rest of your journey; it may be a bit bumpy at times.

⌒ **Chapter 4** ⌒
TEMPERAMENT AND PERSONALITY

Scott was the second child of three in his family. He was relatively quiet and liked to read, and he often played alone. His younger sister was a bit quiet and reserved. She spent most of her time playing quietly with her friends. She was not athletic; her focus was on school. She did well in school, and did not seem to have to work at it too hard. She was five years younger than Scott, and while there were some struggles with her, there were no major ongoing conflicts. Scott's older brother was a rough-and-tumble kid who seemed to get into everything and was very athletic.

Scott liked his environment quieter than his other two siblings, and the three had many conflicts throughout the years about how loud music or televisions would play and how loud friends were.

When Scott was young, he clung to his mother. He didn't like contact with different people, and he cried when strangers made eye contact. His parents tried to get him involved in play groups but Scott never strayed far from his mother, and he took a long time to make the few close friends he had. As he got older, his parents asked his older brother to take him to friends' houses to play, hoping that Scott would learn by watching his brother and would feel safe with his brother present. This, however, often ended in Scott coming home or wanting to come home, and his brother feeling frustrated. Over the years, his patience grew thin, and he and Scott grew further and further apart.

Scott's mother worked to be very patient, recognizing many similarities between them as he grew older. Scott's father, on the other hand, was not so patient. He often played roughly with Scott when he was an infant and toddler, and Scott often cried. After a while, his father gave up, focusing instead on Scott's older brother and his activities. The older Scott grew, the less he spoke to his father, and his father felt frustrated when Scott would not answer his questions. His mother often told his father to be patient, and this apparent "rescuing" by his mother became an ongoing issue between them, creating visible tension between his parents that the family noticed but never discussed. His father made side-handed comments about how Scott was a mama's boy, and occasionally his mother would reply that if he didn't treat him like dirt, Scott might be different.

In high school, Scott had a difficult time with presentations, and his class participation grades were lacking. His teachers tried to call on him, but he sank into his seat, sometimes answering so quietly he could barely be heard. When Scott was in third grade, he was once ridiculed by a teacher for not answering. Overall, his grades were good, and he worked hard in his classes. He had a small group of friends at school, and was not teased very much by his peers. He seemed to be under the radar with most of his classmates.

Scott's story is not unfamiliar. He grew up with a somewhat tentative approach to life. While many different events in his life could be the reason for this approach, none of them point to any traumatic situation by relative standards. But whether or not he *perceived* any of these events as traumatic, given his view of life, is a potential issue. Still, his behaviors were consistent from birth and are more representative of innate traits, or temperament, than those caused by life events. While some events probably influenced his behaviors and attitudes about life, it is more likely that the strategic interaction between him and his environment resulted in the behavior of others and his reactions to them.

TEMPER TEMPER...

What is temperament? Initial research into temperament was done in the 1950s by Alexander Thomas and Stella Chess. The word "temperament" is related to "temper." When someone has a good or bad temper, temper refers to a more changeable state of emotion or behavior; temperament on the other hand refers to the way a person tends to approach life. Is she easy going? Does she tend to create drama around new situations? Does she take time getting to know people? Furthermore, often the definition of temperament is seen as interchangeable with personality.

But temperament and personality are not the same thing. Temperament is a component of personality. Personality is also influenced by life events and comprises attitudes and belief systems that are the result of various life experiences, as well as innate views. The key issue is that while children's disruptive behavior is often seen, by parents and society alike, to be the result of poor parenting or a difficult environment, behavior can often be influenced by a child's temperament, as well as her parents' temperament. Scott's parents are a good example. His mother was more understanding of his needs because of their similar temperament, but may have overcompensated because of her own issues. Scott's father, on the other hand, did not understand, and the differences between his own attitude and temperament and Scott's, likely had a more negative impact on Scott and their relationship.

Some believe that children have to teach their parents about their temperament. This education often starts during the first days of a child's life. The more open the parent is to the cues, the better chance all have at understanding each other. The problem is that most parents are not educated on the idea of temperament. This chapter will address the issue of temperament and various aspects of it. We will also discuss the interplay between a child's and her parents' temperament and provide some strategies about how to remedy these issues when they do not gel. While we don't want you, as the parent, to take on blame and guilt, we do want you to see how you may play into these issues so you can take some accountability and improve your relationship with your children, as well as improving their self-esteem.

Types of Temperament

Children are born with their own personal style of interacting with or reacting to people, places, and things—their temperament. Researchers found that nine traits were present at birth and continued to influence development in important ways throughout life. These traits are: activity, rhythmicity, approach/withdrawal, adaptability, intensity, mood, persistence/attention span, distractibility, and sensory threshold. We will talk more about these later. The interaction of these nine traits contributes to the development of the three common types of temperament. Approximately 65 percent of all children fit one of these three patterns. Forty percent of all children are generally regarded as "easy or flexible," 10 percent are regarded as "difficult, active, or feisty," and the final 15 percent are regarded as "slow to warm up or cautious." The other 35 percent are a combination of these patterns. Figuring out which category(s) your children fall into is not as easy as an afternoon of observation. You have to be aware of daily variability. Over a period of time, it can become very clear.

- **Easy or flexible** children are generally calm, happy, and not easily upset. Their sleep and eating habits are regular. Because these children are so calm, parents and other adults tend to think that everything may be fine with them because it looks like nothing seems to bother them. This is not always the case. Parents need to set aside special times to talk with these children about frustrations and hurts because they won't demand or ask for it. This intentional communication is important to strengthen the relationship and find out what these children are thinking and feeling. You, as a parent, want to be sure to find the balance between distance and over-intrusion. Be willing to ask a few questions throughout the day. We think it is healthy to ask all kids at the end of the day, 1) What was the high point of your day? 2) What is something that you learned from today? And 3) Was there anything you felt hurt by? My child, an easy child, has been an absolute joy. If we had not allowed for structure or hadn't been sensitive to her needs, we could have had a totally different situation. Just because "easy" children don't make a lot of noise does not mean that they require less love and attention.

- **Difficult, active, or feisty** children are often fussy, cautious, and fearful of new people and situations. Their sleep and eating habits are likely to be more irregular, and they are easily upset by noise and commotion. They are often labeled as "high strung," and can be intense in their reactions. Because of their tendency to carry stress around, providing time for vigorous play to work off stored up energy and frustrations with some freedom of choice will allow these children to be successful in other areas of life. Preparing these children for activity changes by letting them know schedules, and using redirection when frustration mounts, will help these children transition from one place to another. This redirection will also help them find productive ways to deal with potential emotional outbursts. Helping them to learn to verbalize issues when they arise is important to keep stress from building. It is also helpful to review the day to see what went well and what could be learned, as well as what they still feel was not resolved. Parents really have to be ready to listen and hear in these circumstances, because issues in these (and any) children can escalate quickly if they don't feel heard.

- **Slow to warm up or cautious** children are relatively inactive and can be fussy. They tend to withdraw or react negatively to new situations, but their reactions gradually become more positive with continuous exposure. Consistency, while important with all kids, is crucial with them. Sticking to a routine and to your word will help build trust and a sense of stability. Also, give them time to establish relationships and adapt to new situations, in order to allow independence to unfold. These children definitely need to meet a babysitter a few times before they are left alone with them. The same goes with daycare settings, schools, camps, etc. Know that you may encounter stiff resistance to change at first, but stick to your guns and don't react harshly or tell them to suck it up. You want to make sure that you plan ahead for these children so that their life seems more stable and predictable to them.

Is it possible to alter a child's temperament? Not really, but you can help to alter their behavioral tendencies, although usually not to the extent of changing a fussy child into an easy one. However, with more understanding and patience between parent and child, challenging kids can become easier. In regards to "training the easy" out of a kid, over time, disruptions or traumas can definitely result in an easy child taking on more traits of a difficult or slow-to-warm-up child. At this point, changes have more of an effect on personality, because trust, safety, security, and confidence may be strongly affected.

THIS PORRIDGE IS JUST RIGHT...

Often, problems arise between parents and children because there may not be a good fit between the child's temperament and the parents' reaction to it. "Goodness of Fit" refers to the ability of the caregiver to understand and meet the needs of the child's temperament in order to minimize possible negative influences. Difficult and slow-to-warm-up children can learn to have an easier time with their environment, but it's the harmony, or the goodness of fit, between parent(s) and child that's important. In a circular fashion, the behavior of one influences the responses of the other.

Behavioral tendencies associated with temperament are not written in stone; family and other life experiences can make a difference. Let's look back to Scott. His father was not a good fit for Scott's slow-to-warm-up style. It felt overpowering to Scott and tended to result in Scott feeling crushed and his father feeling frustrated. His mother, on the other hand, understood Scott's difficulties because they were her own. She tried to meet his needs, but was still limited in knowing exactly how to help him best. In some ways, she may have coddled him a bit. It was this dance between

Scott, his mother, and his father that continued to feed the challenges. Had each parent been attuned to their own temperament issues, while taking into account Scott's temperament, much of the conflict could have been avoided. Parents who are attuned to their child's temperament and their own, and who can recognize their child's particular strengths and weaknesses, will find life in the family more harmonious. The better the match between your child's temperament and the demands or expectations of his environment (family, school, childcare setting), the better their relationships will be. Here are some thoughts to keep in mind as you work to improve this fit between you and your child.

- Be mindful of your child's temperament and respect her uniqueness without comparing her to others.

- Be mindful of your temperament and how the two might be affecting each other.

- Don't try to change your child's basic temperament. You might as well try to swim up a raging river. Adjust your natural responses when they clash with your child's. You have more experience and understanding in life than she does. Seek to find answers and present them with options.

- Communicate productively with your child. Explain your decisions and motives. Listen with an open mind to your child's points of view and encourage teamwork to generate solutions.

- Set reasonable limits to help your child develop self-control. Respect her opinions, while remaining firm on important limits.

- Being a good role model is crucial, because children learn by your example.

- Life is a dance. Enjoy it. If you can't, get some dance lessons.

Many children are diagnosed with various issues such as ADHD, depression, anxiety, oppositional defiance disorder, bipolar disorder, and other issues. The tendency to call extreme behaviors problematic is becoming more common, so many parents look for a quick fix. Sometimes the quickest place to look is no farther than a lack of fit between the temperaments of the child and parent(s). This is an extremely important issue to consider, and one you should talk about with a professional if you are considering any medical diagnosis.

Let's consider another example. Jenny was four years old and was acting out severe temper tantrums at home, at school and at friends' houses. Her parents were beside themselves and tried everything to deal with her. They resorted to yelling, screaming, and an occasional spanking. They also tried bargaining, and often gave up because Jenny's tantrums outlasted them.

When they came for help, they did not know where to turn. In the office, Jenny was a very likeable child and explored things readily. It was not until some limits were put in place that she reacted. At the first sign of guilt, shame, failure, and judgment by an adult, her behavior quickly turned. At first she was quiet, turned away and would not talk. The more we pushed for her to talk, the more she reacted and shut down. Within five minutes, she was in a full-blown tantrum. A better response was to hold her and rock her, reassuring her that she was okay. Although she was screaming to be released, this is what she wanted from her parents; their usual reactions, and the feeling of isolation that followed, were what fed the tantrums. She wanted to control everything and had to learn limits in a safe manner. After holding her until she calmed down a bit, she was then given to her parents to soothe. She responded favorably.

On the next visit, her mother stated that Jenny had had only two tantrums in the last week, a drastic decrease. During the session Jenny had another tantrum, thirty minutes of kicking, screaming, and pushing. We worked on holding her, remaining calm and reassuring, and gently told her that it was important for her to see that she was feeding the tantrum, and we urged her to stop. At no time was she yelled at. At the end of this tantrum, her behavior calmed and she was docile. I explained to her mother that sometimes kids almost go into a trance when they have a tantrum, and it has to run its course. How they respond during the tantrum can feed it, as much as how they respond before.

From a temperament standpoint, Jenny would be considered to be a difficult child. Her parents had not considered the concept of temperament, and their responses were not a great fit for her temperament. When we helped them to see some of the factors in their responses and reactions to her, and they changed their responses, her behavior improved dramatically and quickly.

TEMPERAMENT TRAITS

There are nine factors that researchers considered in defining what makes up different temperament types. Remember that while the three primary types listed previously capture sixty-five percent of all people, others don't fit the mold. The traits below are what make up the various aspects of temperamental behaviors. You might want to consider how your child falls into these individual traits rather than trying to determine her type. Often the more information we have, the better decisions we can make on how to respond.

- **Activity:** What is the frequency of your child's movement patterns? Is she always moving and doing something, or does she have a calmer, relaxed style? Some kids are moving from awakening until bedtime, and even then, they seem to run a few laps around their crib. Trying to throw a lasso around their activity level and always rein them in will only result in frustration for everyone. The key is to manage their energy. Give them some space and time to run around, even if you have to say, "I am going to give you five minutes to run in circles in this room or outside. Run as much as you want, and then I will ask you for some quiet time." Be prepared for the fact that your child will not stop right away and will need a little time to cool down from that. The goal is to help them learn limits and structure while managing their activity level.

- **Rhythmicity:** Do your kids tend to stick to patterns or schedules? Is the child regular in her eating and sleeping habits, or more variable? Some kids are like clockwork, and many pediatricians and advice books believe that as much as you can keep kids on a schedule, you want to do that for your sanity and theirs. However, some kids seem to go for variety. They may never want to eat when you want, and may not go to sleep when you ask. They may be easily influenced by excitement and external factors, as well as internal cues. They can be very hard to figure out. Work to keep to a schedule as much as you can, but don't be so rigid that you are forcing food down their throats or forcing them to sleep. Be willing to work with them, and they may be more willing to work with you. You also want to be careful to not give in to their wishes all the time. Ask them to eat something at dinner and save some for later as a snack. Make sure they are in their bed at a certain time, but if they like to stay awake a little later, make sure they have some books or something to entertain them. Keep the time limited, then lights out. If they are feeling tired the next day, talk about it to help them realize why you want to keep them on a schedule.

- **Approach/withdrawal:** How easily do they adapt to new people? Does your child become fearful around strangers, tending to shy away from new people or things, or is she comfortable with meeting new people? Some kids will approach and say hi to anyone. This can feel frightening to many parents. We all know the safety issues around this circumstance; however, be careful not to scare your child by telling her that everyone should be feared. Talk to her about asking permission to talk to strangers, and let her know that some people out there may be untrustworthy. Your job is to help her figure out how to learn to discern who is safe and who may not be. Some kids hide behind their parents, cry, or even run away from strangers. Many parents feel embarrassed by this, and some will even express anger toward their child. Give your child space and time to get used to others. If you are showing anger or frustration toward her in these instances, she may pair strangers with your anger and tension, further reinforcing her avoidance.

- **Adaptability:** How easily does your child adapt to changes in setting or structure? Can she adjust to changes in routines or plans easily or does she become agitated by transitions and changes in schedules? How does your child react when you have a babysitter come to the house, when you don't have the same thing for breakfast every day, when you can't find her favorite shirt, or when you go on vacation? Some children just don't do well with change. They move into the future kicking and screaming. On the other hand, many more kids almost prefer change and see the future full of exciting possibilities. From early in life, changes never seemed to affect them. These patterns of adaptability stay consistent through to adulthood. When children have a hard time adapting to change, the primary concern should be to determine what impact will any given change have on your child? Are you prepared for her potential reaction? From there, consider how you can make the change a positive thing. Can you present a small reward to serve as a distraction if she behaves well through the change? For example, I know a mother who put a few small surprises in a treasure box for her kids to open after she and her husband left on a trip. This way, the kids were focused on the treasure box and not their parents leaving. If this is not an option or your kids continue to react even with distraction, there are two schools of thought in how to deal with their negative behaviors. The first school is to forecast the change for them in advance. For major changes (trips, moves, guests visiting, school changes) allow at least one week or more for them to digest. For minor changes (clothes, meals, parent coming home late) let them know that day, as early as you might know. If they react emotionally, talk about it. Tell them that their reaction is a choice. If you let them know what to expect, they will trust that when change comes they will know. If they continue to react negatively, stay calm. Reacting harshly only reinforces their resistance to change. Continue to move forward with your plans. If they continue to respond negatively, you may need to use time-out or other non-physical consequences focused on their behaviors, not the change. The other school of thought is to present the change as it arises.

This way the child does not have a chance to get upset, and before they know it, it is over and done. You can talk about it with them afterward. While this may keep the drama down before the event, it does raise issues of trust. You have to remember that as a parent, you are preparing your child for a lifetime.

- **Intensity:** To what degree does your child react when feeling emotionally provoked? Does she react strongly to situations, either positive or negative, or is she calm and quiet? The issue of intensity can be a touchy one. Some kids will resort to head banging, hitting, scratching, punching, or any variety of other reactions, while others barely show any. Just because your child fails to react, though, does not mean she lacks feelings about a situation. You still want to talk with her and look for subtle changes in mood and behavior. If your child reacts intensely, be careful not to react with her. It will only feed the chaos. Stay calm. Many parents can fall into the trap of reacting even before their child reacts, and this feeds, escalates, or even provokes a reaction that may not otherwise have occurred. The first step is to keep your child safe from hurting herself. As noted in the example with Jenny, some young children who hurt themselves when they feel upset respond well to being held and rocked until they can calm down. But keep limits in place and focus on the emotions underneath the child's intense reactions. Talk through the reaction afterward, but don't bargain with her in an effort to calm her down. Be mindful that coddling or bargaining with children expressing negative behaviors may lead them to use these tactics to manipulate you or to gain leverage for getting their way. Keep your cool. Refrain from using negative labels such as "cry baby," "worrywart," or others. A child's abilities to develop and behave in acceptable ways are greatly determined by the adults in her life trying to identify, recognize, and respond to her behaviors. The following are some strategies provided by child development experts at the University of Wisconsin.

- "Intervene early—you can't teach kids something new when they are losing control. Wait until they have calmed down. Then point out what you saw and how they might

73

handle it differently. Try calming activities like baths, quiet time or reading stories.

• Regular exercise is effective in managing intensity in parents and kids, allowing them to "blow off steam."

• Repetitive motion, especially of the jaw, can be helpful. For young children, this might include sucking a bottle or pacifier, swinging, rocking, riding a rocking horse, or riding in a baby carrier. For older children, try drinking from a straw, chewing gum, swinging, rocking, jumping rope, or going for a walk.

• Deep breathing helps calm children who tend to hyperventilate or hold their breath when intensity rises. You can teach them to use deep breathing by blowing bubbles, blowing up balloons, pretending to blow out candles on a birthday cake, or counting to ten.

• Use humor, but avoid sarcasm or ridicule. Try doing the unexpected—give a silly response, use a different voice or use a funny mask or puppet. Have a family "I had a bad day" party with pizza and ice cream and let kids discuss their day.

• Change the scene in order to disconnect from the source of intensity. Encourage sensory activities. Use Play-Doh or Silly Putty; give back scratches or massage; dim lights in the room; use a sensory bucket filled with water, sand, or oatmeal. Other ideas include reading, playing dress up, or water play in the bath or sink.

• Provide a time and a quiet, comfortable space for cooling off. Teach kids ways to calm down, and that time-out is an opportunity to pull out of the action in order to rest, relax, and regain control. Help them feel comfortable taking a break."

- **Mood:** What is your child's typical mood? Does she tend to express a negative or positive outlook? Also, does she have frequent mood shifts, or is she even-tempered? Kids all go through moody periods in life—or sometimes they just wake up grumpy. Some kids see the proverbial cup half empty and others see it half full even when it is empty. These are very difficult attitudes to shift. Sometimes a child's first reaction might be negative. Try talking with her about other ways to look at her options and outcomes, and know that it will take some time to turn this tide. Consider that emotions underlie her moods and try to talk about those, and be willing to get help if the negative moods continue. Be careful not to criticize your child's mood or make comments about it—this only feeds the problem. Look at your own mood also. Many times parents don't want to see themselves as being in a negative mood, but more times than not, the apple falls close to the tree.

- **Persistence and attention span:** To what degree and for how long will your child stick with a task? Does she give up easily when she meets opposition or faces the possibility of failure, or does she keep on trying? Some kids have an attention span that lasts only a few seconds to a few minutes. This can continue throughout childhood and even into adulthood. However, just because a child has a short attention span does not mean she has an attention deficit disorder. Parents need to think of creative ways to maintain attention and use redirection to get children back on task. Patience and consistency are important. Teach children the value of following-through, and work with rewards that may start with a completed short or easy task, and then generalize to longer tasks. Teaching sequencing and order is also important with these kids. Cleaning a room is not just one task, it is a number of tasks in a series. Start early to help your kids learn persistence and follow-through, and know that children's attention spans are typically very short, growing longer as their brains develop. If you have concerns, talk with a professional.

- **Distractibility:** How easily is your child distracted from a task? Is she easily distracted from what she is doing or can she stay focused, even with other distractions? Many factors can influence distractibility from time to time, but some kids are more distractible than others. Just as with attention spans, parents often feel concerned that if their child is distractible, she must have an attention deficit disorder. This is not the case. With ADD/HD, both attention and distraction need to be considered as well as other criteria, and the problems must be causing significant impairment in two or more settings. Some kids are distractible in certain situations, like when watching television or before the holidays, for example. If you pay attention to the cues for a child's distraction, sometimes you can solve the problem. Focus on patiently redirecting her to the task at hand and be consistent.

- **Sensory threshold:** To what degree is your child bothered by stimuli? Do things such as loud noises, bright lights, smells, fabrics or food textures bother her, or does she not seem bothered by these things? Do others get on her nerves easily? Does she complain about tags in her clothes, the feel of dirt on her hands? Many of us have our little quirks that can result in sensory overload in one specific modality, auditory, olfactory, or tactile. Some of us feel overloaded by a number of sensations and others are bothered by just a few. We have known many people who are bothered by tags in their clothes to the extent that they need them cut out of their shirts. We can all probably think of a child who has a low pain tolerance, one who cries or causes a scene every time she is touched. The difficulty often becomes knowing whether or not she truly perceives the situation so painfully, or is just trying to get attention.

After numerous experiences of their child's seeming overreaction, parents may grow weary and can respond with little or no compassion, sometimes even making comments such as, "suck it up," or "I'll give you something to cry about," or even calling her a "cry baby." These comments only make the situation worse and damage her trust in you. Though parents sometimes feel frustrated when their kids have these sensory issues, whether it is clothes, textures in food, or smells, it is important to maintain your patience and understand that we all may feel things differently. If your child is faking her response or wanting attention, you will figure it out sooner or later. Kids often slip up when they are not sincere. The tears may all but disappear when they get what they want, or they may make faces at a sibling as they complain that the sibling hurt them. Be careful not to react with anger if you find that your child is faking. We often find that stories like *The Boy Who Cried Wolf* come in handy in these circumstances. Also, it gives you an opportunity to talk about lying and how it affects trust, especially when it comes to a child's physical safety. Finally, if your child seems to have a low sensory threshold, talk to your pediatrician to get some feedback.

As you have read through these temperament traits, how many stand out to you that may pertain to your child? How many may pertain to you? Does this discussion help you to see your child and yourself differently? Can you see how the two of you may bump heads, given these traits? Some of the traits that may have seemed annoying may be part of her internal wiring. As you can see, not everything your child does is because of what you did or did not do, and determining where your role lies can be tricky. We will now turn to our discussion of personality.

PUTTING THE PERSON IN PERSONALITY

As was discussed in the beginning of the chapter, personality is often an extension of temperament. The behaviors we begin with often stick with us throughout our lives and can become enhanced with life experiences. Many times people have a difficult time distinguishing temperament from personality. Consider temperament as similar to the ability to speak a language. Children are able to make noises from the time they're born, and begin speaking with chatter and echolalic patterns (i.e., la la la, ba ba ba, da da da…). As they grow up, their unique voice tone is determined by their physical attributes. Personality also involves the language they learn to speak (French, English, Chinese), which is in turn influenced by the region where they grow up. Even more, the phrases they use may be unique to the friends and family they spend time with, as well as their own idiosyncrasies. Taken together, the ability to speak, their tonal qualities, the language they use, and how they use it makes that individual unique.

In personality, some unknown factors also contribute to the development of personality. For example, some children live in the most difficult environment—with parents who were abusive, family members who abused each other, parental employment problems, and addiction issues—and grow to be hard-working, ethical, moral and peaceful adults with integrity and honor. There are also situations where the opposite is true. Impeccable and honorable parents and siblings, yet one child in that family develops a somewhat deviant personality. This is part of the unknown, and we are unsure if anyone can truly explain it.

How much of an influence do you have on your child's personality? The jury is still out. It is no mystery that your attitudes and beliefs can become your child's attitudes and beliefs. On the other hand, if your child was born with a more willful temperament, your child may demonstrate beliefs opposite yours, and she may develop an oppositional personality style. Studies on twins demonstrate many similarities in personality traits, but environmental influences are strong. Results of these studies indicate that genetics account for about 40-50 percent of the differences in personality traits, while environment accounts for about 30 percent. Forty to 50 percent of variance may not seem like very much, but statistically it is very large, when one considers all of the other possible influences.

Some of the case studies have demonstrated that twins raised apart have similar behavioral patterns like chewing fingernails, and being neat freaks or more messy, and have similar preferences in cigarettes, cars, clothes, and other items. Other research has found that temperament is very stable and relatively unchangeable throughout the life span. Finally, some research has found that antisocial behavior may be influenced genetically up to a whopping 80 percent. So, if you have an individual(s) in your family with a history of anti-social or aggressive behavior, there might be an increased risk for this behavior in your child (all the more reason to seek help at early signs of a problem).

Genetic research has found that human DNA has six billion base pairs on the chromosomes. There is a 99.9 percent overlap in all of our genes; only 0.1 percent separates us all from being genetically identical. Obviously, the overlap in chromosomes determines many of our physical similarities, but as you can see from these few examples with twins, much more of our personality—and our beliefs, attitudes, and behaviors—may be determined by our genetics than we realized.

Some of the implications of these results could lead us to think that our job as parents and guiding agents of our children is overrated. We could consider that our kids' attitudes, choices, likes and dislikes, and ultimately even their personalities are determined at conception in that magical cocktail of chromosomes and DNA, and nothing we can do will change much. Yes, there is much truth to this. Even your child's sense of humor (and the possible lack thereof) may be determined at birth. Sometimes, even with almost no contact with related family members, there may be an overlap over generations in almost identical mannerisms, behaviors, and attitudes. I have found it interesting to notice the similarity in sense of humor and mannerisms between myself and my nephews. Both of my sisters often call their sons by my name because of this.

If this is the case, then what is the point of writing a parenting book? Other than your genetic influence, your behavior and parenting style should be a minimal influence…right? Well, yes and no. The biggest piece of the puzzle in this equation is that your actions moderate your child's genetic tendencies. In other words, understanding your child's temperament and personality development can greatly influence how you and she react to each other and the world. And as has been alluded to and will be reiterated again and again, your relationship with her can profoundly impact her relationship with others, now and in the future, and by understanding your child's temperament you can help both yourself and her to learn to respond differently. This, in turn, will affect the development of her personality and her attitudes toward you and the world.

To illustrate this, let's consider some research. One research study involved an evaluation of temperament and a nine-week education program for mothers, teaching them what temperament meant to them and their children, and what to do about their behaviors. One session also helped parents devise consequences for behaviors that were unique to their child. The parents were also given "homework" to practice the behavior techniques they learned in class. Parents in this class reported greater satisfaction in relationships with their children, feeling more competent as parents, and experiencing more attachment to their children. Mothers also reported reduced feelings of anxiety and depression, and they felt less restricted by the demands of parenting.

In another study, the mother of twins responded more negatively to one twin than the other when they were working on a task. The child responded to more negatively was more negative, noncompliant, and more active, and responded less positively, less responsively, and less on-task. On the other hand, the child who received more positive feedback behaved more on-task and was more responsive, more compliant, and less active. Sadly enough, this is not an uncommon situation, and the results are often tragic. We have often found that parents are not able to be honest with themselves about how they may treat their children differently, because they don't want to feel their guilt and shame.

Another study looked at the "goodness of fit" between parent and child and found that the poorer "the fit" between the child's temperament and the parent's response, the more behavioral difficulties the child experienced and the less persistent she was when trying to complete tasks.

Finally, Kaiser-Permanente instituted a temperament education program for parents to attend when their child is four-months old. They receive written materials and information aimed at anticipating potential problems. Further support is also offered to those families that are having temperament-related behavioral problems. Video and Internet-based education is also provided. Results were somewhat limited but indicated that children of the parents who attended this program had fewer visits to primary care providers. Is it possible that children who feel happier and more content become ill less often? Increasingly, research is showing that emotional stress causes a stress to the immune system, resulting in the possibility of more illnesses.

The sum total of all of these studies reveals that what we are born with can be modified. With diligence and attention to the needs of our children, we can have a positive influence on them. Clearly, the results of the above studies indicate that how a person is treated in the environment has a large influence on her behavior, stress level, and subsequent physical health. The long-term implications are that understanding your child's temperament may affect the development of her personality and world view. The uniqueness of her temperament and yours must be understood in order to have the most favorable impact.

In the field of psychology, we know that there are critical periods in a child's physical and emotional development that can influence their personality development. For example, Erik Erikson, who lived from 1902 to 1994, identified various developmental stages of social-emotional development that theoretically needed to be successfully resolved in order to move to the next phase of development. These stages were based, in part, on Sigmund Freud's theories. Some of these stages are: Trust vs. Mistrust, Autonomy vs. Shame, Initiative vs. Guilt, and others.

These stages of development occur at certain age ranges, and it is believed that if a child does not successfully resolve a certain stage, she may stay stuck in that phase of growth. It is thought that these unresolved phases may influence personality development. These theories of development have some basis and can occasionally be helpful to consider therapeutically. For parents, Erikson's stages may be helpful to review to see what factors may need to be considered. Other psychological theories to consider are Piaget's Stages of Cognitive Development, and Kohlberg's Theory of Moral Development. All of this information can be found on the Internet using search terms. While we merely introduce this, we highly recommend that you review the information to help in understanding your child's development.

While our family can be a significant influence on personality development, society also affects us. Researchers often look at how cultures behave collectively and how aspects of culture affect personality. Northern European countries and the USA are considered to be more individualistic cultures in that they put more emphasis on individual needs and accomplishments. They are more "me" based. Asian, African, Central American, and South American countries are referred to as collectivist cultures that focus on membership in a larger group, such as a family, tribe, or nation. In this type of culture, members value cooperation more than competition.

Similarly, American children are usually raised in ways that encourage self-reliance and independence. Children are more likely to be included in making decisions about some of their choices in day to day events. Children are also given an allowance to learn how to manage money, often in exchange for completing tasks around the house to teach them how to be responsible for themselves. On the other hand, children in China and other Asian countries are usually taught to think and act as a member of their family, often resulting in a suppression of their own wishes if their wants are considered to be in conflict with the needs of the parents, who are more likely to determine the needs of the family. Independence and self-reliance are viewed as selfish and as a loss of control by the parent, which is seen as an insult to the elders.

Although these and other differences in how children are raised throughout the world result in different personality dynamics, there are also some similarities in child rearing. Boys and girls are treated differently to some extent in all societies. However, in some societies, girls are taught that they are inferior to boys, and in others they are treated with honor. Regardless, boys and girls receive different messages from their parents and others in terms of what is appropriate or inappropriate for them to do in life. The way they are treated, the way they are taught to treat each other, the toys they are given, how they are taught in school, and what they see in the world around them help them to prepare for their future in jobs fitting their gender. When children don't follow the prescribed norms, they are often ridiculed by family, adults, and other peers, often resulting in feelings of rejection, inadequacy, sadness, or other emotions.

An important thing to understand about personality is that much of it not only pertains to attitudes and beliefs, but also that those attitudes and beliefs affect the way we perceive our emotions, which influences how we use them. The manner in which we use our emotions can mean the difference between being liked or disliked by others, and being perceived as strong or weak, good or bad, a winner or a loser. This is the same for our children. How you reward and punish their expressions of emotion could be contributing to patterns that you had not intended. Let's consider an example.

Jennifer was always a little slow to warm up to people, often clinging to her mother, Martha. Martha was able to stay home with Jennifer until she began school. Because of this, Martha often kept her close by and did not expose her to many experiences. When Jennifer began pre-school, Martha volunteered as an assistant in order to be close to her daughter. If Martha was not able to be there for her, Jennifer often cried and was inconsolable by others. When Jennifer started kindergarten, she cried when Martha dropped her off. Even when Martha stayed as long as she could, Jennifer often secluded herself from the rest of the class and behaved quite irritably when Martha left. The other kids in the class tried to play with her, but she seldom wanted to play. At home, her parents almost never went out together because Jennifer had prolonged tantrums if her mother left. Her father often felt frustrated with her behavior because he could not console her. Sometime they punished Jennifer because of her emotionality.

This behavior went on for some time. As she went through the school years, Jennifer became more and more avoidant. She did not want to go to sleep-overs, and the other kids in school did not ask her. When she did have friends over, they often left early because they had conflicts, and Jennifer would shut down. She didn't have many friends, and when she did not get her way she threw tantrums. By fifth grade, she was having a lot of difficulties with her peers, her mother felt burdened with her, and her father had very little interactions with her.

You may see, in this example, the interaction between a child's temperament and her developing personality. A number of issues influenced her behaviors and world view. The primary issue was that while her mother meant well in being home with her, she was somewhat coddling and did not give Jennifer the chance to grow as an individual. In many ways, her mother's need to feel needed and important prevented Jennifer from being exposed to situations early on that would help her develop a sense of independence and competence. Her mother often felt guilty when Jennifer cried, so Martha tended to her and all but excluded Jennifer's father. In essence, the only person Jennifer trusted was her mother, and that was what Martha wanted due to her own need to be needed. Because of this, Jennifer avoided others, and as others reacted negatively to her because of her behavior, it reinforced her idea that others were not safe.

Children need a safe base to explore life from, and it is important to encourage them to go out into the world and allow other people in their life to comfort them. Had Martha been willing to let others, like Jennifer's father, other family members, or sitters, give her comfort—with Martha present—Jennifer would have been able to feel safe and comfortable with others. Then Martha could have tried to distance herself more and more, increasing the time she was away from Jennifer and exposing her to different situations with and without her there to build her confidence and comfort level with change.

Taking Jennifer to school before school started, or even to walk through the school in the springtime and/or play in the classroom, meet the teacher, or play on the playground, may have helped Jennifer get used to the environment. Slow-to-warm-up kids require time to anticipate change. They take time and patience; Martha's unintentional coddling was overkill. The result was the development of greater difficulties over time that were very difficult to change.

In this situation, helping Martha to look at her own needs and issues is crucial. It is likely that Martha had issues with boundaries, and Jennifer was working just as hard to take care of Martha's feelings as Martha was working at trying to make Jennifer happy. These scenarios happen more times than we realize. Again, the parents' ability to be painfully honest is the key to resolving these issues, for everyone's benefit. Furthermore, others in the society around Jennifer reinforced these patterns and beliefs because no one tried to understand the behavior. It is likely that those who did see what was going on and tried to talk to Martha were dismissed, because of her denial toward her contribution to the problem. The long-term consequence of this can be the development of a care-taking, martyr-type personality that feels dependent on others for support, and also a feeling of resentment due to feeling that they have to put their needs aside for others. The behavior may look like someone who can never feel happy in a relationship and may have emotional outbursts when they feel unappreciated and taken advantage of.

Personality Shmersonality

Many of us are looking for some predictability and understanding with our children and with others in our lives. We often feel that if we knew why they did what they did and how they might behave, given their world view, it would help us to make different choices. A great deal of research has been devoted to the development of personality inventories.

Some of these inventories or tools (the Minnesota Multiphasic Personality Inventory or MMPI, for example) are focused on finding emotional problems and difficulties that may arise in personality dynamics and psychological problems. The MMPI helps professionals understand where a person might be having some difficulties in the way she is approaching life, and how that might be causing emotional and/or relational problems. Other instruments (the Myers-Briggs Type Inventory MBTI, for example) are developed to help define differences between people and understand their likes, dislikes, trends, and tendencies.

The MBTI can be used in a variety of settings and has even been adapted for use with children. It has been used in family settings in order to help all family members figure out how their personalities may blend and differ. Instruments like this can help define where families may be having some of their difficulties, based on their similarities and differences. The Myers-Briggs helps to identify four basic dynamics in personality. These are **I**ntroversion-**E**xtraversion, **I**ntuitive-**S**ensing, **T**hinking-**F**eeling, and **J**udging-**P**erceiving. The various combinations of traits (ENTP, ISTJ, ESFP…) result in descriptions of people that can be very telling about their personality and how they may respond toward others, and in different settings. These traits tend to be stable over time, often beginning in childhood and solidifying in adulthood.

More information on these inventories can be found in many informative books on personality inventories and on the Internet..

An interesting research finding regarding personality is that although you may think that family members would have similar personality traits, results have found that, when the effects of genetics and heredity are removed, not as many similarities exist as was thought. This suggests that each person is unique, and that although we grow up in similar environments and have similar genetics, each of us is unique. What you, as a parent, want to take from this is the knowledge that you need to consider the uniqueness of each of your children when giving them guidance and not assume that they will think or respond as would you, your spouse, or your other children. Be willing to recognize each child's uniqueness in a positive way. A child's personality is something that can blossom into a beautiful adult, or it can be stepped on and never be allowed to flower.

SUMMARY

We hope that you have begun to understand the concepts of temperament and personality. These two concepts, though often confused, are unique. Because it seems as though we are born with many traits, and that genetics plays a large part in our development, we could feel that our future is cast on the day we were born. And in fact, research with twins raised apart demonstrates how many of our day-to-day traits are genetically influenced. We want you to consider the influences of genetics in many behaviors. Too many times, parents blame themselves for too much, when some of it is out of their hands. However, parents have to understand and be willing to recognize the ways and instances when they *do* contribute to an unproductive situation involving their children or other members of the family.

We want you to take this information and consider the factors that influence your temperament and that of your child in the context of your ability to parent successfully. The types of temperament (easy, difficult, and slow-to-warm-up) and temperament traits such as Activity, Rhythmicity, Approach/Withdrawal, Adaptability, Intensity, Mood, Persistence, Attention span, Distractibility, and Sensory Threshold are all important to consider when identifying the challenges your child may experience. Through the examples provided, you can see how a poor fit between parent and child can result in an exacerbation of problems. A case can be made for consistency, patience, and understanding, and for the necessity for a parent to consider her own past and present when dealing with a child.

And while it is true that genetics predisposes us a great deal, we also hope that you realize how much you can moderate your children's behaviors. Taking into account the various traits of temperament and how they influence your child can help you to develop more productive strategies to deal with unproductive behaviors. Return to the example of Scott in the beginning of the chapter. He was somewhat slow-to warm up, resulting in a "goodness of fit" issue with his father, some overcompensation by his mother, and difficulties in how he was treated by others. Over time, these challenges likely influenced his personality development. The approach to life he developed could have been altered if his parents had approached the situation differently. The longer the environment remains the same, the longer it takes to change some components of personality. Scott's temperament issues may have predisposed him to always take a slower approach to new situations, but if he felt more confident in himself and his environment, life might not feel so overwhelming.

While temperament is genetically influenced, personality is the result of the interaction of temperament and environmental factors. Life experiences, family issues, societal factors, and other events contribute to our personality. This is where you, as a parent, may have the most impact. What we want you to take from this chapter is an understanding of the power you have to influence your child's personality development and moderate her temperament. Finding the similarities and differences between you and your child, and respecting her individuality, are hugely important for growth—hers and yours. Remember that your job is to raise your child, not control her. As you will by now have recognized, a child's behaviors are often trying to communicate things to you, not make your life miserable. When parents don't listen, the noises get louder. The unfortunate outcome is that no one ends up listening.

You have the power to understand more about your child, not to mold her into what you want but into what is in her best interest.

In the next two chapters we will discuss the process of attachment, which can be a very important influence on personality development. First we will address a "normal" process of attachment and what you can do to foster a healthy attachment. Then we deal with issues that occur when attachment is disrupted. We feel that both of these chapters are critical. We believe that childhood issues are based in subtle attachment problems that have been ignored and/or overlooked. How you—a father or mother—attach to your child can have a profound effect on how your child views relationships. Temperament issues can influence attachment, and the quality of your child's attachment to you will influence some of their temperament traits. This book builds on concepts to help you see a bigger picture in your role as a parent. We hope that you will continue to keep in mind these issues of personality and temperament as you read on.

⊂⊃ **Chapter 5** ⊂⊃
ATTACHMENT... FOR THE HEALTH OF IT

This chapter is devoted to the concept of how children and parents emotionally attach to each other and how to do that in a more healthy way. If people cannot form meaningful attachments, how can they develop healthy relationships? Without attachments to things or people, there would likely be chaos. The strength of our attachments teaches us many things in life, most importantly it teaches us how to love. In an earlier chapter we saw that genetics to a large extent determines temperament and influences personality, with environment playing a minor role. Conversely, environment greatly influences quality of attachment, and parents are the strongest environmental influence in a child's life. Additionally, temperament can influence how easy or hard it may be to form an attachment.

Chapter 6 will continue our discussion of attachment; however, it will address the more challenging side. Many issues related to attachment may pertain to some of the challenges that you and/or your children may have. While it is important to understand how to form a healthy attachment, it is just as important to see the forces that can erode an attachment and/or prevent it from forming. We have broken attachment into two chapters so that we can focus on both aspects and give them the attention they deserve. Keep in mind that we feel that the interaction of temperament/personality and attachment is possibly the most critical issue to consider when parenting your children.

Development of Secure Attachment

Attachment to a parent or caregiver forms over time, not just in the first year or two of life but often continuing into adulthood. However, while attachment is a constantly evolving state, critical issues in early life are crucial to healthier attachment later on. It is crucial that a secure bond of trust between the infant and caregiver develops during the early stages of the child's infancy. This strengthens the relationship and attachment between them. Variations in attachment do not always cause problems later in life, but they contribute to perceptions that influence the child's attitudes and beliefs about the world. A person's developmental history and current situations influence behavior. Past experiences, whether we consciously remember them or not, can influence how we feel about our current situation. Our past experiences influence how we feel in the present.

There are at least two opposing lines of reasoning on attachment. One says that most children are resilient, and as long as parents are consistent, attachment problems should not exist. The other camp would say that if some aspects of attachment are missed, and/or there is trauma and/or neglect, this could result in difficulties. Both groups support their beliefs with research, but often people see what they want to see and support their beliefs only with data that supports them, ignoring other input. In reality it seems that the most accurate approach is a combination of the two beliefs. It is true that most children are resilient; however, events in their early life can influence relationships throughout their life, even if they cannot remember these events. The core of these attachment issues relates to trust, safety, security, and the ability to form deep meaningful attachments to others.

Attachment involves a series of exchanges between parent and child that enables the development of a sense of trust, closeness, safety, and security. Children form a more healthy attachment when there are personal, intimate interactions between the child and caregiver, and a loving bond develops. The parent offers many things to the child such as love, support, safety, and comfort, and the child, in return, offers love to the caregiver. This equitable give and take is crucial to the child developing a sense of self and sense of empowerment. The consistency and quality of the care offered to the child is very important. Children can easily overcome a few missed opportunities at having their needs met, if they have secure attachments to caregivers.

Healthy attachments also require a stable interactive presence with a caregiver. The child needs to develop a sense of a secure home base from which it can explore, as he grows older. Research shows that children will not develop healthy attachments without a stable and interactive presence. However, children who do not receive proper care and treatment, even those who are mistreated, will form attachments, but the attachment is unhealthy and flawed. This lack of attachment and/or unhealthy or flawed attachment can affect a person for a lifetime.

As a parent and child develop a relationship, the caregiver learns to identify cues from the child. The child may cry, smile, grunt, or any number of things, and the caregiver learns what these signals mean and then responds to the child. Thus, the infant develops trust and security, which contributes to the health of the attachment. Through experience and exposure to each other, something that we could call a "sixth sense" can develop between our kids and us. Contrarily, if a child feels that the people and environment around him are not meeting his needs, she won't develop trust in either the caregivers or surroundings. This can lead children to feel responsible for their own survival.

Differences in attachment are not solely due to traits of our children or us. Instead, they develop through time and experience between the two. Early experiences are important, and parent/child interaction from early childhood affects the development of children's relationships with peer groups from an early age and throughout their entire lives.

Time is in short supply for many of us. We may believe that as long as we feed, change, and bathe an infant, we are meeting his basic needs. After all, what else does an infant do other than eat, sleep, and, well . . . you know? Some parents feel that as long as someone addresses those needs, it doesn't matter who. Many parents feel torn between trying to make ends meet and giving as much as they can to their children. Meeting these needs is just the tip of the iceberg. When children are born they start learning almost immediately, and their environment sets the stage. Infants learn from those who care for them, and they develop a sense of how the rest of the world will treat them based upon these experiences. If children feel safe from the threats of the world as they develop and grow, they can then venture out and learn more. If children do not feel that they are a significant and valuable part of this world, their ability and willingness to learn may suffer.

The degree of interaction and love they receive from the world is critical. We communicate love through the process of feeding, changing, and bathing. Love also comes through communication, play, holding, caressing, comforting, singing, and some would say that it even comes through a sending of energy or the intent of loving emotion. All of these factors contribute to a healthier attachment.

BUILDING BLOCKS

As mentioned earlier, the attachment between us and our children sets the stage for all their relationships in life. After parental relationships, the next stage of development involves forming relationships and attachments with peers. These relationships are interdependent. Early experiences influence and add to later experience. In other words, the health of our relationships with our children contributes to the health of the development of their relationships with their peers. Relationships with peers affect future relationships with spouses, bosses, co-workers, neighbors, and even our children's children. So, a child's relationships with peers do not replace the parent-child relationship: they complement each other. The quality and health of each of these relationships predicts a person's social skills throughout life, although temperament and personality will also be an important influence. Early relationships affect self-reliance and the ability to show empathy for others later in life. If our kids have a healthy parental attachment, the chances increase that they will have healthier, more intimate relationships later in life. Healthier peer attachment predicts better skills in social interactions.

In the mental health field, some feel that children should not be coddled, overindulged and spoiled, and others feel that children can never get enough love and support. Evidence to support both attitudes exists. Caregivers can over-stimulate a child and try to meet every need leading to the child feeling a sense of entitlement. These situations have more to do with the caregiver's issues rather than the child's needs; infants do not ask for indulgence. The question is, "How much love is too much to give?" It's all about understanding limits. Love, trust, and consistency do not spoil children or their ability to form secure attachments; and sensitivity to a child's needs grows through experience and practice. Through these experiences we may raise our awareness of what love means to us. That may be the most important lesson our children can teach us.

Fears and anxieties surround our experience of having and raising children. Can the level of parents' anxiety affect the attachment process? Absolutely, and as we have discussed, it also influences temperament. To develop a healthy attachment, the emotions of the caregiver must be addressed. The caregiver is a model for the infant and represents all other humans he may come into contact with. Caregivers also serve as mirrors as infants develop awareness and express emotions. If we feel anxious, fearful, and nervous when interacting with an infant, he can sense these feelings at some level of awareness. Infants do not have words to communicate so emotion is likely the first avenue of communication. Underlying emotions are hard to mask and hide, and children may be much more aware of them than we know.

Periodic fears and anxieties are common in parents, and they are not of great concern. However, the enduring anxieties, fears, and worries, both obvious and underlying, are more important. Children are resilient, but if a caregiver has a chronic state of fear or anxiety, it could contribute to an insecure and anxious attachment, which can then affect resiliency. Showing no reaction is just as unhealthy, though. Emotions are crucial to attachment, and while love is the most important, the goal is to find a balance. Maintaining a sense of underlying calmness and peacefulness when interacting with a child, is critical to forming a healthy attachment. Being aware of where our fears, frustrations, and/or angers may lie and working them through with someone can help us to achieve this balance.

People learn through the interactions of behavior, and it follows that infants learn when they sense a caregiver's anxiety. Let's assume that our children can sense the emotions of the people around them. More specifically, let's consider that our children come to understand what each emotion means, even before they can speak. And since infants may feel a caregiver's fear, anxiety, or anger each time they interact, these emotions can influence the child. Whether your child is easy, difficult, or slow-to-warm-up, temperament will influence this to a degree.

How do a caregiver's emotions affect the developing child's sense of self? There is no way to measure this, but often our reactions to children have no relation to what they say or do. Instead, we are reacting to our own issues...but a child has no way of knowing the difference. For this reason, it is very important for caregivers to be aware of their feelings when interacting with children.

Infants often respond to the voice and sounds of their caregiver. Children tend to learn to associate a certain sound, or other sensory input, with some following action or other elements in their environment, especially with a parent or other caregiver. It is important to think of the sounds that caregivers make in terms of voice and tone, abruptness, softness or loudness. Sounds and smells (especially perfume) can create associations a child will keep into adulthood.

TALK THE TALK

Talking to an infant is a very important part of forming attachment. This involves an exchange of energy between the two people and exposes the infant to the sounds of the caregiver(s), which breeds familiarity and comfort. Try to consider these things when talking to infants and small children.

1. Use descriptive words. Many professionals feel that it is important, when talking to children, to use proper terms

rather than slang or more immature language. Remember that they are learning their language from us.

2. Consider the voice inflection of your speech. Be aware of tone, (happy, calm, stern, angry, abrupt, etc.) pitch (higher and more excitable or lower and more soothing), loudness or softness, pace (fast or slow).

3. Pay attention to the times when you call the child by name and use nicknames, even when they are infants and toddlers. Many parents address their children by their first and middle names when the child is in trouble. Even as adults, some people get shivers up and down their spine when they hear their first and middle name called. Some nicknames feel demeaning to a child, and sometimes children outgrow a nickname. If a child does not like a nickname, stop using it. Give children the power to determine their identity and respect their wishes.

4. Singing to a child can be very soothing, whether it is at bedtime, in the car, or while doing other things; it lets them know we are there and that comfort is close by.

LOOK INTO MY EYES

Eye contact and gazing is important with infants and children. Think about what people do when they feel shame, guilt, mistrust, etc., emotions that result in a feeling of weakness…people look away. And we often look for reassurance in someone else's eyes. For these reasons, eye contact is a factor in forming healthy attachments. Pay attention to the extent to which eye contact affects your feelings of comfort, safety, love, and empowerment.

In some cultures, and in the animal world, eye contact is a sign of disrespect and a direct challenge to authority. Children gain empowerment through a healthy dose of eye contact, and we should look our children in the eye when speaking to them. However, it's not a good idea to stare at children, since you don't want to violate their boundaries and you don't want them to learn to stare at other people.

WALKING THE LINE

Understanding boundaries is critical to developing a healthy attachment. Failure to respect boundaries is a mistake often made by intrusive or overly stimulating parents. Abuse, neglect, coddling, competitiveness, conspiring, teasing, flirting behavior, and outright sexual abuse are all boundary violations that will negatively influence attachment. The results of some of these boundary violations do not begin to emerge until the child is older, but the roots often begin in infancy. Research shows that children whose boundaries were violated demonstrated boundary violations with their own children. It is very important to support the independence of a child, rather than encourage him to behave as the parent does.

Refer to a child as "he" or "she" instead of "we." For example, a mother may say of her child, "We still aren't using the toilet, and sometimes we still wet the bed." This can be very destructive to the child's sense of self, and the child can take advantage of this situation by avoiding responsibility for his actions. (In this example, it would also be important to consider that communicating issues about sensitive issues such as potty training or bedwetting, or similar topics that may feel humiliating or embarrassing to the child, to others in the family or outside of the family is also a boundary violation.)

Coddling is sometimes a tough issue to define because parents who coddle often see themselves as very loving and protective of their children. From their perspective, they feel that they are just giving their child what he needs, but others often view the parent as overprotective, overindulgent, and preventing the child from living life and sometimes not acknowledging the child's failures or short-comings. It is important to be willing to give your child space to explore, but also set limits for him. It is also important to give children appropriate feedback on their performance. Finding the balance of constructive feedback and compliments can be difficult, because you also have to weigh in your child's temperament. You can't prevent your child from experiencing painful feelings, but you can help him to understand them and talk about them.

Meal time is an important part of family time and an ongoing attachment. This is a time to talk, share, and catch up. There is ample research that demonstrates the benefits of family meals. It can also be an important part of setting limits with your kids and sending an important message that even if your family is busy, some family time is a priority.

TIPS AND FACTS

1. Be responsive to your child's needs. For example, our rule of thumb is if your infant is crying for more than ten minutes see if something is wrong or if the child needs something. Sometimes what is thought to be colic is not always colic. *The Happiest Baby on the Block* by Harvey Karp is a great book/DVD to use as a resource for difficult infants.

2. Be aware of your emotions when interacting with your child.

3. Talk to your kids even if it is to just hear yourself talk about what you are doing when they are infants.

4. Be conscious of your voice tone and body language.

5. Remember to use and maintain eye contact with your child when talking with them, no matter what age he may be.

6. Be consistent.

7. Set firm boundaries and limits.

8. Eat meals together.

9. Remember that attachment is a lifelong process.

BEHAVIORALLY, RESEARCH SUPPORTS THE FOLLOWING OBSERVATIONS ABOUT CHILDREN WITH SECURE ATTACHMENTS.

1. They are more resilient to change.

2. They show higher levels of self-confidence and independence.

3. They often form good friendships with other peers and more intimate relationships with significant others later in life.

4. They tend to be better able to learn.

5. Others view them as being more likable.

6. They show fewer signs of psychological dysfunction throughout life.

The task of helping your children develop secure attachment does take work, and the rewards last a lifetime, not only for your children but often for their children, as well.

☙ Chapter 6 ☙
ATTACHMENT GONE WRONG

We will now address the other side of the attachment issue. We mentioned some of the difficulties that can occur with attachment in our last chapter, and we will spend some time addressing additional issues here. While there are obvious issues that can affect your child's trust, we will discuss a number of issues that may be overlooked with children that can impact them in any period of their development. We will address these issues through the story of David.

Then we will discuss Reactive Attachment Disorder (RAD). While RAD may not be as much of a concern in most families, the reason that we discuss it is due to our view that attachment is not about having a problem with it or not, it is about a continuum from having a healthy attachment to more problematic issues. For foster and adoptive families, this chapter will be of special significance, because of the more common occurrence of attachment issues and disorders in foster and adoptive children.

All of the information in this chapter will help you understand the most critical issues and the seriousness of the concept of attachment. It is important for us, as parents, to understand the issues related to attachment. As we have tried to impress, a child's age is immaterial when considering attachment issues. Even minor attachment issues that occurred in infancy and early childhood may not become evident until later years, sometimes as late as adulthood. In reading the forthcoming story of David, you'll probably see similarities and differences to your own situations. However, the key is to consider all of the subtle issues that may have contributed to David's behaviors.

THE STORY OF DAVID

David was twelve years old and the middle of three children. He had an older brother and a younger sister, and they were all about two years apart. Their parents had divorced two years prior, and the children lived with their mother and visited their father about one weekend a month. David's mother sought help for David because of behavioral problems that were increasing at home including problems at school starting about a year before our first meeting.

David had been diagnosed with ADHD and a few psychiatrists had thrown around the word "bi-polar." To summarize David's patterns of behavior, he lost interest in school, abused animals, manipulated his teachers, and threw tantrums and outbursts when he failed to get his way. While "bi-polar" and ADHD may explain a couple of the symptoms that David expressed, we need to look at the bigger picture with the family to more accurately see some things that may have contributed to his behavioral issues.

David's mother had been abused by her father, physically and emotionally, and mainly married David's father because he didn't shout at or hit her as her father had done. When her daughter was born she knew she'd have to treat the children equally, as best she could. She made every effort, but David felt resentful toward his sister and there would eventually be much friction between them. After fifteen years of marriage, David's mother divorced his father.

David's father was a hard-working man who provided for his family financially, but was not outwardly warm or loving. He worked long hours and often spent his spare time reading or playing tennis. No one in the family felt that he was emotionally available, and they usually tried to just leave him alone and "give him his space." In turn, he largely removed himself from interacting with the other family members and failed to involve himself with his wife and children on a personal level.

With her husband working long hours and unavailable to help tend to the children, David's mother, who also worked a full-time job felt pressed to care for the children single-handedly, and she often felt harried and exhausted. When the children were pre-school age, she often had to put a tape in the VCR while she did house-work, and after the children were school age, she had to rush from work to pick the children up, make dinner, bathe them, and get them to bed. Again, during this time period, the children were left to play video games, watch movies, and listen to music without supervision or monitoring from their parents.

After the divorce, the children only saw their father once a month, and often that consisted of watching him play tennis. Otherwise, they watched TV and listened to music, unmonitored, at his house. When his father became involved with a new girlfriend, David didn't get along with her children, and didn't enjoy going to his father's house for visits. As time passed, he eventually refused to speak to his father on the phone and David's father didn't seem bothered by this situation.

By the time David's mother brought him for therapy, she felt, among other things, confused, frustrated, and a deep sense of fail-ure. While some may say that "all David needed was a good spank-ing," she'd tried every plausible means of punishment that she could imagine, and nothing worked. The fact that her other two children were well-behaved only added to her feelings of confusion and be-wilderment. David's father would not attend any of the therapy sessions and said that therapy was a waste of time. He also made negative comments about the children's mother in front of them.

At this point, David hated his parents, his siblings, and the world. He didn't know why no one liked him, and he acted faultless in all matters. He told fantastic lies about things that happened to him at home. His mother felt concerned over the fact that people some-times believed the things David said, and she feared that the child protective agency could come and take all of her children away.

David told his stories with conviction and sincerity. Was ev-eryone lying about David and his misbehavior? He said they were. He maintained his attitude of guiltlessness, even when confronted with eyewitness accounts of his exploits. David eventually admit-ted to many of his actions, but only after presentation of the facts and lengthy discussions about the things people saw him do. How-ever, at home, he often showed little sense of conscience or remorse.

After being in therapy for a good deal of time, David slipped up and the truth about his stories and behaviors became more evident. While in the beginning he acted friendly during counseling, his attitude deteriorated to the point of violence as the truth emerged. David had outbursts in the office and then acted as though nothing happened. When he did express anger, he said whatever he wanted to say, and on several occasions he threatened to throw things. He sometimes spit, kicked, and punched at the therapist.

What could cause these behaviors? It would be easy to label David as the problem and blame him for all of his actions, lies, and manipulations. There were obvious situations in his life that might have caused some of his feelings (his parents' divorce, family relationships, and school problems), but earlier therapy to address these issues had produced no results. Similarly to Hillary (discussed earlier in the book), David should benefit from strict behavioral management and stern parenting, shouldn't he? However, his mother had tried to implement as much of this as she could, and nothing seemed to work. What ultimately led to these behaviors, and what approach to parenting could prevent this outcome?

If you asked ten mental health professionals (psychologist, psychiatrist, social worker, school counselor, etc.) what was wrong with David, you could probably get ten different answers. These differences in interpreting David's problems may explain why someone diagnosed David as having ADHD and possibly bi-polar disorder. David showed many behaviors and symptoms that overlap into many different diagnoses. In recent years, more and more children and teens show behaviors similar to David's. Many kids and adolescents receive a variety of diagnoses from various mental health professionals, and the numbers and types of medication prescribed to them are disturbing.

The issues with David do not lie in the behaviors and diagnoses; they lie, for the most part, in subtle, easily-overlooked issues in his history. Taken individually, these seemingly small acts did not yield much information about the degree of David's behavior. Collectively, however, little things explained a lot and will be explored later in the chapter.

In assessing a child's issues, it is more important to focus on how she views the world instead of trying to figure out what is wrong with her. The only way to help children find their way in life is to go where they are and see what they see. Their actions are in reaction to how they see the world around them. For them to continue to behave as they do, they must feel upset about something. Furthermore, many of these kids do not understand why they behave as they do; they just know that they feel angry and upset. At this level, it seems that many of their behaviors come from the subconscious. David's collective issues, and those of kids like him, may pertain to interruptions and/or distractions from their attachment to caregivers. Disruptions in attachment do not have to be significant to result in problems for children as they grow into adulthood, and many times, the parents of children with these issues often have a history similar to those of their kids.

ATTACHMENT DERAILED

What happens when infants do not get what they need from a caregiver? Whatever the cause, whether the child is habitually neglected or abused, if they are in an institutionalized setting with multiple caregivers, or if they have parents with emotional problems, etc., these infants lack what they need to develop any attachment, let alone a healthy attachment. We will digress from our discussion of David to introduce the most serious side of attachment issues and return to David later in the chapter.

Reactive attachment disorder (RAD) is a psychological issue that has gained increasing attention in recent years, especially in situations that involve children living in orphanages overseas. However, RAD can involve a number of different scenarios including interruptions in the early bonding cycle, abuse and/or neglect, multiple placements, painful medical conditions, frequent separations such as recurring hospitalization, chronic family situations, lack of nurturing and love, and orphanage/institutional care. Failure to form healthy and proper attachments can strongly affect an individual's behavior throughout life.

Signs and symptoms suggestive of
Reactive Attachment Disorder are:

- superficial charm,

- lack of conscience,

- lack of cause-and-effect thinking,

- uncontrollable rages,

- obvious lying,

- preoccupations with fire, blood, and gore,

- stealing,

- indiscriminate affection with strangers,

- cruelty to animals/people,

- abnormal eating patterns.

These symptoms do not mean that a child has an attachment disorder, but indicate that there may be, in the least, issues to address.

Researchers did some hallmark attachment research using monkeys. The researchers removed infant monkeys from their parents and placed some in a cage with a metal frame shaped like a monkey with milk bottles to provide nourishment. The researchers separated another group of infant monkeys and provided that group with a metal frame shaped like a monkey with carpet attached to it to make it easier to hold onto and cuddle. These experiments found that both groups of monkeys had difficulties relating to other monkeys later in life. And the monkeys with the uncovered metal framed "parent" that provided the milk had more difficulty adjusting.

Data collected on children raised in orphanages and who did not receive individualized care often noted that children had what is called "failure to thrive" syndrome. This occurs when an infant does not receive much physical contact, human interaction, or feelings of love and comfort from others, although the child's physiological needs, such as nourishment, clothing, and diaper changes, necessary to sustain that child, were met. These children do not grow and mature as other children do, and the condition delays the development of their cognitive skills. In many cases, the situation degrades the child's immune system, along with contributing to other physical deficits, and sometimes contributes to death. Children with "failure to thrive" syndrome may continue to be undersized compared to their peers and often have developmental and learning difficulties. Additionally, they are likely to have many emotional difficulties and dysfunctional relationships as they grow older.

As mentioned earlier, attachment to a caretaker occurs when an infant has a consistent, loving attachment for a regular caretaker or caretakers. According to Erik Erikson, a well-known psychological theorist, trust is the first phase of psychosocial development. If children do not develop trust at an early age, trust issues can linger for a lifetime—unless the issue is resolved. Since an infant cannot tell anyone that it does not feel trust, then as caregivers we must do our best to provide an environment that enables the child to feel loved, safe, and cared about, and to know that her needs will be met. If a child does not feel trusting toward her caregiver, and this mistrust lingers for an extended period of time, it can lead to a more lasting sense of insecurity and underlying fear, which affects the attachment process and the child's sense of self.

Reactive Attachment Disorder occurs when a child either lacks an attachment to a consistent caregiver, or forms a dysfunctional attachment with a caregiver(s). If no assurances exist that a child's needs will be met, the child begins to psychologically turn inward, depending upon herself for survival. Internalized emotions are often fear, abandonment, rejection, neglect, mistrust, anger, rage, and hatred, as well feeling unloved. It is unlikely that the child fully understands these emotions until later in life, but they are deep and enduring. Many children with RAD do not know why they behave as they do; they often act out impulsively.

When children develop Reactive Attachment Disorder, they are very difficult to treat, and treatment requires a great deal of cooperation from parents, teachers, doctors, and others in their environment. Some of the most important aspects of this work involve reparenting which often involves backing up to do what was missed. Consistency and structure are critical. The phrase "A steel box with a velvet lining" is appropriate in describing the behavioral approach needed. Many naïve foster and adoptive parents feel that these children just need love, and that love and understanding will make everything better. Love is just one of many ingredients that are needed to help children with attachment issues, let alone RAD, to heal. Children with attachment issues often run roughshod over adoptive or foster parents who believe that "love conquers all." Children with attachment issues learn, early on, to do whatever they feel they must in order to survive. It is important to understand that they carry a great deal of anger that is not readily evident. It is fairly common for these children to destroy possessions and relationships (especially prized possessions of others) and soil themselves, lie in the face of obvious truths, manipulate, and steal things (often things they have no need for).

When working with children who have RAD, logic or love alone do not work. Neurologically, research shows brain development in children with RAD is lacking in certain areas. Effectively treating RAD can involve neuro-feedback and other types of cognitive rehabilitation to help the brain recover some of the lost opportunities for development. To ignore these neurological issues in the treatment of RAD often translates into an incomplete healing and continued problems for all involved. This form of treatment is expensive, and often difficult for many families.

Understanding the development of anger and rage are important to understanding children with attachment disorders. Emotions become "activated" through experience, although the child may not understand them. Most people feel that anger and rage are useless and unwanted emotions; however, anger and rage are adaptive emotions that help to ensure our survival. Many people who care for children with attachment issues believe that their reactions of anger, rage, and destruction are ridiculous, and have no place in a child's life, when in fact this may have been the only thing that ensured their survival when they were young.

When someone confronts a child with RAD about her anger, the child usually does not know how to respond and either shuts down or reacts even more strongly. She probably doesn't have a clue as to the origin of these feelings. Like rage, anger is a protective emotion. People use anger to cover up and hide other, more vulnerable feelings. When people are unable to feel safe with anyone, anger and rage keep them safe from feeling hurt by others. Anger pushes people away. Therefore, if a child shows anger and gets a negative response from others, the idea that there is a need for protection is reinforced. For example, if a boy with RAD feels angry toward his mother, he may intentionally break her favorite lamp. If his mother shouts and verbally assaults him, making him feel threatened, then his initial feelings of anger seem justified and this reinforces his feeling of need for protection. Sadness, fear, shame, unworthiness, guilt, rejection, and other, similar, emotions do not protect the child—and can result, in fact, in more hurt and pain, so they learn to hide those emotions even more. If we have to protect ourselves, we are not concerned with coming across as good and right, just with being strong. Sadness, fear, and the other emotions listed above are viewed as bad, wrong, and weak. How do they help us win anything? They don't in our culture. Therefore, children with RAD learn to bury them deep down inside and continue to push others away.

ON A RAINBOW OF ATTACHMENT AND HOW WE LOOK AT PSYCHOLOGY

Many people who visit mental healthcare providers, speak with the provider, and then ask, "Okay Doc, what's my diagnosis?" or, in essence, "What am I? Am I ADHD? Am I bi-polar?" We feel very strongly that it is inaccurate to use diagnoses to identify people. They become labels that can become very damaging to that individual. A better approach involves identifying the issues that led them to where they are now. However, diagnoses aid in communication between people in helping professions, with insurance companies, and in the legal system. For example, if a mental health professional mentions that Depression or Anxiety might be an issue, then people often believe that they must have this problem and they call themselves "depressed" or "anxious." Regardless of the person's age, in many cases, the diagnosis becomes a part of her identity. Often parents will tell people that their child is depressed, anxious, or ADD, and we have seen the damage of this too many times.

Diagnoses, in our current model, fall under what we call a categorical model of diagnosis, which basically means "all or none." So, under this model, Depression, Anxiety, Schizophrenia, Reactive Attachment Disorder, etc. is either present or it is not; there is no middle ground. Many clinicians have a problem with this type of classification system because it is not always easy to say whether someone is experiencing Depression or Anxiety. To complicate matters further, a person could experience Depression and Anxiety simultaneously. Which label is more accurate? People and their issues do not fit neatly into categories or labels; they in fact often exhibit a number of behaviors and symptoms, and to varying degrees. What do we do about these?

The dimensional model of diagnosis affords a means for the healthcare provider to consider degrees of issues. In other words, a person might not just be considered depressed but instead she might be mildly, moderately or severely depressed. Overall, this can provide more information. For this reason, it is a viable alternative to the categorical model of diagnosis. The main argument against this is that it would likely result in a much more blurry assessment of people's emotional conditions than the categorical model. However, a dimensional model, in many ways, makes more sense in describing human behavior because it accounts for varying degrees of symptoms or actions. We must be cautious in how we look at the labels that we attach to others, especially children. Labels are often inaccurate in describing the entire person.

To return to our issue of attachment, our overview of RAD was offered as a reference to the diagnosis. Again, this is an uncommon diagnosis in its true form. While many of the issues children have could stem from attachment issues, it is not to the degree, nor is it often even close to the severity, of the abused and neglected kids who experience the extreme symptoms of RAD. A large number of children who have dealt with divorce, absent parents, observed abuse (verbal, emotional, physical), and/or have been in daycare from early ages, also display symptoms similar to RAD. Common symptoms often take the form of aggressive defiance, impulsiveness, acting out, habitual lying and/or manipulation, difficulty in forming relationships, sabotaging relationships, apparent unwarranted levels of anger and rage toward parents, and difficulty trusting many adults. The current trend is to diagnose many of these children and adolescents as having Bi-polar disorders. And as recently as ten years ago, mental health professionals may have told these same people that they had ADHD. In any case, these individuals received prescriptions for various medications, sometimes amounting to a cocktail of assorted chemicals. While in many ways our advancements in science have helped us to evolve to higher levels of health and longer life spans, it has also helped to prompt us to look for quick fixes and sometimes to avoid the cure. We will discuss the diagnostic issues in Chapter 11; however, it is important to understand some diagnostic issues in relation to the discussion on attachment.

Could it be that the answers to our children's problems are so easy? Could it be that their behaviors result from a few missed opportunities to bond? Definitely not. However, the shades of gray are important for us to address when we look at our children and their attachment to us. On the other hand, neurochemistry and other life experiences, outside the realm of attachment, may explain many behaviors and issues, as we discussed in Temperament and Personality. Children with RAD display issues that we know resulted from situations that occurred years earlier, even before the child could speak. Therefore, it is important to have the same perspective when we consider our own children and their behaviors. We must ask the question, "Can early life experiences affect an individual's behavior years before the behavioral issues occur?" If these early life experiences affect children, what can we do to change them? How did these experiences affect their trust in us and the world? From this discussion, parents should consider the choices they are making and their priorities when parenting their children. If feelings of guilt, shame, or failure as a parent are present, don't allow yourself to feel mired down in these emotions. Instead, use those emotions to prompt change and growth. The intent of this discussion is to educate and challenge, not to blame.

Let us consider a single event that sheds some light on the previous discussion. A father had taken his eight-year-old son Bobby to several therapists, behavioral specialists, and psychiatrists, and the son was on various medications. Bobby had a history of behavioral problems that resulted in uncontrollable rage. Although the rages often centered on his mother, sometimes he channeled it toward his father and brother. Bobby had physically hurt his parents in the past, and they did not know what to do with him. Everything they tried had failed, and Bobby's parents did not want him to depend upon medication for the rest of his life.

They said that he often seemed to go into an altered state when he expressed his anger. They also said that it almost seemed as if Bobby's "trance" had to run its course before he could calm down. Bobby did not know why he felt or behaved as he did. During therapy, he was very agreeable and easy to work with. In looking at the family, there were some hierarchical issues to address and the family tried several recommendations to remedy some of the problems. One of the suggestions involved hypnosis to see if there were any subconscious issues prompting Bobby's behaviors.

Bobby was responsive to hypnosis, and his subconscious evoked an experience that helped him understand his behavior. Without prompting, he said that he felt very small and scared, and he went on to say that he did not understand why he felt this way. He was asked to view his life as a movie and back up in time to before he felt scared. He said he felt warm and safe and then things started changing. When asked if he felt that there were others around him, he said that he felt his mother's presence. Bobby stated that he felt her feelings change, and she no longer felt safe. As he moved through this, he said, "I think I am being born." He said that something was wrong and that he remembered feeling cold. Then someone pulled him away from his mother and strangers surrounded him. He said that he felt sad, scared, alone, and then angry with his mother because he thought she should have protected him. He was asked to see himself as he was at eight and imagine him taking care of the little boy that was just born. He seemed to like this idea. Although the infant could not talk, he and the infant could communicate through their minds. He saw himself holding the infant and being a big brother to it.

When asked about his history, Bobby's parents said that they could only think of the complications that occurred at birth. They said that he almost died and that the neonatal care unit treated Bobby immediately after birth. Bobby didn't know of any of this, since his parents never discussed it with him. After this session, the parents noted a drastic reduction in rage and anger. Since hypnotherapy, Bobby has not expressed the rage reactions that he had expressed before. It is important to note that this was a rare case where the child was very responsive to hypnosis. There were still a number of other issues to address in his behavior, but this single experience, when resolved and understood, resulted in a drastic improvement in his behavior.

As we get further into this discussion, we should consider that many factors in a society could influence the behaviors of children. Research on the effects of television, music, video games, and the media, just to name a few, and how these affect our children and their behavior is extensive. However, it is difficult to prove causation. Is it TV, song lyrics, graphic violence in video games, or other factors that lead our kids to behave violently? It is important to avoid rushing to judgment—correlation does not prove causation; just because two issues may be related, it does not mean that one event causes the other. For example, studies have shown that people with myopic vision (near sightedness) tend to have an IQ slightly above average. However, there is no basis to conclude that near sightedness causes people to have a higher than average IQ

People tend to jump to the conclusion that if two children listen to heavy-metal music, and are suspended from school for doing drugs, then it must be the music that caused them to do drugs. However, it is important to consider other factors they may have in common: they come from divorced families, a history of drug or alcohol abuse in their families, both had a history of conflicts with their parents and siblings, etc. Many people, especially parents, tend to ignore these other issues and see what they want to see.

The tendency to come to a false conclusion, such as the one regarding music, is called a spurious correlation. Simply put, people make a connection between factors that may seem related, but the connection between those issues is not as strong as it would seem to be at first sight. A more common example of a spurious correlation is the belief that planes are not as safe as cars. People may falsely believe that planes are unsafe because we see every plane crash on the news and they stand out in our minds. But car accidents happen at a ridiculously high frequency and we see virtually none of them. Similarly, many people listen to heavy metal music or watch violent TV shows or movies and never do anything to harm themselves or others.

ISSUES THAT RELATE TO ATTACHMENT

In our discussion of David, which issues that could contribute to the problems in his life stood out to you? Before you read further, take some time to re-read the example and make a list of all the potential issues that could be a factor. Then read on.

1. BIRTH ORDER

David is a middle child. Research finds inconclusive results about whether birth order in itself could cause issues, but it is likely an issue when it involves other variables in the family (gender, mental health of parents, economics, etc.). It should never be ignored when looking at the individual.

2. DEMANDS ON THE PARENTS

In today's society parents feel many demands. We may feel pressured to keep kids active, maintain a household, cook for the children, ensure economic stability for the family, and help kids to be competitive in academics, sports, and other activities. All of these factors create an overload on many parents. Because of this, we can feel exhausted, short-tempered, unappreciated, overwhelmed, resentful, etc. Sometimes parents exert this effort for their kids, and other times they do it for themselves. In our minds, our children's success may depend upon our success. We should find a balance between what we must do, what we can do, and what the children want us to do.

Our stress will affect how we treat our children. We must consider the quality of the parent/child relationship for what it is—not in terms of what we want to do for our children. Do we play the martyr role with the child? Do we believe that feeling tired or being busy provides an excuse for shouting at the kids, failing to keep promises we've made to them, or treating them disrespectfully? How much resentment do we feel? Do we say that the kids are ungrateful and selfish? These are just a few questions to consider.

David's mom felt that she had to work, and she returned to work soon after he was born. She also felt that she did not have much help from her husband. She felt spread very thin and felt constantly tired. This is a critical factor, because her fatigue probably affected the amount and quality of time that she spent with her children. Furthermore, if she stayed tired, she may not have been as sensitive to his needs, or the other children. Is this a major factor contributing to David's issues? It is likely one of the collective factors affecting how David feels about himself. While David's mother may not have always been sensitive to the needs of all of the kids, he was likely only aware of his perceptions.

David's father may have been very busy, too. Often, mothers bring their kids to counseling or therapy sessions and fathers are less commonly involved, at least initially. When fathers do turn up for a family member's counseling, another side of the story often emerges. In some situations the father is uninvolved and doesn't care about the family. However, sometimes a father feels branded as a persecutor and he then fades into the background in his relationships with his kids. Sometimes, the father works diligently to provide a living for the family but never feels recognized. The mother may feel that her role is to care for the children and never expresses her needs for help and support with the kids to the father for fear of causing conflict. The father's outside activities (golf, tennis, hunting, etc.) may result from a sense of deserving to have recreational time, without a clear recognition of the wife's responsibilities in the home and at her workplace outside the home.

As the resentment increases between the wife and husband, the children may turn against their father if their mother portrays him as being self-absorbed, cold, and uncaring. The father, on the other hand, may feel that his behavior is appropriate since he provides for his family and needs a break. In these scenarios, fathers are often responsive to change, but change requires a shift in the perception of power on their part and a willingness to become a part of the team. The mother also has to recognize that she has played into this dynamic possibly by assuming too much responsibility and/or surrendering her power to her husband. This change process takes time and coaching, but it can happen. The shift has to be toward an equity model; the father must take on more of the tasks in the house, and the mother must let the father share in the tasks.

The dual demands of work and home often fall on the mothers in our culture; therefore, it is understandable that they feel overwhelmed and unappreciated. Mothers tend to take on a martyr role in order to receive recognition for their work and efforts. However, sometimes mothers don't ask for needed help, for many reasons. Fear of confrontation is a common reason, and some mothers take on too much responsibility because of feelings of hopelessness and futility. Sometimes they work too hard in order to meet the needs of all. In these cases, the mothers' busy schedule helps them to feel important and valued.

In David's situation, it is not clear what his father and mother's workload involved. However, most roads lead to the conclusion that David's father has some responsibility to bear, and he sorely neglected his role over time.

3. Psychological/Emotional Health of Parents

Research in childcare studies indicates that the psychological well-being of the parent (more often mother) is a very powerful factor contributing to attachment. Having a few days of the blues, or feeling anxious about paying the bills, or about a relationship issue, is not significant to this discussion. However, attachment problems may arise when a parent experiences chronic depression or significant anxiety that affects how that parent interacts with the child and/or the child's environment. Also, parents may have personality disorders, such as Borderline, Narcissistic, Histrionic, Psychopathic, etc. In these circumstances, the parent often focuses on her own issues to the point of allowing them to interfere with healthy attachment and bonding. Entire books are devoted to successfully covering this arena.

Parents who have psychological or physical problems often feel a great deal of guilt. Discussing how their illnesses or issues may affect their relationship with their children can add fuel to the fire. Therefore, addressing these issues to parents with known difficulties is a delicate matter. Parents with mental or physical difficulties must realize that heaping more guilt upon themselves will only result in more distance and pain for all involved. Taking care of ourselves must be a priority for all parents, and this is especially true for parents with physical or mental illnesses, since they must heal so they can care for their children. Quite often, the child's issues improve as the parent's issues improve.

We should consider the situation wherein the parent has a long-term illness and the child acts as the caregiver. The child begins to believe that in order to get love and attention she has to help the parent heal. The child may fear that the parent could die, which creates a great deal of underlying fear. These patterns of caring for a parent sometimes begin in childhood and continue into adulthood. It seems that many children who have to care for their parents tend to grow up with a knack for finding people who need "fixing," and they devote their lives to "fixing" others and never feel that they get what they need. As a result, they often find themselves ill later in life and someone ends up of taking care of them, if allowed to do so. Their illness or physical problem often has roots in the feelings related to repressed earlier life experiences. We will address this again in another chapter.

Many of us can benefit from therapy. Too often, we, the parents, put our children's needs ahead of our own. The irony is that it is often much easier to take care of your children's needs after you take care of your own. Additionally, resolving personal issues enhances our relationships with our children. If we don't fully understand ourselves and how we feel, we cannot understand our children and their needs.

In David's case, his mother knew that she was feeling unhappy when he was born. She had formed some conclusions about her marriage and her life that negatively affected her mood. We don't know whether there were any post-partum issues, but from the history, it does seem clear that there was some depression. For how long, and to what degree, is only speculation.

4. GENDER ISSUES

Parents, whether consciously or unconsciously, often prefer children of one gender or the other. Sometimes this is glaringly obvious and the child hears about the parent's gender preference throughout her life, and other times it may be very subtle. The most obvious way this is expressed is through a parent discussing her preference for either a boy or girl child. This can influence the parent's relationship with a child and the child's developing attitudes toward herself. If the child enters the world with a disappointed parent, a lasting emotional separation can result. The effects of a parent's disappointment may be subtle in the beginning but it can have profound effects on the child's self-esteem and self-worth, especially if she knows the parent's preference.

In David's case, it was not obvious that his mother had wanted a girl when he was born, but it became clear that this was the case after his sister was born. David's father's wishes were unclear because he was not assessed. However, after David's sister was born, his mother's attitudes changed drastically. Therefore, it is likely that David sensed this change in energy and felt confused and possibly rejected. This rejection could have led to anger, which he then took out on his siblings, especially his sister.

116

5. COMPETITION AND DEVELOPMENT OF SIBLING RIVALRIES

Often, the birth of other children is a non-factor in issues of attachment. In larger families, other siblings can help in building a strong attachment for the child. On the other hand, in some instances the birth of a child can result in the disruption of a secure attachment for an older child, especially if the older child is only a few years old. This discussion is not about glaring attachment disorders but a spectrum of attachment issues. These issues can result in behavioral and emotional problems for children throughout childhood and sometimes beyond.

Sibling rivalries are nothing new, but sometimes the rivalry can become extreme. A new family member can disrupt the hierarchy. A newborn can divert attention from the youngest child who likely got the most care and attention prior to the new addition to the family. In this situation, the arrival of a newborn can bring a great deal of fear and disruption to the other children's sense of safety and security.

When a newborn enters the family, the parents may become short-tempered with an older child—parents feel that the older children must understand that the baby needs to be cared for. An older child may perceive this message as, "You are not important anymore," or "You've been replaced." The disruption for the older child can result in fear, threat, insecurity, jealousy and envy, which may then result in anger, rage, hatred, and other protective emotions. Depending on how the parents handle the older child's emotions, these rivalries may continue unchecked. Feelings of frustration, helplessness, sadness, guilt, and failure to meet the needs of all of their children often lie beneath a parent's reaction of anger.

Jealousy and ensuing rivalries can become dangerous when they result in aggression and violence. A child feeling jealous and angry may lash out at the object of her jealousy with violence and aggression. In extreme situations, children have caused serious harm and even death to siblings due to feelings of jealousy. In these situations, we must be aware of how we respond to our own jealousy. Has the child seen, learned, and adopted our reaction to jealousy?

If we punish the jealous behavior, the child will often place the guilt, shame, humiliation, and then subsequent anger onto the new sibling, which worsens the problem.

When rivalries occur, we have an opportunity to help our children understand that we still love them. We can do this by discussing what they are feeling and why they are feeling jealous, threatened, angry, etc. Children may not completely understand the issue, but a discussion often plants a seed for them to begin to understand the different layers of emotions they may feel.

David's mother showed a clear preference for his younger sister, because of her gender, which created competition for their mother's attention. The rivalry ensued and continued for some time. David sometimes harmed his sister, and it seemed that neither parent tried to help either child understand the reasons for these feelings. Instead, their parents punished David for his actions. Part of David's hurt and frustration was taken out on animals, because of his misplaced rage and hatred. David's mother realized, to some degree, that she was showing favoritism toward her daughter, but did not do much to change her behavior. She felt frustrated with her husband because he didn't help with the boys; therefore, some of the frustration she felt toward her husband was taken out passively by favoring their daughter. The boys did not understand why this was happening. Children often attribute these situations to something about themselves but take it out on others.

David's brother, Jordan, took a stronger role in caring for him, possibly to compensate for his own feelings of neglect. The attachment between David and Jordan may have compensated for some of what was missing between the boys and their parents. However, then Jordan started spending more time with his friends and David likely felt abandoned once again, and his problems compounded. Jordan's distancing himself from David may have solidified David's belief that no one could love him and everyone would ultimately leave him.

6. ABSENTEE PARENT

Many reasons and situations may prevent a parent from being involved with the children, even if the parent resides in the household with them. For this discussion, an absentee parent is a parent that lives in the family home but does not spend much, if any, quality time with the kids and is emotionally unavailable. Historically, fathers are more likely to be an absentee parent, but mothers sometimes fit this description. Often, fathers aren't involved with their kids because they lack parenting skills and/or do not understand the child's emotional needs. This situation is often handed down from one generation to the next. A child may form a secure attachment with an emotionally present and available parent, but may blame himself for the poor relationship with this absentee parent.

Our society more readily accepts a father's absenteeism because his traditional role as that of the provider sometimes dictates that his career must come first. It then follows that mothers are often guilted and shamed into being the caregiver. When mothers are viewed as unavailable to their families, society is more likely to judge them to be dysfunctional than a father in a similar situation.

Both parents should be willing to form a deep and meaningful attachment with their children. As parents, if this is an issue, we should have the courage to address our issues and face them head on. Parents may find that they have residual attachment issues left-over from their own infancy or childhood.

It appears that David's father was absent. While no information was collected from him directly, enough evidence points to it. David's father's absence and the influence it had on David was significant in combination with the other factors in this case. The father became one more person who rejected David, and this rejection led him to feel even less lovable. The interactions that David and his father had seemed to be more punitive than loving. So, David perceived that males are more likely to pose a threat or behave judgmentally instead of being supportive and loving toward him. David will probably carry this belief system through childhood, and it may carry over into his belief systems as an adult. These belief systems could eventually affect David's relationship with his children. Lack of perceived trust and safety are key issues that create walls and defenses.

7. DAYCARE

For millions of families in the United States, daycare is a necessity. In 1999, about 8.9 million children under the age of five (children with employed parents represent seventy-three percent of this figure) were placed in a non-parental childcare setting. Twenty-eight percent were in center-based care, relatives cared for 27 percent, 14 percent were enrolled in family childcare, and babysitters or nannies cared for 4 percent. The years from 1998 to 2003 showed nearly a 55 percent increase in the number of licensed childcare providers, from 193,044 to 300,032. Sixty-two percent of the mothers in the workforce have children under six years old. Fifty-eight percent of the women who give birth in the U.S. return to work before their children are one year old. In 1985, 34 percent the nation's three to four-year-olds were in childcare—by 2001, the figure had risen to over 52 percent. There are many reasons that childcare has become a way of life for so many. In many cases, however, it seems due to the financial necessity of having dual incomes to meet financial obligations. Whether real or imagined, both parents tend to feel that they must work at least part-time if not full-time.

SELECTING CHILDCARE

Childcare is a very serious issue and can cause many parents much distress. Whether you choose to have someone in your home, take your child to their home, or to a childcare center, there are many questions that you will want to consider and things you will want to check out.

When you visit a center, try to go in the middle of the day. Don't make an appointment before you come to the center. You don't necessarily want them to expect you. Use all your senses when you enter the childcare setting—sight, sound, smell, gut feeling, etc. Does it look clean? Does the food smell good? Is there dust or caked on dirt on tables, floors? How do the bathrooms smell and look? Does staff wear gloves when changing diapers?

Some questions to ask:

- Is your center accredited? By what organization? How often do you go through accreditation?

- Has your center ever been cited for any violations?

- What are the educational backgrounds of the teachers and do you support their training and education? Who does the training? Is there quality assurance for competencies?

- What is the average tenure of your staff? Incentive programs for staff that stay? Do you perform national background checks on all of your staff?

- Do your teachers move up with the students?

- How do you handle issues with inappropriate behavior of your staff?

- What are your teacher-to-student ratios for your different ages?

- Do you use observation cameras, and are they linked to the internet?

- How often are classrooms observed by administrative personnel?

- What is your sanitizing process for toys, furniture?

- What information do you require on my child and how is confidentiality protected? This may include health needs, allergies, medications, family emergency information, names of persons authorized to remove the child, and etc.

- Do you have an open-door policy on parent visits?

- What are alternative arrangements for care if the program closes? On what holidays is the center closed?

- What is your policy on communicable diseases? Chicken Pox, Pink Eye, Ringworm, lice, etc.

- What's your policy on delivering medication?

- What is your policy on allergies and food allergies? How will the staff know? How will substitute staff know?

- What are your procedures if my child is injured when in your care?

- What is your policy on caring for sick children?

- Under what conditions are children permanently removed or asked to leave from your care?

- What are your policies for sending children home for the day for misbehavior, illness, emotional problems?

- Do you provide written progress reports or evaluations on my child?

- Do you send home written daily sheets for children under 2? List could include what and how much food consumed, nap time and duration, diaper changes #1 & #2.

- How are children grouped? By age? By interests or abilities?

- Do you welcome children of varying ethnic, cultural, and religious backgrounds to the program? Do you include children with special needs? Are your teachers specifically trained, or are there those that can come in to provide services to your children with special needs?

- Do you have emergency drills, and what is your emergency plan?

- What is your discipline policy? (Offer "what if" scenarios to elicit responses to situations that could arise. For example, if a child hits another child or throws a tantrum over a toy someone else is playing with, what should the consequences be?)

- How will you provide new experiences to enhance my child's mental and physical development?

- What are the opportunities you can offer for my child to experience art, music, group and individual play, and indoor and outdoor play?

- How would you handle toilet teaching? At what age do you begin training?

- What is your policy on children taking naps? What if they don't nap?

- How would you handle separation anxiety?

- How do you monitor children on the playground? How old is the equipment and has it recently been inspected?

HERE ARE SIGNS TO LOOK FOR IF YOU SUSPECT THAT YOUR CHILD IS BEING MISTREATED:

- The caregiver has lied to you or stolen from you.

- He or she does not answer questions about the daily routine.

- You come home to find your child unsupervised.

- The caregiver does not respond to your child.

- Your child becomes moody or withdrawn or has problems eating or sleeping.

- Your child suddenly becomes upset when left with the caregiver.

- You simply have a bad feeling about the caregiver.

This is by no means an exhaustive list of questions and issues, but it is a good start. Should you choose to ask these questions, observe how the caregiver responds to the extensive list. If they are impatient with you and your questions, how might they be responding to your child? We know that placing your child in childcare can feel extremely stressful, but we hope this provides you with a little more peace of mind.

Quality childcare can substitute for some of the parents' missed opportunities. Many factors pertaining to childcare can have a positive or negative effect on children. As of this writing, a long-term national study conducted by researchers around the country is underway. This study seeks to evaluate the effects of childcare and other factors that influence children; however, the behavioral data from this study are most pertinent to our discussion.

What are the major concerns regarding the effects of childcare? If a child, especially a child younger than one year old, spends extended amounts of time with non-parental caregivers, what effect does this have? What about a revolving door of caregivers, in a single setting or in multiple settings?

At this time, the children involved in the previously mentioned study are twelve years old. It will be interesting to see the results of this research as they reach adolescence. Largely, the results thus far, neither prove nor disprove the negative impact of childcare. One finding, however, suggests that the mothers whose infants and toddlers spent more time in childcare were less sensitive to the child's needs and less positively involved with the children. Furthermore, mothers who were less sensitive to their child's needs at the age of six months often showed even higher levels of negativity with their child at fifteen months of age. When these children were between the ages of twenty-four and thirty-six months, the children and mothers were less affectionate toward each other than children who spent less time in daycare.

These results indicate that there is an interaction between a mother and child that contributes to an attachment from both the child's and mother's perspectives. In other words, parents can feel rejected by children just as children can feel rejected by parents, and the amount of time that children spend with their parents, even from a very early age, is an important factor. This data implies that parents must consider their issues and behaviors toward their babies in order to understand and accurately interpret the child's behavior. The findings of the study also suggest that parenting requires practice.

The study found that aggression and other dysfunctional behaviors in children increased as the time spent in childcare increased. (This research did not take into account the quality of parenting or other important factors.) An Australian study suggests that mothers who felt comfortable about returning to work after giving birth were more likely to have secure infants. This Australian research also found that early and predictable separations in the first year were less disruptive to attachment than later, more sporadic separations. These findings allude to the importance of the emotional state of the parent, and a mother's ability to communicate confidence to their children.

Quality of childcare does, as mentioned earlier, make a difference in a child's level of emotional well-being and sense of security. Higher quality childcare has a positive impact on the quality of interactions between the mother and child. Additionally, children's cognitive development benefits from high quality care. So, to sum up the research to date, quality of childcare is a key variable that can affect relationships between parent and child. A major benefit of quality childcare seems to be that children receive more structured cognitive stimulation, which can aid in their development.

An interesting finding of the research has to do with a correlation between family income and quality of childcare. Interestingly—and counter intuitively—families with low incomes are often receiving subsidies, which allow them to place their children in higher quality daycares than lower-middle income families.

For many reasons, parents may frequently change daycare providers, a cause for some concern. It is important to screen the daycare setting and the staff in order to ensure suitability and minimize the chance of having to change providers again, and to ease in transition. Adjustments for some children are quite difficult, depending upon temperament and attachment issues. Parents often rush their children in and out of the daycare. Each time a child enters into a different daycare setting, the child must adjust to new caregivers while leaving behind others with whom they may have already bonded. If parents must change the childcare arrangements, they should consider ways to help prepare the infant/child for that change. An important aspect of making this involves allowing the child to warm up to a new person or place in the presence of a parent. This consideration also applies to in-home care situations.

Some daycare centers are realizing the importance of consistency and attachment with children; these providers recognize that they are spending more time with the kids than the children's parents are. In response to this realization, some daycares are adopting a policy of allowing children in their care to remain with the same caregiver throughout their pre-school years. Ideally, we, the parents, would be the main source of attachment, but it's also true that children need to have meaningful, secure attachments in educational settings which can promote a better learning environment.

looping!

David was put in daycare at an early age, as were his siblings. He had conflicts with kids but cooperated with the staff and felt emotionally attached to some of them when he was younger. He cried when some caregivers left or when he changed classrooms. As he grew older, he expressed increasing indifference, and he seemed hardened to the staff. He sometimes behaved disrespectfully toward those staff members whom he had known longest. David's mother wanted to put her kids into a better quality daycare, but could not afford it for all three, so she kept them together. David complained during the summer, because many of his friends were at home; sometimes he tried to sabotage his ability to stay at the daycare by causing problems with others and getting into trouble. When he got too old to be in daycare after school, his mother was leery of leaving him unsupervised.

In David's case, daycare may have fostered some attachments but unfortunately those relationships ended. And his attitude about daycare was certainly a factor in how he handled being there. As for the care itself, many unknowns exist, as is common in child-care settings. Mental health professionals often help families deal with events that have occurred in daycare. Many conflicts and situations occur between children, but some problems pertain to the way a staff member treated the child. Clearly, some people in the childcare field do not belong there, just as in any other occupation. These unsuited childcare providers can cause a great deal of damage in a short time, having a profound effect. A child's problems with a caregiver should not be pushed aside or underrated. As parents, we should try to find out what we can about the situation. At the least, this sends a message to the child that we support her and are willing to do what we can to protect her.

8. Divorce

Divorce is a painful reality for many families, and its impact varies from family to family and child to child. Some of the biggest factors include the age of the child at the time of divorce, the relationship between the parents and the turmoil in the home, the relationship between the custodial and non-custodial parent and child, living arrangements and visitation, consistency of environments, attitudes, maturity, emotional health of the parents and child, and quality of interactions between the parents. All of these (and more) factors are important. Countless studies uphold one particular fact regarding children and divorce: children of divorced parents often have issues with commitment to others and fear rejection. The influence of divorce on other emotional and personality issues depends upon the individual.

We need to remember that kids usually know when their parents are feeling unhappy. Sometimes divorcing and moving on with life sends a better message to the kids than staying trapped in an unhappy relationship. A couple should work diligently to resolve problems in their relationship, but whether the marriage is wrought with conflict or not, when a relationship cannot be saved, it may be in the best interest of all to move on. If the parents can work together and maintain a cooperative parenting relationship apart, the outcome can be much more favorable than staying together. The message here is that sometimes a relationship needs to end because it is hopelessly damaged or destroyed; this is far different from the attitude that marriages should end simply because life gets a bit tough. Couples should seek counseling to try to heal their differences for the sake of each other and for the kids. Parents who stay together for their children often put guilt on the kids for the misery of their parents' relationship.

It is inevitable that children will take on some of the traits and mannerisms of their parents. Often, a child will have many of her parents' physical characteristics. Additionally, children sometimes make a facial expression, verbal comments, or other subtle gestures similar to a parent. In a successful marriage, these similarities may seem endearing, but what happens when the relationship between the parents is conflicted?

Parents sometimes take their frustrations out on the children that remind them of the other parent, resulting in comments such as, "You're so much like your father, I can't hardly stand to look at you!" or, "You get your smart mouth from your mother, don't you?" This behavior can range from mild—being emotionally distant or short-tempered—to physical and/or emotional abuse. These reactions can happen in divorce situations if parents do not resolve their conflicts with each other, and also frequently occurs when unhappy marriages remain intact.

Negatively comparing a child to a parent or other family member can be extremely detrimental to attachment, because the child has no power to change the opinion (or the past) of the parent. This feeling of helplessness can strongly affect the child's self-image, confidence, and competence. It is crucial for parents to be clear with their issues and separate their spouse's or other family member's traits from their children.

In David's situation, the divorce of his parents was just one factor of many that contributed to his situation. Since his father was an absentee parent, the impact of his leaving was not as painful as it could have been, but the fact that his father remarried did become an issue for David. David may have felt that his father was one more person who left him and then found more happiness without him. Additionally, his parent's relationship remained as contentious after the divorce as it had been. We don't know to what degree David's mother was affected by the divorce, but there was a significant financial impact; her job became even more important because it became the family's major source of income. The additional burden of being the breadwinner for the family increased her level of stress, and influenced her ability to be emotionally and physically available to her kids. David received even less attention and his mother lost her temper more easily. His father still seemed non-existent. So, in David's eyes, no one was there to protect, care for, or rescue him. David had physical and personality traits that were similar to his father's, and as David matured, these traits became more pronounced. After some therapy, David's mother realized that as she saw him acting and looking more like his father, she sensed more anger within herself.

9. Unrealistic Expectations

Sometimes parents have certain expectations for their children—that they "should" become a doctor, lawyer, or athlete, take over the family business, etc. In these situations, the parents' interactions with their children, from birth, may consistently center on their own wants and dreams. As long as the child lives up to the parents' expectations, the relationship works. However, the child must continue to meet certain conditions in order to maintain a high level of worth in the parents' eyes. Parents who foster these expectations often hold these hopes even before the child is born. Therefore, the depth of the attachment from the parent to the child depends on the qualities of the child. Most children who feel as though they don't live up to their parents' expectations view themselves as being damaged and this self-image often lasts for a lifetime.

Children may internalize their emotions when they do not live up to the parents' expectations. During a child's first years of life, parents commonly brag about the child's milestones such as walking and talking, and children often thrive off the attention. However, parents sometimes refer to a child as "My little quarterback," or, "My genius" or apply similar labels. Additionally, measuring children's progress relative to siblings can be just as damaging as labeling them. If these labels and expectations become part of a pattern, children may deeply internalize feelings of inadequacy, affecting their ability to feel worthy of love and acceptance. This situation, in turn, affects the depth of the child's attachments to others. Feeling unable to live up to parental expectations is one side of the coin; is there less pressure placed on the child labeled the "goat" than on the "golden child"? This is more a question to consider rhetorically for our own growth. Is either label fair to any person? There is no harm in hoping for our children to succeed, but when these wants and dreams are a part of our interactions with them, it leads to problems.

Children should receive exposure to a variety of experiences in order to learn where their strengths lie. As they find their strengths and gifts, careers and other life choices will fall into place. Setting conditions for being loved is very damaging. The result of feeling that love is conditional during childhood often has one of two outcomes. Some people come to believe that they must surrender their wants and needs for everyone else in order to feel accepted and loved. The other common outcome often leads the individual to push everyone away and refuse to take advice from anyone, because they resent feeling that others are judging them. When we, as parents, set these expectations, either we want our children to be like us, or better than us, instead of letting them be who and what they are.

It is unclear whether David had any expectations placed upon him. Sometimes his parents compared him to his siblings, often when he was not living up to their standards. This became a source of competition and a reminder of how he was falling short. Although this competition was not a major factor, we can add that to list of other contributing factors.

SUMMARY

As was discussed in these last two chapters, many issues can contribute to and negatively influence a child's ability to form meaningful attachments with others. It would be a good idea for you to do some of your own research on this topic if you see some things that concern you with your child. The Internet offers many opportunities for learning if you search under keywords "child development and attachment." Although there are key stages to consider in helping your child to form healthy, secure attachments, the process of attachment continues for years and not only includes us, as parents, but also many of the people (adults and children) our children interact with. Overall, children with secure attachments tend to be resilient when experiencing potentially adverse situations. However, some issues and situations can disrupt the attachment process, and these disruptions can influence development, relationships, and learning, which lingers. It is critical for us, as parents, to take responsibility for our mistakes and get our children the help necessary to resolve these issues.

Despite the information in this chapter, do not feel tempted to second-guess yourself so much that you live with fear and guilt that you have permanently damaged your children. Missed opportunities may come and go, but even if you learn enough from this to catch a potential problem, the issues can be remediated and relationships can be healed. Remember that past events and current circumstances influence behavior. Past events affect the attitudes and beliefs which, in turn, affect perceptions of the present. If people can understand their pasts and resolve the hurts, then they can change the attitudes that contribute to their perceptions of the present. With children, this process of change usually involves growth and change from the child's caregivers.

Sigmund Freud once said, "Sometimes a cigar is just a cigar," meaning sometimes things should be taken at face value. However, sometimes we can miss the obvious if we view situations too simplistically. Attachment issues can be mistakenly misdiagnosed as a broad range of conditions. Understanding all the pieces of the puzzle is crucial to a proper diagnosis.

Humans can be simple in some ways, but very complex in others. Yes, many kids just need some discipline and structure—as do some parents. In these situations, there is usually information that parents can learn about their children and, more importantly, about themselves that help them to understand the depth of the issues. Usually parents' growth comes from seeing how earlier events in their life affected their behavior later on.

No parent or child is perfect. The issues presented in this chapter are intended to help bring attention to the choices parents make, and how they can affect their children. Understanding the process of attachment is just one of the more important stops on the path to the empowerment of you and your family.

⊂⊃ **Chapter 7** ⊂⊃
THE MANY FACES OF THE FAMILY

Tony was a typical nine-year-old boy and the only child of Jean, a homemaker, and Greg. When Jean and Greg suddenly divorced, it created stress for all three parties, particularly Tony. He felt hurt and confused because he missed his father and did not understand why his parents divorced. He also sensed that his mother felt much bitterness and anger toward his father—and indeed she felt isolated and friendless—making things even more difficult. Tony still loved his father but thought that it might upset his mother if he expressed or displayed this love in front of his mother.

Tony lived with Jean but saw Greg on weekends, and Greg remained involved with coaching Tony's Little League and Pee Wee football teams. Still, these were difficult times for Tony and Jean as they tried to come to grips with adjusting to living their day-to-day life depending only upon each other. During this adjustment period, Tony came to feel quite attached to Jean and to having her undivided attention. Jean still had her bad days when she cried over the lingering sadness and loneliness of the failed marriage. Tony tried to console her and felt as though he needed to take care of her. He worried about her and felt scared and sad when he saw how badly this divorce had hurt her. Tony often felt sad and lonely too, but he usually tried not to show it because he did not want his mother to worry about him.

This situation lasted about a year, until Tony was ten, and then Jean decided it was time for her to start dating. Tony tried to make himself believe that the men that his mother went out with were just friends; he didn't like the idea that his mother had boyfriends. Although he understood that his parents were not married anymore, he still felt a growing sense of betrayal when it became clear that his mother's "friends" were romantically involved with her. He started out feeling that his mother's dating was a betrayal of his father but as time passed he began to feel that her time spent dating meant that she was betraying him.

After his father left, Tony came to feel that his mother was the only person he could count on to take care of him. Suddenly, he felt that his mother's social engagements and boyfriends were more important than spending time with him. He felt as though he was being dumped off on friends and relatives so that Jean could pursue her new social life. As this happened, Tony felt more and more anger toward Jean. He felt fearful that she would stop loving him and that he might not fit into her new life. As Tony's feelings of resentment, anger, and fear increased, he started expressing these feelings by behaving rudely toward his mother and her boyfriends, several times, screaming at or occasionally punching them when they kissed her. Although he finally managed to learn to control these outbursts, as a result of being punished for these behaviors, the feelings persisted until his mother remarried a few years later.

Tony is now a grown man with a family of his own, yet he still finds it hard to form and maintain lasting relationships. He worries that the people he cares about will abandon him, and he doesn't stay in close contact with many people. He has felt this way ever since he can remember, but never realized why he felt this way or where these feelings came from.

Tony's example is one of many different types of family scenarios, none of them perfect. For most, a "perfect family" would be something like the families we have seen on TV—the Cleavers or the Huxtables, to name a few. Statistically, this is not the case. More often than not, families do not consist of two parents in a first marriage living in a house with only their children. In this chapter we want to address situations that may be more common in today's society than you might think. We hope to help you find various ways to manage these situations. We will start by looking at issues that can arise in any family, including sharing and competition, the Black Sheep, living the parents' dream, and others. In this chapter, we will also cover some of the alternatives to the intact family such as divorce, step families, extended families, adoptive families, and foster families. Much of the following material in this chapter is excerpted from our first book *The Art of Managing Everyday Conflict.* A more thorough discussion of the family and power struggles can be found in that book.

FAMILY ISSUES

MEETING THE NEEDS OF ALL

A child's desire and competition for affection, recognition, and attention from one or both parents is the source of many power struggles in families. It isn't realistic to believe that a parent can give even one child everything he needs, let alone multiple children, so it's obvious that sometimes a child's needs will not be met. A parent who cannot meet a child's needs is likely to feel frustration, guilt, shame, failure, and/or various other emotions. As time passes, it is not uncommon for parents to feel resentment, anger, annoyance, and even rage toward their children, as the children seem to continually seek attention or frequently have needs. These feelings typically are covering up the underlying feelings of guilt and other emotions.

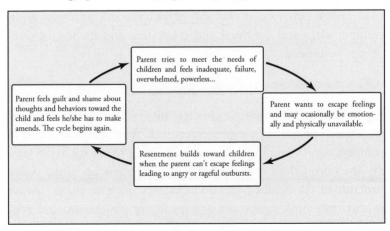

Figure 4: Guilt-Resentment Cycle

135

These emotions are often not really about the child, but more about the parents feeling inadequate in their roles as parents. Even so, the child is often the recipient of these feelings. As the parent lashes out at the children, the children often respond in such a way that their parents feel guilt and other vulnerable emotions for the way they've treated their children. This pattern of interaction will be referred to as the guilt-resentment cycle. Many families have this guilt-resentment cycle, regardless of the family arrangement, and in many instances it generates the perception that inequity is present.

Through observation, children begin to learn that they can manipulate their parents by saying things like "You're mean" or "I don't like you." The idea, from a child's point of view, is that the parents will try to gain approval and try to win him over. However, it's more common that parents will feel that their status power has been violated or disrespected and so they retaliate by punishing the child. Afterward the parent may feel guilt, but may use justification and rationalization as a defense.

One of the behavioral consequences of the guilt-resentment cycle is that often the party feeling guilty feels the need to make amends for his actions. Commonly, parents are not consistent in how they respond to a child's unproductive behavior, or they may try to bribe love out of the child. Parents often resort to these behaviors because they fear being "too hard" on their child. Needless to say, when parents aren't consistent with rewards or punishment, children often feel confused and frustrated, and inclined toward defiant behaviors.

Share and Share Alike

In families with multiple children, the children closest in age are most apt to experience the greatest conflict. Why? These kids tend to compete to move up in the "pecking order" or hierarchy in the family. The unconscious reasoning may be, "If I move up in the power structure of the family, Mom and Dad may love me more." Power is often measured in number and quality of possessions, and even young children learn this. Young children view the number of possessions as more important than their quality. Abstract ideas of value, such as denominations of money, are lost on small children. A small child, for example, would likely choose to have four nickels instead of one quarter. Instead of seeing abstract value, children relate to things they can touch and feel or that have some mass or visual quality.

Since children relate material items with power, it can be a challenge to teach a child the value of sharing. Giving part of his possessions to another child may feel as though some power is being given away. Commonly, children must see some positive result of sharing before they can make the connection to its value—maybe other children treat them more nicely when they share. When the child understands this cause and effect relationship, the motivation to share is reinforced. Many of the "me first" attitudes some children display point back to the child having unresolved issues with sharing. While adults may easily understand concepts such as "compromise" and "sacrifice," these aren't things that children instinctively grasp. They can be difficult lessons to teach, and there is no way to force understanding.

The issue of sharing most often causes conflicts between siblings, but these conflicts naturally tend to ripple through the rest of the family to include conflicts between a child and parent or between the parents. Problems with sharing often grow from being unwilling to share toys to being unwilling to share friends or parents.

A feeling of scarcity is often at the heart of sharing issues. When a child believes that there is not enough of something to go around, he may feel he must hoard that thing. This feeling comes from fear and mistrust. If I perceive that something is scarce, I may fear that there will not be enough to meet personal needs, or fear others taking advantage of me, or that I may have to fend for myself because I'm not being provided for. It is fruitless to punish children for not sharing. Punishing children for selfishness only teaches the child to avoid getting caught, and the punishment just breeds resentment toward the parent and often toward the would-be recipient.

WHO'S NUMBER ONE?

Scarcity is also the underlying motivation for kids to compete with each other, in the sense that only one person can be first, and when people compete, they all try to be the best. Some parents encourage their children to compete—for grades, sports awards, scholarships, etc.—feeling that knowing how to compete will be an asset later in life, and that competition is a good motivator to perform better. However, the children may equate these competitions as a quest to become the child most deserving of love and acceptance. Sometimes, parents even compete with their children to gain the affection of the other parent. In still other cases, one parent may leave all of the "dirty work" of discipline to the other, or may make a special effort to shower the children with treats and bribes in an effort to be seen as the "good guy." In either of these cases, internalized, unresolved family issues regarding love and affection may lead a parent to feel that love is a scarce commodity, and to get it, one must compete. In other words, if a wife feels that there is only a fixed amount of love to be had from her husband, she may feel compelled to compete with their children for his love. At the other extreme, a parent may put himself last and then feel rejected or abandoned. Sometimes, however, a parent may feel that because of his status as a parent, he is more entitled to the time and attention of the spouse and should come before the children. Either way, the parent will likely experience feelings of resentment, insecurity, fear, and maybe even some guilt. This interplay of emotions often fuels a pattern of conflict between the parents that radiates outward to the rest of the family. This, however, is only one small example of subtle competitions that can contribute to mild, moderate and severe family conflicts.

Children often believe that a sibling is better loved by their parents. Sometimes this feeling is well-founded but more often, parents simply have a different—not "better" or "worse"—relationship with each child. This difference in how the parents respond can lead the children to focus on their own feelings of inadequacy, and a child may come to believe that the only way to gain more love from the parents is by competing, or "winning," that love and approval away from his siblings. This is what we know as sibling rivalry. Sibling rivalries do not necessarily disappear with the passing of time—if they aren't resolved during childhood, they will carry over into adulthood. While physical violence may be an extreme consequence of sibling rivalry, it is more common to see siblings competing for achievement in school, athletics, etc., and then as adults compete for the best job, the most successful spouse, the nicer car... Many parents estimate their own success by judging the success of their children, and then compare the success of their children with the success of their siblings' children.

It would be misleading to say that competition within a family is wholly bad or harmful. The value of competition, however, is best determined by the motivation behind it. In fact, competition can in some ways assist in growth and learning. This can only happen, however, if each family member can recognize what he is learning about himself and realize the gifts and talents he has. When family members understand the lessons and issues surrounding the need to compete, learning and working toward resolutions can take place. Here again, the family's ability to work together and grow often relies upon the parents being aware of their own issues.

Parents should understand that their children often don't know their parents' issues and usually want to see them as perfect (enjoy it while it lasts, by the time the child reaches age thirteen or fourteen, you'll probably begin to feel that the children believe that you're the most imperfect being in the world!). When children mature and the brain becomes capable of more complex thought, their attitudes will certainly change, and they will see their parents as human beings. Whether we can see it or not, as parents we are likely to influence our children with our own issues through our behaviors and our emotions, and how we model them. Not every emotional problem a child has is automatically the parents' fault, but everyone in the family benefits when parents know their issues and work to resolve them.

While most parents want the very best for their children and love them deeply, many are still unwilling to accept the idea that their issues may negatively influence their children. Vulnerable emotions such as guilt, fear, and insecurity may cause a parent to avoid an honest confrontation with his issues. To ward off these emotions, he might use protective emotions such as sarcasm, arrogance, anger, or flippancy. A parent must then figure out how long he will allow his problems to be "the family's" problems, before he is willing to do something about them.

LYING

Lying is a big issue. Parents feel betrayed when their children lie, and they often overreact. However, they spend very little time trying to understand why their children tell lies. Lies are often told to avoid feeling shame, embarrassment, humiliation, and getting in trouble. Kids (and adults) think that if they can keep others from finding out the truth, they can avoid taking responsibility for their actions. Remember that kids want to avoid having their parents think less of them, and they also want to avoid pain. Adults are not so much different from that.

We feel it is crucial for parents to recognize that telling lies may be something that most kids try and is not a psychological issue, but continued lying is a symptom of much more. It can be a sign of low self-esteem, attachment problems, anxiety, impulsivity, and in many cases is just an extension of the parent's own problems with lying. Many times parents lie as much as, if not more than, their own kids. Yet they hold their children up to standards they are not willing to live up to. We also have to recognize that our culture is surrounded by exaggerations, cover-ups, and outright lies, whether in our homes, from our politicians, or in our media. So although we don't accept it in our children, we do accept it with ourselves and in our society, and we end up sending mixed messages to our children that can be destructive. We take a "Do as I say and not as I do" attitude, and the accountability that we hold our kids up to becomes a lie. It has to stop with us; we want to help our kids to see that lying only leads to more problems.

We don't agree with telling a lie to help someone feel good, though we do feel that if you don't have anything good to say then don't say anything. If your child brings a piece of artwork in to you, you may not like it, but you can find the positive aspects of it. You can ask him what he likes about it. You can let him know you feel proud of his efforts. You can teach your kids to be respectful of others and honor their own truth.

We stop our children from believing that lying works by example, by helping them see the wisdom in living honest lives. You cannot control whether your children tell lies, but you can manage the outcome. When kids tell a lie, there have to be immediate consequences. Often a letter of apology to the person they lied to is appropriate. Discuss the process of lying and ask them why they felt it was necessary. If they have told a lie to cover up something they did or didn't do, then two separate consequences should be given and you should clearly explain what each consequence is for. Too many times kids "get into big trouble" for doing something and lying about it, but parents forget to explain that the consequences would have been much less severe had they told the truth about it. Remember that lies are told to protect. They are told out of fear, shame, guilt, and rejection. If your child trusts that you are not going to overreact to issues or humiliate him for his mistakes, it will be easier to tell you the truth.

BIRTH ORDER

For years, experts have been trying to figure out whether birth order carries psychological influences; they have never reported a conclusive link. However, there is evidence to indicate that birth order can contribute to psychological issues within the hierarchy of a family. We saw earlier that competition, and needing to have needs met, can be related to birth order, and birth order almost always factors into the formation of a power structure in a family. In a family hierarchy, most children will struggle to maintain the status they feel has been imparted by their birth order, and then may try to advance higher from there. When status power is deemed to be a matter of high importance in the family, conflicts often arise because a person's status is not guaranteed. When parents do not make a big fuss over birth order or recognize status that way, then there is likely to be less conflict between siblings. In other words, if status is not a big deal to you, then it probably won't be a big deal to your kids. Parents may not even realize that they are assigning value to each child's status, but children will know.

141

Conflicts among siblings are unavoidable, and they are also an important part of life. Through conflicts, children learn how to express their wishes and communicate their feelings. It should not be a parent's goal to eliminate conflicts, but instead, to guide the children to finding a resolution and mutual understanding.

When we analyze the cause of most sibling conflicts, we find that birth order and the perception of power are often the driving force behind the situation. These childhood sibling conflicts lead us to form ideas about how to best respond to conflicts as adults. Therefore, if kids can't resolve issues related to birth order while they're still kids, they carry over into adulthood.

Certain tendencies that follow birth order lead children to be inclined toward particular behaviors. Older children often have greater responsibility although they have a choice to rebel against or accept it. New parents tend to aspire to be perfect when their first child arrives, and this often means that they also have very high expectations for that first child. Certainly, this oldest child senses these high expectations but may respond in various ways depending upon many factors. The child's self-esteem, his perception of the support system in place, his outlook on life, and still other factors will influence how he responds to the high expectations of his parents. Each child has the ability to try to live up to the parents' standards, or reject them.

Experience is a great teacher, and through experience parents become wiser in realizing their expectations of themselves and their children as additional children enter the family. As such, parents may have lower expectations and standards for the younger children. This lower standard for the younger children may not feel fair to the older children. At this point, parents need to explain, and help the children understand that they have evolved as parents.

A common sibling conflict arises when younger children realize that older children have greater responsibility. This often leads the younger children to seek more responsibility from the parents. Often, this is actually a mission to undermine the tasks or responsibilities of the older child or to disrupt the older child's ability to carry them out. It follows, then, that the older kids recognize this as a challenge to their power, and this breeds conflict.

Playing the role of the victim is yet another way that children may seek to gain power. If a child gives up all of his power and plays the role of the victim, it sets the stage for him to then call upon someone with more power (the parents) to rescue him. Which children seek increased power through responsibility and which try to gain power by being rescued can be influenced by birth order, but there are also other factors at work.

Factors ranging from biology to socioeconomic status and many things in between can influence a child's attitudes and actions. For this reason, the significance of birth order on a child's issues must be viewed. It is far more important to consider that each child is an individual and help him discover who he is, and identify his individual needs. Although birth order often plays into the motivations for a child's behaviors, it should not be viewed as an overreaching factor that provides a simple explanation.

THE ONLY CHILD

Naturally, if there is only one child in a family, he doesn't have to share power, status, toys, love, a parent's attention, or anything else, with siblings. For this reason, the only child does not have the benefit of experiencing sibling conflict and, therefore, may not learn certain aspects of resolving conflicts. It follows that only children, if they don't learn to share, may be more self-centered and unwilling to compromise, and this can follow the child into adulthood. These kids are seen as being spoiled, self-centered, stingy, or uncooperative but their attitudes and behaviors generally stem from social learning, or lack thereof, and the pattern of habits present in their homes.

Only children often feel a great sense of power, and it would be very difficult, in our culture, for any of us to want to give up power that we've enjoyed as a part of our day to day life. When a child has no siblings, he should socialize with other children early in life and regularly. Learning to function in a group of peers is important; it allows the child to learn valuable lessons regarding sharing, cooperation, acceptable social behavior, and many other things. Play groups can also provide an excellent outlet for a child to interact with other children and learn about mutual respect and team work.

GENDER

Power issues in families as they pertain to gender are often strongly influenced by the parents' notions and attitudes concerning gender. In families where the parents still believe in male dominance, males are likely to enjoy more status power than females, regardless of birth order. Sensing that males have more power or higher status can lead girls to feel a sense of powerlessness, which contributes to learned helplessness. In these families, girls are expected to do tasks traditionally considered to be female-oriented such as cooking, sewing, and laundry, while the males are expected to do traditionally male tasks such as mechanical work, lawn maintenance, and carpentry. Dividing tasks according to gender can cause several problems on several fronts. In the first place, dividing tasks by gender doesn't take personal choice into consideration. Maybe a boy wants to do some cooking or a girl is very good with and enjoys working on mechanical things. Secondly, many of the things that have been labeled "male jobs," such as lawn work, are seasonal, whereas "female jobs," such as cooking, are required on an ongoing basis. When seasonal tasks leave free time, sometimes children assume that it is okay to sit around while others continue to work. This situation is easily avoided by dividing household tasks without regard for gender. Allowing children to become exposed to all tasks, allows them to be well-rounded, and in turn they do not expect that only certain tasks are only suited for males or females.

Many parents already have a gender preference before a baby is born, even if they are reluctant to admit it. Along with this preference comes hopes and dreams for the child and visions of him accomplishing wonderful things. If a child isn't the gender that was hoped for, most parents can put their original hopes aside. Still, some parents have a difficult time accepting the fact that they didn't get the boy or girl they desired. These parents often experience feelings of anger, emotional distancing, or outright rejection toward the child, or they favor their other children who are, in their minds, the "right" gender.

Children of the "wrong" gender, or otherwise unwanted children, typically feel that their power is lessened because of their gender and, perhaps, feel as though they've done something wrong because they are not the gender that the parents hoped for. Sometimes this occurs when the parents project a sense of their own failure (to produce the 'right' gender) onto the child. But perhaps having a child of the gender opposite that we had hoped for will teach us something about our ability to accept the gifts handed to us, without reservation and without questioning why things happen as they do.

THE BLACK SHEEP

Often, families have a "black sheep." This label is applied to a child who did not follow the expectations of the parents and rebelled to the point of being ostracized from the family unit. The Black Sheep tends to be the eldest child, perhaps because of parental demands although any child can deviate from what the parents had envisioned.

If a child doesn't feel that he can find empowerment and positive recognition as the parents expect, he may seek rewards in a different area or by different means. Along these lines, some kids (and adults) choose to adapt, and become "good at being bad." When children don't feel capable of succeeding at "good things," they may turn to exploring ways of screwing up or pushing people's buttons to find power. As this pattern repeats, the child may recognize that he is better at "bad things" than good things, and even if these "bad things" get him into trouble, he still feels that least he's good at something. Often, both children and adults who have been, or who feel they have been, labeled Black Sheep, have experienced a certain sequence of events that led them to their belief system. A different perspective exists in children who believe that their parents are "bad" or "wrong" and they are "good" and "right." When this situation exists, the child feels that she is upholding a belief in what is correct, and the showdown with the parents is a matter of principal. In this situation, both sides (the child and the parent) believe they are "right" so the conflict centers around power instead of objective truth. Many times the parent(s) is resolved to not lose the battle, which often leaves the child no choice but to rebel or feel crushed.

Often the authoritarian parenting style ("my way or the highway") in one or both parents breeds a Black Sheep. The system of logic is that failure to live up to the parents' expectations is a foregone conclusion, and failure is "wrong" and if someone is "wrong" then he is also "bad" and "weak." So the Black Sheep seeks to counter these feelings of weakness, vulnerability, and wrongness, with anger and resentment and, eventually, by various acts of defiance. As time goes on he continues to find his own ways to "be right" and seeks out others who believe similarly, which often further distances him from his family. Why do you think kids get involved in gangs and other similar groups?

The role of Black Sheep also influences siblings, who can fear guilt by association if they try to maintain a good relationship with the Black Sheep who might be out of favor with the parents. Siblings may feel torn between trying to keep up a good relationship with the Black Sheep, or remaining in the parents' good graces by shunning him. However, parents are the providers and children recognize it would be in their best interest to ally themselves with them. Because the Black Sheep is associated with conflict and anger, most family members seek out ways to distance themselves physically, behaviorally, and emotionally. The perceived message from the parents is, "Either you will submit to my power and my way of doing things, or I will stop loving you and taking care of you." Such a message can make a deep and lasting impression on a young child and may influence his ideas about love, acceptance, and self that may last a lifetime.

Often a void is left in the place in the family that the Black Sheep would have occupied. The parents may then fill this hole with their feelings of sadness, failure, and shame, while protecting these feelings with rage or hatred. As this happens, family relationships are diminished because of an underlying fear that anyone could be replaced or rejected at any time. Therefore, each of the Black Sheep's siblings feels that he must avoid any weak or vulnerable emotions and appear strong in order to maintain his position; under this façade, communication within the family suffers.

Additionally, the siblings often feel forced to submit to their authoritarian parents to avoid the same fate as the Black Sheep, even if they resent doing so. This situation may continue until the kids believe that they can take care of themselves or can find someone else who will. In any case, these kids will likely remove themselves from their home environment as soon as possible, then could experience feelings of guilt for abandoning their family and/or siblings. As they grow up and leave the home, the kids' relationship with their parents may further deteriorate as communication breaks down as parents feel that they've been rejected, misunderstood, and probably unappreciated.

This situation with the Black Sheep is saddening because it is often simply a matter of the parents and child each trying to do their best, but the misunderstandings and breakdown in communication causes the relationships to unravel for the whole family. Despite all of the conflict surrounding these people as children, they often seek approval from others—bosses, friends, and even spouses—in their adult life to compensate for feeling unaccepted by their parents as children.

Through therapy, we often find a wounded child inside a parent who feels rejection, loneliness, sadness, and failure. Finding resolution between the child and parent would be simple if both parties were willing to drop the power struggle and lay down their emotional defenses, and open their minds to understanding and accepting each other. As is true in so many cases, the matter cannot be resolved until parent and child first make peace with themselves.

LIVING THE PARENT'S DREAM

While parents often want the best for their children, they often determine their perspective of "the best" through their own eyes. They often feel they must choose many aspects of their child's education, friendships, activities, sports, and career planning. Young children do require some direction and are not cognitively able to make the educated choices necessary to choose pre-schools and other toddler-age activities, but parents must have some awareness of how the choices they make for their children can affect them and their choices throughout their lives. Some parents direct their children's lives to fulfill their own dreams and/or recover for their own perceived failures (For example, the parent who wants his son to be a professional football player since he seriously injured his knee playing college football). Whether or not parents are conscious of the influences their choices have on their children is debatable, but this control of their children's lives does have an influence on the children's actions, choices, and perceptions of power.

Varying levels of control are exercised by parents in the choices they make for their children. Even when parents try to teach their children how to choose correctly, they often may control the choices so closely that the perception of choice is an illusion. Sometimes, the child's best interest gets confused with what the parents want for themselves.

Consider the three and four year-old children who are dressed up like dolls by their mothers, and entered in beauty pageants. A similar issue with males relates to choices in sports that many fathers make for their sons. In both situations, the child becomes the conduit for the parent; the parents live vicariously through their child. When the child does not live up to the parents' dreams and expectations of success, sometimes physical and verbal rejection, verbal abuse, and even physical abuse occur. Sometimes parents seek to blame other sources for their child's perceived failures, often voicing these opinions in front of the child, thereby teaching him not to take responsibility for his behaviors. The child learns the victim role, never learning from opportunities.

These issues are not only limited to childhood. Many times the choice of college and career is made by parents to the degree that if the child does not attend the college of the parent's choosing, or major in the preferred subject area, the parent(s) will not pay for the child's education. The child in these situations often feels forced into the choice and may comply to avoid rejection, keep the peace, or even to protect other siblings.

In all of these situations, the wants and desires of the child, at any age, are often neglected or knowingly disregarded. A parent's choices are made from a hierarchical power perspective, assuming that the child is not capable of making decisions in his own best interest. The parent is potentially placing an inordinate amount of pressure on himself to make correct choices, and many times the parents communicate only the final decision without engaging in the discussion of possibilities. Communication is probably the most important feature of a parent/child relationship, and parents ignore it to their own—and their children's—detriment. While parents, in their minds, might be seeking to make life easier for a child, the child may actually feel more pressure by having to live up to expectations they may not agree with.

Many times the parents are perpetuating what their parents did. One danger is that unresolved anger and resentment for the choices made for them may be taken out on their own children. What is transferred from parent to child across generations is that I cannot express my emotions to the proper source (my parents), since they are more powerful, so I will express my anger toward those less powerful (my children)."

When parents choose friends or relationships for their children, it is often because of an emotional enmeshment between the parent and child. While the parent sincerely cares for his child, he has a difficult time placing a boundary between them. The child's pain becomes his pain, and depending on the communication pattern, the parent's pain can also become the child's. Because the child is not as aware of boundary issues and is following the parent's model, the child often does not feel invaded until it is too late. The point when the child begins to develop friendships that separate them emotionally, physically, or attitudinally is usually when the parent begins to feel threatened and may seek to undermine the child's relationships with others. Parents also may see their own failed patterns in friendships and relationships their children are building, and would like to prevent them. But the child may only learn through his own experience.

Even though children recognize as they get older that their parents are only doing what they think best, the reality is that major choices in their lives are being made for them. Emotional implications of these choices can range from feeling helpless and misunderstood to resentment and anger. Whether the child communicates these emotions, verbally or behaviorally, to his parents depends on a number of issues. The main determination will be the child's perception of how receptive the parent is to feedback. If the child feels that he is unable to approach his parents about making his own choices, regardless of the parent's openness, then the child may feel powerless. Some children/adults seek to regain control of their lives in various manners; some not only surrender to parents, but surrender to life and allow others to make choices for them throughout. In some extreme situations, children have chosen suicide in order to regain an ultimate sense of control and/or in order to quell the unending feelings of shame and humiliation they feel for not being able to live up to their parents' perceived and real wishes.

Emotional, Physical and Sexual Abuse

Forms of abuse have existed for as long as people have learned to abuse their power. We are not going to focus on the different types of abuse, but common underlying issues. It is my belief that all types of abuse come from an underlying belief that the abuser has insufficient power to control some aspect of his life. Abusers are often seeking power and control of some form, and often express their power with those they see as weaker than themselves. Abuse is a disempowering, humiliating and shaming experience. Interestingly, while the concept of abuse has been put in legal terms, it is often up to the abused person as to whether or not they interpret a particular action as abuse. In other words, a parent who hits his child may feel he is trying to help the child learn something, while the child feels that the parent's behavior was abusive. Even if the abuser recognizes that what he is doing is "wrong," he may not change his behavior or take responsibility, since such actions means facing his feelings of guilt, shame, wrongness, weakness, and emotional pain. It is ironic and tragic that most forms of abuse occur toward those who we are supposed to love and care for the most, our family members. And many people who become abusers have been abused.

Many discussions about discipline with parents center about the fine line between discipline and abuse. As long as parents feel that they are helping their child learn through discipline, they feel that they can justify almost any behavior as being in the best interest of their child. As soon as the idea of abuse is brought up in the context of the extent or degree of disciplinary action, parents can feel very defensive, protecting feelings of guilt, shame, and remorse. In most situations, parents do not believe that their actions are abusive; in their own mind, they are doing what they are doing because they love their children. Their defensive reaction is understandable, since if they recognized their actions as abusive, they would feel guilt or wrong, which would likely feel disempowering and would result in them questioning their true motivations as a parent. Yelling, hitting, spanking, screaming, emotional manipulation, even sexual behaviors and physical deformation of the body, have been justified in the names of love. We will not critique these techniques, but, we will ask parents who engage in any or all of the behaviors to ask themselves whether or not they truly believe that their child is being served in their best interest. Ask yourself if you would like to experience what you may be doing to your child. Even if it was done to you, remember back and ask yourself how you felt when it was done. At the least, get some help for you and your child, immediately. If you truly love your child, you will have the courage to do what is best for him.

DIVORCE

As was stated, divorce is an unfortunately common occurring situation in our culture. The dynamics that can happen in these settings are too numerous to cover in this book, but we would be doing parents a disservice if we failed to address some of the more serious issues. Some divorces happen for what may be the best interest of all, and it is hoped that when two parents decide to go their separate ways, they can resolve their differences and look to the needs of their children. We do have to remember that we are human, however, and objectivity is not easy when it involves painful emotion.

Primarily, we want to address the manipulation between parents that often occurs with children. Messy divorces are often more about the parents trying to settle a score with each other, than about children's best interest. The problem is that both parents want to avoid seeing their role in creating the conflict, and often both feel victimized. Too many times, children become the pawn of one or both parents and the implications of this can last generations. Parents pump their children for information, tell them to keep secrets, buy them whatever they want, take things away given to them by the other parent, limit contact during visitations, bad mouth the other parent or children living with the other parent, and the list goes on.

The most difficult situation is when a parent subtly manipulates a child who is not old enough to understand. Children often have a feeling that something is not right, but if they ask the parent questions about this, it can result in another manipulation and the child is not sure what or who to trust. Many times manipulations can involve promises made but not kept, and too many times one or both parents are behaving worse than their children.

Many times a parent continues to hold on to so much anger and resentment that he continues to undermine the other parent's efforts to have healthy relationships with their children. The resentful parent often finds subtle and passive-aggressive ways to get back at the other parent through the child. Being open about his aggression would make a parent look like the "bad parent" and he would not be able to claim victim status. Parents may do things like change rules, be late for appointments, not deliver messages to the other parent or even to the children from the parent, not communicate important dates or events, let his kids have more freedoms to be liked more, and find many reasons to keep expensive litigation continuing.

Money is also a common tool used to manipulate. Whether it is with expensive toys, cars or even educations, parents often try to buy their children's love, but sometimes try to make it appear that they are doing it for their child's benefit.

A resentful parent needs to maintain the role of victim and/or rescuer in the eyes of others. He cannot be seen as the persecutor or instigator. The other parent can be left feeling hopeless and helpless, fearing that their children and others will see her as a horrible failure. We advise parents who feel this way to maintain honor and integrity, and remember that their children will live a long time, probably long enough to realize that their other parent has issues. While this does have an impact on the child, it is better for the parent to be there when his children need him, rather than alienate them and create a situation where the child feels like he has to rescue a parent and/or take a side. Parents who behave in these ways should look closely at, and have the courage to heal, themselves. Your child is not a trophy to be won and put on your mantle.

Usually one parent will try to explain to his children why the other parent may not show up for visitation, make phone calls, or send presents. It can feel like a heavy burden to carry not only your own emotions, but your children's. Instead, help them to talk about their feelings, and find someone to talk to about yours. Professional counseling is a good option. Remember that your children's place is not for you to lean on their shoulders. Let them know that you understand what it feels like to feel let down and abandoned, but don't give them a running list of what their other parent may have done to you. Personally, we feel that every family who goes through a divorce should go through some counseling to help them work through issues and improve communications. It is not uncommon for us to work with both parents and the children after the divorce to help resolve some of these ongoing difficulties and challenges of everyone involved. Just know that your children do need their own space to talk about some of their issues that shouldn't involve either parent.

FAMILY SETTINGS

THE INTACT FAMILY

The intact family consists of a mother, a father and children. Depending on the dynamics of the individual family members, an unlimited number of different power issues can affect the intact family. They may stem from parents assuming too much power or not enough, inconsistencies between parent behaviors and belief systems, conflicts between the children, emotional issues of any family member, favoritism between parent(s) and child(ren), and many other combinations of issues. Some of the biggest conflicts stem from inconsistencies between behaviors or belief systems of parents. Many times, the conflicts between parents are played out with the children. Children, being as astute as they are, often pick up on this and may learn how to manipulate one or both parents. On the other side of the coin are the children who feel put in the middle of the parent's conflict, may feel manipulated by their parents, and feel helpless to affect the conflict.

It is essential for parents in any family setting to understand and accept each other's perspective in trying to come to a mutual agreement on how to manage reinforcement and guidance of their children. In respect to the hierarchical nature of families, it is important to address situations where one or both parents feel a conflict with the status level they have achieved or been placed in. Parents often command the first and second positions in the hierarchy, but may wish to command the status level that the other parent has obtained or has been placed in. Sometimes, through both subtle and obvious ways, children may self-select the status level of their parents. The amount of exposure the children may have to either parent, the manner in which the parent responds to the child(ren), and the manner in which one parent responds to the other may all affect how the children respond to either parent. Responses are not measured only in verbal exchanges, but are registered in body language, eye contact, and voice tone. These are only a few of the more subtle issues that not only often strongly influence communication, but also aid in the determination of status in many power structures.

Many times conflicts that may occur within families regarding parental status involve the working parent and the parent who stays home with the children. In this situation, the children may regard the parent at home as having more power to determine and deliver rewards and consequences. However, the parent who works to provide financial support may view his role as powerful and integral to the survival of the family and may want recognition for his sacrifices. When the working parent is home, he may expect the power structure to shift to acknowledge his perceived status, which can result in significant disruption in the family. The parent at home may experience feelings of both resentment (that the working parent seems to come home and take over the power) and guilt (understanding the sacrifices of the working parent). The conflict for the stay-home parent is often between capitulating to the working parent, or asserting the role as the primary caregiver. The need for the working parent to affect the status quo of the family often stems from insecurity within that parent and a dependence on others to "feed his power." These dynamics can feel both confusing and frustrating to children and the spouse.

Sometimes the stay-home parent may be seen as more powerful by the children as the disciplinarian; but this parent might then feel the pressure of always being "the bad guy." On the other hand, the working parent may want to be closer to the children and may feel hesitant to discipline them. In this manner, the working parent sometimes becomes the "fun parent" and the stay-home parent becomes the "bad parent." In any case it is important that the parents respect each other and their respective roles, and model that to the children.

EXTENDED FAMILIES

Extended family includes grandparents, aunts, uncles, and cousins, as well as friendships that may approximate the closeness of blood relatives. Depending on the closeness of the parents with their adult siblings and parents, extended family members can have a significant influence on the family unit. More role confusion can occur when extended family lives in the home, if the boundaries between family members are not defined.

Issues of power often arise with extended families when it comes to discipline and child guidance. Parents feel they should have the authority to reprimand and guide their children but often family elders want to guide those interactions and correct or redirect the parents. This is confusing because a child may not understand who has the true authority or "status." The child can also learn to manipulate parents and other family members. For the parent, interference of other elder family members can feel frustrating, humiliating and disempowering. These feelings of disempowerment can result in feelings of anger and resentment which may erupt toward the other family member and/or the child, or may be internalized. Often this disempowerment can trigger childhood memories, and "child identities" inside may emerge causing difficulty in making rational parenting decisions. In this case, they are often trying to recover a sense of power instead of reasoning what is in the best interest of their child.

In extended families, the parents should be the central source of guidance. If other family elders feel that the parent is not parenting wisely, they may want to make suggestions when the child is not present, keeping the balance of power intact.

It may happen that family elders may discipline and guide the children "their way" when the parents are not around regardless of what the parents' wishes and directives are. This is often due to passive-aggressiveness and power issues. When parents feel that other members are not guiding their children in productive ways, they can remove the child from the elder's care, since the parent is ultimately responsible for the care of the child.

When conflicts arise, it is often in the long-term best interests of all concerned to set guidelines to follow for the other elders. In many situations it can be helpful to seek guidance together from a professional, not only to help determine guidance and discipline for the children, but also to resolve old issues that may be affecting their current relationships.

SINGLE-PARENT FAMILIES

Many situations might cause a single parent family, including divorce, death of a parent, age, choice of single parent to not have a spouse, and other situations. In each of these scenarios, different issues will arise that will affect all parties. When divorce is the cause of the single-parent family, very powerful dynamics will arise with both the single mother and single father, especially depending on who the primary caregiver is and who may be attributed to be the cause of the divorce. Regardless of those issues, the children (and parent(s) often go through a grieving process. Often, increased conflict occurs as family members raise their defenses to protect themselves and their feelings of vulnerability. In addition, the single parent often feels stressed and overwhelmed by the demands of parenthood and may feel that he has no one with whom to share the stress and emotion. This may continue to build and result in either the emotion being taken out on the children and/or it being internalized, resulting in emotional and physical consequences.

Being a single parent for either desired or undesired reasons can be an extremely harrowing experience, since that parent is solely responsible for financial, physical, emotional, medical, and hygienic support systems. While parents are often able to elicit help from their children, often just the stress of feeling like the only parent is overwhelming. From a perspective of power, the children may not be able to play parents off of each other, leaving no opportunity to develop a "good parent/bad parent" situation. The single parent also becomes the primary decision-maker. With only one parent, there is more of a demand for the children to resolve their conflicts quickly since that parent is the primary source of support. With two parents, the child is able to create a "good parent" and "bad parent," letting unresolved conflicts continue with the "bad parent." Having to seek this resolution with the single parent can be very healthy, if the parent is receptive to conflict resolution, because it teaches the child to address conflicts with others they perceive as having more power than themselves.

Other confusing situations can arise in single-parent families when the parent's emotional issues result in him not being truly able to fill the parent role. Older children can sometimes feel pressured to take on parenting roles, and even feel forced to parent the parent, or take on the role of the missing spouse and be a supportive parenting agent to the younger children. While many power issues can arise from this role confusion, some parents are more than willing to accept the role switch, since it results in the parent being able to relinquish responsibility and thus, feelings of failure for things gone "wrong or bad." When a single parent experiences significant psychological issues such as depression, anxiety, or alcoholism, stress is increased on both the parent and children. The parent may feel excessive guilt, shame and responsibility because of their issues, making it more difficult for him to resolve those same issues due to the stress. Children may feel insecurity, fear, frustration, and resentment about their parent's issues, and/or at early ages may also feel confused about the cause, sometimes feeling responsible, themselves, for their parent's psychological condition. The child's perception of cause and effect does not mean that the parent should feel more responsibility and guilt for their child's perceptions, but instead help their child understand the true cause.

TEEN PARENTS

Teenagers becoming parents has been a fact of life throughout the fabric of time. How society viewed the age of the parent has changed, however. In past (and some present) cultures teen parenthood was a more accepted practice, especially when life-expectancy was much shorter. In many twenty-first century cultures, however, there are certain "appropriate" ages to become a parent. Most people equate age with varying levels of maturity, i.e., the older one is, the more mature they are presumed to be. Furthermore, most people believe that the earliest ages for parenthood should be after the age of legally determined adulthood. While it is true that most early teens (ages 12-16) do not have the emotional and mental maturity or the financial means to handle the stresses and responsibilities of parenthood, there are also many adults who have limited parenting skills and financial means to support children. And, many teen parents have guided and raised their children very successfully, and many of the children of those parents excel beyond the aspirations of their parents. However, teenaged parents encounter various issues that affect their perceptions of themselves, their life circumstances, and their belief in personal power.

The first issue to consider is whether or not the teenaged mother has support or assistance from the father of the child. In the United States, many surveys have reported the grim statistics about how few teen mothers have physical and/or emotional support from the fathers of their children. Reasons for this lack of support may be unwillingness to take responsibility, either or both parents' demands, or when the mother may not know the father. When the father is not present or is not able to provide support, this can generate feelings of abandonment and/or resentment. The mother may feel lonely, betrayed, and unloved. How the mother deals with these feelings is essential because her emotions can be transferred to the child, especially if the child has a number of physical features that remind her of the father. Sometimes the emotions the mother feels toward the father are taken out on the child, and both the mother and child can feel powerless, and victimized by those in their environment. The mother's feeling of victimization may stem from life before the pregnancy, feeling abandoned by the father and/or feeling overwhelmed with the caretaking demands of the child. The child's victimization may stem from the mother's behaviors and quality of attention and care, as well as possibly feeling unloved and abandoned by his father.

The second issue is whether the teenaged parent is still living at home with his own parent(s). In this case, the parent is still often regarded as a child in her parent's eyes. The teen parent, from the start of her child's life, many times does not feel she has the "status" to fulfill the role as parent. This in turn can affect the child's ability to believe in the authority of his parent, especially as the child grows older. Involved in the teenage parent's ability to believe in her authority is the degree to which her parents may interact or interfere with guidance and discipline.

Other issues that affect the teen parent and her child are socioeconomic status, education level, parent's marital status, and age of the teen parent's siblings. Each of these issues can have both positive and negative effects, but it is up to the teen parent how she handles the issues that affect her life and the life of her child. The teen parent must understand that she has the power to understand and address her issues. While we all often have to live with difficult circumstances in our lives, it is up to each of us to decide how we will address those issues. Just as with a parent of any age, the teenage parent is still the most significant model in her child's life, and the child will learn much from her, her attitudes, and her beliefs.

STEP-FAMILIES

Because of the high divorce rate in our culture, many families are comprised of children from one or both spouse's previous marriages. Added to this, often the new couple with previous children have children together. Because of the potential presence of multiple parents and step-parents, the dynamics and power issues in step-families are more evident and more abundant than in any other family scenarios.

One of the primary issues that occurs in a step-family is that the step-parent is often not given the status of parent, and thus, some of the children may not want to comply with his demands. As has been discussed in the Control-based Parenting chapter, in a family that has developed in a hierarchical power model, members of the family seek levels of status and try to maintain the highest level they can command. When a step-parent enters the family, a potential shifting of power can occur depending on the level of status that the step-parent wishes to command. In most situations, the step-parent will want to assume the first or second position of power and may call on status power to justify their assumed position in the hierarchy. If the children allow this step-parent to assume this superior role of status, they may feel that they are giving their own power away, which they may have had to work very hard to obtain. The children may also feel conflict about the other parent's (the divorced parent no longer in the immediate family unit) power being usurped. Many children develop feelings of confusion around family loyalty, and one or both parents often contribute to the confusion. If the divorced parent outside of the relationship feels threatened by the step-parent, he may pressure his children for information and/or deliberately interfere with the children's relationship with the new step-parent. Interference from parents in these situations is often based in feelings of fear; of losing status in children's eyes, of what is in the children's best interest, of losing the love of their children, of their children being treated fairly, and other fears and threats. The entry of a step-parent into a family often prompts conflicts over power and hierarchical status throughout the family.

A step-parent often enters the new family with fear and trepidation. Often, before the marriage, the children and other (non-resident) parent may have made their objections known behaviorally and/or verbally. And sometimes the step-parent may perceive conflict where there is none, and will likely react to protect himself, which can meet with confusion and opposition from other family members. It also may be the case that the step-parent may not want to be a parent, but only a husband or wife. Furthermore, depending on his own issues of self-confidence and past family issues, the step-parent may feel threatened by the parent's relationships with the children and/or ex-spouse.

The step-parent may also resent being put in the role of parent. This resentment may or may not be openly expressed, but often children will sense it. Regardless of the step-parent's emotions and motivations, children can also be oversensitive and/or have ulterior motives in reporting conflicts surrounding the step-parent. Because a child often feels threatened by the entry of a new person into the hierarchy, it is important to acknowledge possible concerns and try to understand the motivations of a child's issues. If the issues are able to be addressed early in the relationship, and all can reach a level of understanding and acceptance with the life changes, often this means less conflict and more feelings of respect, safety, and security.

FOSTER FAMILIES

Many people provide homes for children who have nowhere else to live. These foster care settings are often temporary placements lasting from a few months to years. Children in foster care settings may have been placed there because of deceased parents, debilitating illness of a parent, child abuse, parents' inability to care for them, a parent's illegal actions, and other reasons. In most situations, these children have experienced significant emotional trauma or chronic distress which has affected their feelings of safety and stability. They may have developed inappropriate coping strategies which work but are relatively destructive in a family unit. Additionally, entering a new foster family means entering at the bottom of the hierarchy and they are prepared to do what need to do to protect themselves, or to advance in the hierarchy. Problematically, all of the children in the foster family are seeking more power, especially the family's birth children.

Many times foster parents are sensitive to the child's fear and distress when they first enter the family; how they address the child's issues can make the situation more pleasant for all or an absolute nightmare. It is also essential that the child understands his power in the process of acclamation to the foster family. Some children enter foster settings with the intent of seeing how long it takes to disrupt the family enough to be removed. These children are seeking control over who abandon them, and more often than not have significant attachment and relationship issues. Underlying many foster children's lives is a sense of powerlessness. Because they often fear that no one else is looking out for them, they try to take matters into their own hands by whatever means they have. Children who purposely disrupt their living situations often believe that controlling who they won't live with is their only shred of power. Because foster children realize that they are in temporary placements and realize that their caretakers are being paid to take care of them, they may not trust the foster parents.

While many people become foster parents because they deeply care for children and want to help them succeed, it cannot be ignored that there are some foster parents who do house foster children for money and/or for their own gains.

Even those who truly intend to help children often approach that desire from their own perspective. They might see these children as being disruptive and disrespectful, or excessively needy and submissive. While it appears obvious that the needy child feels powerless in many ways, it may elude the caretaker that that the disruptive child may feel the same way underneath his façade of defiance.

We often find that asking a defiant child questions about his perspective and telling stories of personal experiences can help break the ice. The child may not respond at the time the story is told, but it plants a seed and gives him power to digest the information at his own rate. Foster children are very adept at testing others to see if they are safe, or to test their power. Because there are numerous tests, and all a person has to do is fail one test to be crossed off the child's list of "safe people," it is important to be consistent. Challenges to power can be seen as healthy, if the child learns to direct power in productive directions. Many foster children are seeking recognition of their value. In order to not be drawn in and react to defiant children in an aggressive manner, it is important to be aware of your own emotions and to challenge how and why you may want to respond. At the core of the interaction lie both internal and external power struggles that you can ignore or seek to resolve, for the benefit of all.

While we have discussed children's attachment issues, we have not addressed the attachment issues of the foster parent. Many times, foster parents develop a deeply caring and loving relationship for their foster children. The longer the children are in the home, the more comfortable the family may feel, and the parent may care for them as if they were his own. Many foster parents are looking for children to love. Feelings of abandonment and rejection can occur when the child is placed in a permanent setting or moved.

Any time a person enters or leaves our lives, there is a period of emotional and physical adjustment. We believe that it is important for all of us to honor this adjustment.

ADOPTIVE FAMILIES

Adoption is often seen as one of the greatest gifts you can give to a child. It can also be the greatest gift you can receive. Many adoption stories have happy endings—parents who want to provide a loving home to a child or children adopt, and everyone wins. These parents did their homework, had structured settings, support systems, behavioral plans, and a home filled with love. The results are heart-warming. In some situations, however, this is not the case. Adopted children may come into a family and absolute havoc may result. What is the difference between the families that succeed and those who don't?

Sometimes, nothing is different. As we talked about in the chapter on attachment gone wrong, adopted children often times have significant issues with attachment disorders. The situations that set up the problems began before adoption, and many may not surface until long after the adoption is complete. The adoptive parents are often not prepared to deal with these issues and the problems continue to mount. Many times these cases necessitated multiple therapies and interventions. In any case, the parents still bear a responsibility to the child, and blaming pre-adoption trauma does no one any good.

In our experiences with adoptive families, parents bring their own issues into the situation. Similar to foster parents, adoptive parents may feel that they have rescued a child and that the child should love them unconditionally as a result. They feel that this child owes them something. When the children grow older, this attitude, whether it is communicated verbally or not, can contribute to conflicts and feelings of mistrust. Because parents do not want to think that they would feel this way about their child, they have a hard time admitting this belief, but it comes out in subtle ways. We have seen that when the parent is able to acknowledge his underlying beliefs, the child senses a shift and his reactions change.

Where we have seen some of the most destructive relationships with adoptive families is when there is an authoritarian, "my way or the highway," parent who tries to run a tight ship, combined with a child who has a controlling, attachment disordered, personality. In any family this is a problem, but in an adoptive setting, the parent wants to consistently seek absolute submission from the child on almost any issue, and the child wants to manipulate his way around it. In fits of anger, both parent and child may say they wish they could go back to the world before they were in the current family situation; said in anger, these comments have lasting effects, especially when the parent says them.

As you have seen throughout the book, you cannot demand submission from someone who has a history of mistrust. And if you got that submission, it would be as dangerous for the child as it would be if he fought tooth and nail for independence. If he is submitting to you, he will submit to others. Realize the importance of teaching them to find a balance in believing in and asserting themselves, with open communication and building trust. To reach this end, you will likely need the help and support of a good therapist to guide both of you through the process. Finding the balance is a very difficult tightrope to walk.

Because adopted children often carry a deep feeling of abandonment, a few risks can arise in current and future relationships.

The first one is that they become dependent in relationships and give too much of themselves away because they fear rejection. Because of the possible traumatic history of your child, you may need to coach him to know that if a relationship cannot be resolved in a way that preserves his integrity, it may be time to end that relationship. The other possibility is that he might not feel close to others or allow themselves to experience the ups and downs and risks and rewards of relationships, because they fear rejection. The end result is the same, but the behaviors look different. Look for some of these tendencies in your children and be willing to talk to them about them. Have the patience to plant some seeds and see them grow. Listen closely, and you may see these children open up. Remember that everything you have done to build trust can be undone in one careless moment.

Often before you adopted your child(ren) you went through your own painful process of trying to have children. The resultant emotions can feel very painful and are often surrounded by failure, shame, guilt, inadequacy, hopelessness, and anger. When you bring a child into your family, you are often looking to him to heal or fill a painful place inside. Children feel this emotional pull, and the underlying message is that they are there to fix something in you. This can be a big burden for a child to carry, and if the parent continues to need that fix, it can drive a deep wedge into the relationship over time. The child often feels that he needs to escape the relationship, and the parent is fighting to hold him close. Remember that you adopted your child to improve both of your lives. Getting to this level of honesty with yourself on many of these issues can be difficult, but will benefit all involved. We would suggest that you and your spouse explore your reasons for adoption and any issues that may surround it before you move forward.

These are only a few of the issues to be considered in adoptive families, but we hope that they help to introduce some of the factors that could be contributing to the challenges you may be having. We believe that you ultimately find the perfect child for whatever you may need to grow from. Just as any parent should, see your child as a gift to you.

SUMMARY

This chapter was meant to provide some insight and overview of various issues that can affect the family, as well as to apply what we have been discussing to a variety of family settings. We have addressed some issues that are seldom discussed, and others that are very serious. At the least, we hope you will consider if any of these issues are impacting you and/or your family. At the most, we hope that you may take these discussions to heart and see how they can help you grow as a parent and a person.

A family is a family is a family. It is made out of love, trust, and support, not genetics. Each has its own unique qualities, and most, if not all, of the issues have the common denominator of emotions that can occur in any family setting. By taking a fresh look at this chapter, and addressing other issues in future chapters, we hope you will see how to contribute to the creation of the family you have dreamed of.

ᖛ Chapter 8 ᖚ
Follow My Lead: The Road to Better Behavior Is Paved by You!

Whether you like it or not, you have an incredible amount of power in influencing your child's behavior, not only by what is said, but also by what you do. In this chapter, we will address how to understand your child's behavior better and how to guide her toward more productive behaviors. The key is that you understand that your child sees you as a pathway to what she wants to be like. As she matures, she may do unexpected things. The irony is that she probably saw you do it or heard about it in some form. Kids often do not mimic behavior just after they see it, though they may demonstrate similar behaviors days, weeks, months, or even years later.

When a child misbehaves, she is often trying to achieve one or more of five main goals—to get attention, to get a need met, to get revenge, to explore her sense of power, or to express feelings she does not understand. A child seeking attention often says, "Watch this!" or "Look at me!" If you don't comply with your child's request for attention, she may feel motivated to do something inappropriate in order to force the issue. If all else fails, she may choose to have a temper tantrum—something you cannot ignore. In this case, the tantrum is simply an escalation of your child's need for attention. After all, negative attention is better than no attention at all.

A child's effort to initiate a power struggle may express defiance or uncooperativeness. The child struggling to feel her sense of power may tell the parent "no" when a parent requests that she clean her bedroom or do some other chore. She doesn't want to feel as though she has no choices. An argument usually ensues as the child tries to challenge the parent's power, and the parent tries to get the child to do what is expected. Power struggles produce the perception that someone "wins" the conflict. However, as a parent and a model, try to attain mutual respect and understanding and avoid power struggles altogether. No one truly wins, and refusing to engage does not mean "losing." Being aware of your child's temperament and developing personality is important in these situations. Keep in mind that you do not want to crush your child's will, you want to elicit cooperation. We will address techniques to deal with these issues later in the chapter and the book.

Children seek revenge for the same reasons adults do: they feel hurt and want others to feel hurt, too. In essence, they feel that their power has been taken away, and they want it back. This can happen when a child breaks a rule and does not want to take responsibility for the consequences. A child feeling a need for revenge may say things like, "I don't love you anymore," or "I hate you," or some other comment meant as retaliation for her disappointment or pain. While many parents do feel hurt at such comments, displaying this only reinforces the child's efforts, and anger only reinforces that the parent is not safe to trust. The most productive approach to this situation involves simply telling the child that you are sorry she feels hurt or upset, and that she must deal with the consequences if she breaks the rules. This is a better approach than showing outrage, hurt, or some other emotional response. If the child does not get the sought-after results, then this behavior loses its appeal. Stick to whatever consequences you feel are appropriate for the misbehavior, and let the matter drop. If you are not sure of what consequences to use, hopefully you will have a better idea after reading this book. Children quickly lose interest in long-winded explanations or lectures, so it is important to get to the point and say what you need to say.

Children often try to explore their power, watching how people react to them. Sometimes they feel out a new person by trying to push some buttons. How that person responds will set the stage for how the children treat her in the future. One of the more common examples involves substitute teachers. At least one child will want to see how far she can push the sub, exploring the environment to establish the hierarchy of power. Discussing this child's need to try to manipulate power is often the best way to handle the situation.

The last of the four main behaviors involves a child expressing feelings she does not understand. Usually, when kids feel failure, frustration, and inadequacy, they may express anger and defiance to protect their perceived weaknesses. This type of behavior is often expressed with sentences that begin with "I can't..." usually followed by some act of aggression, anger or defiance. "I can't tie my shoes" will be followed by throwing the offending shoes across the room or stomping off. "I can't figure this problem out. This is stupid. I quit. " or "I can't color inside the lines" might be followed by the child ripping up a picture and possibly breaking her crayons. A child may use these types of comments to get the parent, teacher, or caretaker to feel sorry for her, and help with the project, or in hopes of avoiding the task entirely. She doesn't want to face her feelings of failure, and is playing the victim, hoping someone will fix the problem.

Children sometimes encounter things they really cannot do, and many times they fear their own failure and judgment from others. They try to come across as helpless either because they want someone else to do the thing for them, or they want some sort of sympathy. Simply telling the child, "Yes you can do it," is not necessarily the best approach. Neither is making the child feel stupid or silly for her inability. Instead, encourage the child to do the best that she can, and to try her best.

This does not mean refusing to help a child with homework, or leaving her to solve all her problems on her own. We want to give children the message that they can do some things if they give an honest effort, even though it may be difficult. The goal is that they practice and learn. If parents rush in to take over and do things for the child each time the child says, "I can't," then the child may begin to lose confidence in herself, and simultaneously learn to manipulate those around her and feel dependent upon other people to fix things, instead of trying to do some things for herself.

We have provided the tips sheet on the next page to deal with challenging children. Sometimes the biggest help we can get when trying to figure out what to do in a situation when our children are behaving defiantly is to take a quick look at some strategies that can help us step outside of our own emotional perspective.

DEALING WITH CHALLENGING CHILDREN

The following is a list of suggestions for helping you to deal with children when they are having behavioral challenges. Whether it is your child's behavior or not, they are important points to keep in mind.

1. Always remember that the child's first priority is often to protect herself…at any cost. If she feels threatened, she may fight back.

2. The child's second priority is often to please her parent.

3. If the child is about to do something impulsive or danger-ous, try not to yell at her to get her attention (sometimes you have no options). Remember, yelling often evokes fear and not learning.

4. Set up guidelines in advance with your child. Anticipate both positive and negative outcomes and possible alterna-tive choices. Teach her to problem solve and your job will be easier.

5. Be willing to recognize that children are often a mirror for their parent's issues.

6. Some parents may get into power struggles with their child because of their own issues, not the child's.

7. Some parents may revert back to their childhood when deal-ing with their children. Fear and resentment are often key emotions acting in the parent.

8. Parents often protect their image as successful and "power-ful" parents. Take a few deep breaths, find your power, and

believe in yourself. Children are very forgiving and understanding, but it is important to take responsibility for your errors. You are a model to your child. If she is doing what she observed you doing, you may want to change your behavior.

9. Be willing to entertain what the child wants and repeat what you hear back to her before you tell her why it may or may not work. Then offer a solution.

10. Realize that if your child has an attention or learning problem, you may have one also. This can create problems with attention, impulsivity and comprehension from both parent and child perspectives.

11. Your child is not an adult and will not understand as an adult does. She also does not listen like adults. Be willing to relate to her at her level (eye level, emotional level, and intellectual level).

12. Just because you are a parent does not mean that you can't learn from your child a new way to do something. Children often teach us much about ourselves if we are willing to listen.

13. Don't feel as if you have to have all of the answers all the time. You are human, not perfect. You most likely did not take a course to learn parenting before you became a parent. It is okay to not know about something and get back to your child when you find what you need to know, but be sure to follow up.

14. If you feel that an interaction with your child may be stressful or confrontational

   a) Go for a walk beforehand to get your thoughts together.

   b) Imagine yourself in a peaceful, relaxing scene.

   c) Talk about the sources of your stress with a friend and seek guidance.

d) Be aware whether or not your issues are playing into the stress.

e) Explore the sources of your stress:

   i. Is your stress based in the present or past?

   ii. What are all the emotions you are feeling?

   iii. How are you expressing the emotions associated with your stress?

   iv. How powerful/powerless do you feel related to the source of stress?

   v. Are you taking your stress out on others or your child?

   vi. How can you increase your sense of power related to the stress?

   vii. Look for options to reduce your stress. Often when one recognizes that they have choices, they are able to choose to feel less stress.

15. Ask yourself if the child is being served in her best interest.

DISCIPLINE OR TEACHING?

We have all heard parents say, or said ourselves, something like "I'm going to have to punish you to teach you not to do that anymore," when a child misbehaves or breaks the rules. We certainly need to guide our children and help them learn to behave well and follow the rules. But, how do we go about this? In many ways, we live in a culture that strongly believes in punishment for wrongdoing. Which word do we naturally want to use to fill in the blank in the phrase "crime and _____"? Now, we certainly aren't likening a household that employs punishment to a prison. But if we think about attitudes toward "punishment" in the penal system, we find something that shows us a basic truth about how we deal with improper behavior of children.

In the not so distant past, our "correctional system" relied upon the idea that locking people up for some period and letting them rot in a prison cell would serve as a deterrent to crime. The criminal would fear the consequences of her actions and not make the same mistake again. On a large scale, this proved to be incorrect. Studies show that prisoners we teach, counsel, and show the error of their ways, stand a much better chance of staying out of future brushes with the law than those who are simply punished and left to think about their actions. If the person doesn't know why it was wrong in the first place, thinking about it won't help. Many times people knowingly make choices to abuse, harm and manipulate, but even these individuals do not always know why.

What does treatment of criminals have to do with teaching a child who makes a mistake or misjudgment? The similarities are greater than we might at first believe. Children who draw on the wall or shout at the table are not criminals and do not compare to someone who commits robbery or who burglarizes homes. But even criminals receive a fair trial. Many times, children are judged quickly and consequences doled out without considering the reasons behind their actions, or even if they committed the acts they were accused of. Essentially, we want our children to learn that they must behave in the manner that fits in line with society. Punishing a child without having her learn how and why she should not repeat the act often only serves to reinforce the idea that getting caught brought on the consequences, not the thing she did. This can promote further lying and manipulation. From this standpoint, we may begin to see that punishment often teaches kids to try harder to get away with, or take greater care to conceal, improper behavior.

Some parents invoke forms of punishment that border on bizarre. Some make their child stand in the corner on one leg, some make a child balance a book on the backs of their hands for uncomfortable periods of time, and some literally wash their kids' mouths out with soap. These forms of punitive and corporal punishment were very much en vogue in generations of the past, but do they really teach the child anything? Sure, punishing a child by making her do something unpleasant may make her want to avoid being punished in the future, but does it really reinforce the understanding of the reasons why she should not misbehave in the manner she did?

An important step in addressing and correcting misbehavior requires that the parents have a clear definition of what constitutes misbehavior and identify it when it happens. By seeing and considering the situation as it happens, a parent can often figure out the child's purpose or motivation. In order to change the child's behavior, the parent must change her own response. This process of learning how to respond to the child's misdeeds goes back to the overall learning process—on the part of the parents and the child—that we mentioned earlier. For example, if a child throws a temper tantrum and it does not garner any attention, then the purpose for that behavior has been defeated. If the parent simply walks away, or says, "I will talk to you when you calm down," the child has no reason to continue this ploy to gain attention. The problem comes when the child escalates her behavior. Often escalation won't occur unless it has worked in the past. We need to make sure of giving the child attention when she behaves properly and does the things she's supposed to do, and guide her unproductive behaviors in productive ways. The child will gauge how she is or isn't supposed to act, and what she chooses to do, based upon the reactions she receives from us, the parents.

Although we have entitled this section *Discipline vs. Teaching,* we purposely used these words to evoke the more commonly considered definition of the word discipline: "control by enforcing compliance or order." We want to raise your awareness to the origin of the word. Its original meaning had little to do with control or compliance; it had to do with teaching and learning. One origin of the word is disciple, which means pupil or student; therefore an alternative definition of discipline is "to teach." Your children are disciples of your teaching. We wanted to evoke a comparison of the terms, to show the differences between the two words. With this explanation, we hope you will consider that even in discipline, the goal is teaching and guiding your child with meaningful lessons that will promote productive learning and growth, leading to more productive behavior.

FAMILY EXERCISE

Give each family member a sheet of paper with a circle in the middle, and a pencil or crayon. Have the family members draw lines extending out from the circle like sun rays and have them write the names of people, groups, or entities they feel have been supportive or represent a positive influence in their lives. In addition to family members or friends, the list may include religious affiliations, teachers, or social/service organizations. When the lists are complete, identify each person or group on the list and have the creator of the list talk about how each person represents something positive in her life. Have everyone also talk about how each person or group may have influenced their behavioral choices and talk about ways they can think about the influence of those people in future situations.

The main purpose of this exercise is to increase communication and help you all understand more about each other. Many times parents and kids are not aware of who is having an influence on their children and how. Parents often find that their children are influences on their behavior, and this can feel very empowering to a child. The second purpose to this exercise is to promote positive behaviors by using past behaviors of self and others as examples to promote future behaviors.

1-2-3, YOU'RE OUT

Time-outs are one of the more popular forms of consequences for children (and parents) that help to shape behaviors. They have been the source of humor and criticism over time, and often those who are more control-based have the biggest bone to pick with them. Time-outs are not meant to be a quick fix for problems; they are a stepping stone to guide a child's behavior and teach her limits.

They are a form of punishment, and often a way to give both parent and child a break from each other. Used consistently, the results are often positive, but time-outs are not always the best consequence for children. The most common way to institute the time-out is to count "One," "Two," and "Three" for EACH INFRACTION, not for each second that they do not listen. Say nothing more than "That's one," "That's two," or "That's three." You don't want to lecture or demand and you don't want to count too fast. Kids need a chance to respond and often do not have the behavioral control to stop what they are doing in one or two seconds. This means that if a child is touching something she knows she is not supposed to, that would be a "One." If she touches the same thing again or does something else she is not supposed to do, that would be a "Two." The same for a "Three." A time-out is then the result and is typically five minutes in her room or in a pre-determined place if not at home.

When in time-out, a child is not to talk or be talked to, there is not to be eye contact, and siblings are not to be interacting or instigating further problems. There will be plenty of time for discussion after the time-out is complete, and many times parents benefit from the time to reflect on what is occurring. The flip-side of the time-out is that the parents should be willing to call themselves for a 1, 2, or 3 if they engage in an inappropriate behavior. The willingness to count yourself shows that you, as a parent, are willing to model what you expect from them. While children can inquire if you should count something, we do not suggest that they count you. Many younger children want to count their parents for everything. Sometimes they have a point. When I am working with families I will purposely do something to get counted so that I can demonstrate to parents and children that I am willing to live by the same rules they are. Ask yourself where you run into difficulties with your kids and realize that it is often when they think that there is hypocrisy on your part.

Some children may actually respond to get a time-out so that they can get a needed break, and others who are looking for negative attention may also seek to instigate conflict in order to be noticed. In either of these situations, parents/caretakers need to look for the motivations a child might have to purposely initiate a time-out. If a child is looking for a needed break, let her know that she can ask an adult for some time alone if she needs it. For the child who is looking for attention, find other positive ways to give it. We suggest noticing things that children do well, and verbally reward them. For example, if a child tends to run out toward the street and you are constantly reprimanding for this, tell her she did a great job of staying in the yard, even if you know she may be getting ready to run toward the street. This may change her original intent.

But we digress.... Time-outs require patience, a non-controlling voice tone, consistency, and follow-through (wherever you may be). The purpose of a time-out is to decrease the occurrence of "stop behaviors," behaviors that you want your children to stop doing. "Start behaviors," on the other hand, are best increased through reward systems such as the *Comprehensive Behavioral Program* we discuss later in this chapter. Patience is important because your children often capitalize on your lack of patience and sometimes count on your lack of time when misbehaving. For example, some children are notorious for acting up just before it is time to go somewhere or when they are out in public. They know that their parents will not do anything about their behavior except maybe yell or bargain with them. The parent does not have time to go through the time-out, and the child holds her parent hostage. The answer is to be willing to be late for some things and follow through with the time-out.

A variation on the time-out option is to delay the same amount of time that you were delayed when it is time to take your child somewhere she wants to go. For example, take Zach. Zach is consistently slow to get his shoes and socks on when it is time to go somewhere. Because of this, his mother is constantly feeling frustrated and delayed. The more she demands, the longer Zach takes to get ready. One day, Zach quickly gets his shoes and socks on and is ready to go to a birthday party, when his mother says, "Oh no Zach, not so fast. You take about a half-hour to get your shoes on all the time, so that is how long it is going to take today." Zach cries and argues and pleads, because he is going to be late for the party, but his mother follows through and Zach shows up late for the party. After that experience and a few others, Zach gets the message about delaying his mother and is much quicker to be ready. While this is not your typical time-out, it is a form of the tool, and can have a very powerful effect.

How do your kids know when they are getting on your nerves and what might drive their defiance? Your voice tone. Always be aware of your voice tone, and work to keep it as calm as possible when counting. Even be willing to apologize to your child after counting if your tone sounds stern or angry.

How about where you enforce the time-out? We are strong believers that wherever your kids make unproductive choices, you have to be willing to administer a time-out. When children are in a mall, a restaurant, a store, another person's home, you can always determine a time-out location, together. Your child realizes that you mean business. Children often act up in public to try to embarrass you and mess with your power. If they end up in time-out a few times in public, and you stand firm and are willing to see the long-term benefits of teaching them responsible behavior, consistency, and limits wherever they go, you will all be better off.

How about the amount of time for the time-out? There are a few schools of thought on this. One is to have the time-out be one minute for each year of the child. Another is to have the time-out be the same for everyone. We believe in the latter. At age two and above we feel that five minutes is an adequate time for kids. Remember, a time-out is administered to let the child think about her actions and get away from escalation patterns. If you choose to do one minute for each year, that is fine too. Be sure to pick a strategy, stick with it, and be consistent.

What behaviors should you count? You want to figure out what behaviors are "countable" before you start counting them and have some agreement with others who will be counting your child. You want to be sure that everyone is counting the same things. Your children will capitalize on confusion, and/or it will add to everyone's frustration. If a behavior occurs that you feel is countable make a note of it and make others aware of it. Before you start counting a behavior, let your child know that you will be counting it from here on out. Interrupting, talking back, touching things without asking, name calling, and not following directions are just a few of the behaviors that could be counted. Hitting, swearing, or threatening others would be automatic time-outs. At older ages, consequences for these last behaviors may evolve into essays, which will be discussed later. The key to counting a behavior is to count it as consistently as possible. If you make a mistake and count something that has not been counted before, be willing to acknowledge it and reverse your judgment. Just don't let your children take advantage of your willingness to reverse a judgment.

So at what age should you start using time-out. I started using 1, 2, 3 time-out with our daughter when she was eight months old. This is considered somewhat early by some people's standards, but our daughter was able to learn this successfully. It took about one week for her to get the hang of it, and she soon stopped what she was doing and would look at us after a one, two or three. The time-out for her, at that age, was different than for kids older than two. The action was to remove her from the object and put her on the other side of the room, turned away from the object to redirect her attention. She was then free to explore again to find another activity. Before we counted with her we would say, "No Touch." We would then start counting. For those items she could touch but not put in her mouth we would say, "No Eat." and then count each time she put it back in her mouth, totally removing the item from her after a 3. We then moved on to "no rough, okay gentle" (when she would pull or bang on things), and so on, slowly adding to her vocabulary. Consistency was the key, and within a few weeks her behavior was much more easily guided. There were short tantrums, but these were ignored, and hugs were offered when she was ready for them. We were also able to teach her which books (children's vs. adult's books) and other items she could touch and which ones she couldn't. The goal was not to limit her behaviors, but to steer them in more productive directions. Older infants and toddlers can become frustrated and throw tantrums when too many of their behaviors are limited and they are told "No" to everything. Let them know what you don't want them to do, and then guide them toward a more acceptable toy or activity. Let them explore their environment and learn limits with your guidance. Don't remove every opportunity for learning from them.

We have intended to provide an overview on time-outs and a cursory course on its use. For more information on time-outs and counting, there is a great book called *1-2-3 Magic*, by Thomas Phelan. There are some philosophical differences in the manner in which the message is delivered; variety is the spice of life. While we believe strongly in the message we are promoting, we also understand that each child is different and may respond to slightly different techniques.

PROBLEM SOLVED

Too many times, children are told what to do by parents but are not encouraged to figure things out on their own. Most children do understand the choices they make and often do not want to be lectured; however, their impulsivity can overwhelm their ability to make better choices. We want our children to be able to slow down to make better choices. Telling them what to do does not accomplish this. Instead we suggest a technique similar to the 1-2-3 time-out technique—teaching them three questions. 1) Is what I am going to do (or did) a good idea, 2) could it hurt, harm, or interfere with anyone, anything or myself, and 3) is there a different or better way to do it?

When kids learn to ask themselves these questions, they have learned to slow down enough to think about their choices. The questions are designed to teach children (and adults for that matter) how to problem solve. This will make your job easier. The sooner you can help your child adopt these skills, the better you will sleep. When a child is able to work through problems on her own, you can feel more assured that when she is out in the world, at whatever age, she will make better choices for everyone. When an individual works through these questions, she finds that they guide her through a process. Question one leads them to question two. If her action does interfere, hurt or harm another, then it's not a good idea. This then guides her to evaluate the different and better choices to make. Some parents think that the questions are too complicated and multi-layered for a child, but the key to these questions is repetition. The more she rehearses and uses the questions, the easier it comes. You want to encourage the repetition of these questions, and use them with a 1, 2, or 3 count toward a time-out. For example, if your child is counted with a "One" for not following directions, you can remind them to use their questions you taught them by saying something like, "That's a one. Remember your three questions. What is the first question?" It is always helpful to have triggers to help children remember tools for their success.

The reason for phrasing question 3 as "different or better" is so that children will think of the different choices they can make without evaluating them. Some of the ideas your children may come up with may seem totally outlandish, but they will eventually be more reasonable. In the learning stages of this process with your child, you will want to walk her through it and help her to answer the questions, see all the angles, and understand who might be impacted and how by her behaviors.

How old does your child need to be before she can start using these questions? At the time she can begin to talk and understand. You might want to give her some visual triggers for these questions to help her remember them, and incorporate as many senses as possible into learning. Remember not to undermine your child's ability to understand and use these skills. Just be willing to give her the tools. Visual and auditory cues combined often enhance learning. Here are a few suggestions for some visual cues that you can give your children.

Figure 5: Visual Examples of Three Questions

COMPREHENSIVE BEHAVIORAL PROGRAM

A large part of empowered parenting involves not only consistency, but ensuring that your child (and other family members) knows exactly what her chores and responsibilities are, how to do them, and when and how often these tasks should be performed. For this reason, many families find it useful to create a schedule that identifies who is responsible for which task, when and how often it should be performed, and what the rewards or consequences are for doing or not doing it. It can be helpful to attach a system of rewards to the task list to encourage productive behaviors.

This comprehensive program can be customized for the whole family. In order to increase the possibility of success, the family, but especially the parents, must be dedicated to seeing the behavior program through, from start to finish, before starting it. Setting up the program is the most important stage. Failure to accurately identify the issues, difficulties, and problems that may arise when instituting such a program may create many problems that could undermine its success. If set up properly, the program can prove to be a very powerful success for everyone involved.

Although the rewards and consequences used with the program may change over time, families can modify and continue to use the program for an unlimited period of time. This task list will help you and your family develop organizational skills for both the present and throughout life. People who follow lists and write down goals are 80 percent more likely to complete those tasks and goals than those who do not write them down.

WHY THE WHOLE FAMILY?

In order to communicate a sense of equity, decrease conflict, and provide a good model for your children, you should be willing to follow this program along with them. If you aren't willing to participate, why should they? When parents cooperate and participate in the program, they have found it quite helpful. Many parents realized, in retrospect, how disorganized they had been, which had contributed to the disorganization of their children. We, as parents, have to be willing to accept our responsibility in our children's issues. Our efforts to learn and grow are important because our willingness to improve ourselves reinforces the value of learning and growth in the eyes of our kids.

GENERATING THE TASK LISTS

It is important to have a comprehensive list of tasks in behavioral programs; this will aid in making sure all the tasks are completed. The whole family can participate in generating the list of tasks, or the parents can make the list and then solicit input from the rest of the family. It is very important to have the entire family participate so everyone feels that they had some say in this process. Your children's feeling of empowerment, from the start, is a key to the success of this program.

To generate the task list, review the day or week and ask yourself what tasks you and your family do, from as small as packing a bookbag to as significant as going to work or paying bills. When you brainstorm and list all the activities, you may eliminate some but add others. The other important issue is considering tasks that may be more complex. Complexity depends on the interpretation of the task by the individual as well as the number of steps it takes to complete. For example in cleaning a bedroom many steps are involved, from picking up clothes and stripping/making beds, to vacuuming and emptying trash cans. Telling children to clean their room without splitting that into steps can set them up for failure instead of success. Break down tasks that may be considered complex into simple steps that can be completed and checked off one at a time. Completing homework assignments and cleaning a bedroom or even doing the dishes may be examples of tasks that could be broken down into simpler tasks.

The next step is to define the task from completion to end. This is different than breaking down complex tasks into simple ones, because the complex tasks are written on the chart, whereas the definition of tasks is written on a separate sheet to be referred to if necessary. Defining the task involves writing down directions to be followed to obtain a checkmark for the completion of the task. For example, vacuuming the floor involves:

1. taking a vacuum cleaner out of the closet and into the room to be vacuumed,

2. vacuuming the entire floor in orderly fashion, almost as if cutting the lawn,

3. moving furniture and vacuuming underneath and behind the furniture (if necessary) and returning the furniture to where it had been,

4. wrapping up the vacuum cleaner cord and return it to the closet.

The reason for such detail is that children are infamous for doing only part of a job and wanting all the credit. If there is a direction sheet that can be referred to, it decreases the chance for arguments. All family members sign off on the directions, indicating their understanding and contractual agreement concerning the completion of the task.

LISTING THE TASKS

After you've generated a list of tasks, it is important to put them in the order in which they will be completed throughout the day. If the task is to be completed more than once a day, such as brushing teeth, it should be put on the chart as many times as it will be done. For example, brushing teeth is often one of the first and last things done in a day.

Some tasks will not be performed every day, but on the days they are performed it is important to list them in the position that they would be completed.

If you are having a child as young as three or four and up to the age of seven or eight use the task list, you may want to consider using pictures in place of or next to the written task. The pictures will help the child understand what the task is. This will help build a sense of independence and self-confidence in the child, as well as to decrease the chance of developing a dependency on others for instructions or advice.

Children often blossom and feel very empowered when they recognize that they are able to do things on their own. It gives them many more opportunities to believe in themselves. If you are going to use pictures instead of or included with words, you may want to take a picture of your child doing the task with a smile or while enjoying the task. This will communicate to her that she enjoys completing the task.

TIME LIMITS ON TASKS

Some tasks need to be done by a certain time or the purpose is lost. For example, if we need to brush our teeth twice in a day, then technically we may wait until the evening, do it twice and mark the task completed. Also, kids are famous for putting things off until the last minute, and you may find them rushing around the house trying to get things done before they go to bed. This is probably not a good idea.

In order to prevent this, put a time for a task to be completed next to the task. In setting a time, be reasonable, but not so casual that the tasks could be put off too long.

DAILY VS. WEEKLY TASK LIST

Do you use a daily or a weekly task list? One option is a master chart in a central location that everyone can refer to. The problem is people have to return to the task lists to remember what they need to do if they do not have a copy with them. Since most people have a computer, a chart made on the computer can be reused, edited and easily printed.

Each person is responsible for carrying her own list. In some very competitive family environments, one child or another may try to hide or destroy another sibling's task list so she can be seen as doing better or "winning the game of getting positive attention." If this happens, it is a definite power issue to be discussed and resolved.

A daily list can be helpful to show which tasks do not need to be completed on that day. However, a weekly task can be helpful because the child learns to develop the habit of carrying that list with them, checking off the tasks as they go long. This gives her a visual reference to her success at every point in the day and shows the tasks or challenges that lie ahead.

If you have a master task list, as well as a progress chart, you will want to mark each person with a different color (or different stickers) so it is easy to tell who has completed which tasks.

HOW LONG DO WE HAVE TO DO THIS?

This is a ten-week program and is repeated after every cycle. In the first ten-weeks, the goal is to gradually build confidence in completion levels to get rewards. In order to receive the ten-week reward, participants have to reach the weekly goals in eight out of ten weeks. The "Performance Levels" in the last column of the "Progress Chart" on [page 193] give guidelines for the necessary percentages of tasks to be completed, and show the number of tasks necessary per day, to reach the daily rewards and to obtain a weekly reward. For example, if Jim completed 60% (6 out of 10) of his tasks on a Tuesday and the performance level was 55%, he would get his daily reward. If he completed 50% (5 out of 10) of his tasks on Wednesday, he would not get his daily reward. If his weekly performance indicated that he earned his daily reward on five out of seven days, he would receive his weekly reward if the performance level was four out of seven days. The percentage of the completion of tasks increases to get the daily reward over time (from 55% to 95% over the initial 10 weeks), just as the number of daily rewards increases (from 4 out of 7 to 6 out of 7) to get the weekly reward. After the first ten-week period is completed, the program is started over, but the performance levels are maintained at 95 percent of tasks completed in a day and six out of seven days that the task completion percentage is reached.

A critical part of the program is that the participants must successfully complete the tenth week in order to earn the ten-week reward.

The program is built on a combination of short-term, intermediate-term, and long-term rewards. One of the difficulties with most children is that they cannot delay gratification. This system teaches them that it takes time to work for some goals, and that many goals are attainable with persistence, dedication, and self-discipline. Once they learn this, they will hopefully internalize that information and continue to develop productive attitudes and beliefs that will last them a lifetime.

Be aware that it takes time, energy, and effort to follow such a program. But remember the long-term goals; you are teaching your children skills that will last a lifetime. The short-term benefit is that it will make your life much easier in the present. For example, asking a child to complete a task generally means asking more than once, and waiting between requests to see if it gets done. This process takes a great deal of time out of everyone's day and can add a lot of unnecessary stress. The task list and ten-week program take time to set up but the time will balance out. You are likely to spend much less time than if you did it the old-fashioned way.

BUILDING CONFIDENCE

As was discussed in the last section, the behavioral program starts by setting easily obtainable levels to reach success. As the participants' confidence is built the performance levels are gradually increased. Once again, please observe the changes in the performance levels on the Progress Chart on page 194.

When performance levels in a behavioral program start out with inflated expectations, the chances for failure increase. This means that the participants may quit because they do not want to feel failure and don't believe they have any chance of succeeding. 55 percent, as a starting point, is often an easily reached goal. Remember that you are working toward long-term success, not immediate compliance. Many of us, as we get older, often want too much too fast and need to remember that our children learn to walk first by crawling and then taking one step at a time.

Many times parents are hesitant to start at 55 percent because it seems too easy and the kids can manipulate the program. This may be true in some instances, but we have observed that when the family is doing the program together, the children often end up competing with each other and complete most of the tasks, rather than only completing enough tasks to get the rewards. If the kids do feel the need to be so manipulative as to only complete the number of tasks requested, then that may indicate more significant issues that go beyond the behavioral plan.

You will also notice on the performance levels that we never ask for 100 percent of tasks completed or seven out of seven days that they've reached their goals. It is important to allow for one task to be missed and for people to have one rough day in a week. We don't expect perfection, nor do we think it is wise to ask that of anyone. We are all human, and we make mistakes. It is crucial to remember that. What we have found is that kids get in the groove of getting their tasks done and generally earn their rewards every day.

If a participant does not complete the same task two days in row, she will not get rewarded. If she does not pick her clothes up, for example, or does not vacuum or complete tasks on two consecutive days, then no matter what else she did, she does not get the reward. Otherwise, a participant could deliberately not do a task that they just didn't want to do but still get the rewards for the program.

REWARDS

Again, this program involves using short-term, intermediate, and long-term rewards. Short-term rewards for young children can occur for each task as they go through the day. However, for most, short-term rewards are recognized only when the daily goals are met. Daily rewards may mean earning the privilege to play outside, watch TV, play video games, etc. Sometimes these rewards are delivered the following day, because the last task often would not be completed until bedtime.

Weekly rewards are more intermediate-term rewards and may involve anything from having a friend over on the weekend, renting a video game, or even earning a weekly allowance. It is important to take the child's inputs into account in choosing all rewards, because if the rewards have no meaning to her, she will not have the motivation to complete the tasks. If a weekly allowance is involved, you might want to keep that in place throughout the program. However if the reward is having a friend over, renting a video game, or renting a movie, then it may be decided each week. This should be decided on a case-by-case basis, but with some consistency.

The ten-week reward teaches delay of gratification and is a long-term reward. It is something they are willing to work for, and that is worth waiting for. It can be anything from a computer game, an I-pod (on the pricey side), or even a season pass or trip to an amusement park. Once again, it is very important to select a reward that has some importance to the child.

Select the daily, weekly, and ten-week rewards before the program starts so that each person knows them from the beginning. Imagine if your boss did not tell you how much you were going to get paid before you started a job. Would you have the motivation to work to the best of your ability? For intermediate and long-term rewards, we may borrow an idea from a practice used by some employers. When an employee receives a positive comment or letter of commendation from a customer, management gives the employee a "Thank You" card. When the employee collects ten of these cards, they can be redeemed for a paid vacation day. A similar strategy could work with rewarding a child. Parents may choose to use gold stars or stickers or some other means of indicating and measuring the child's success. When the child has accumulated an agreed upon number of stars or stickers, then she receives an agreed upon reward.

There is a difference between intrinsic and extrinsic rewards. An "intrinsic reward" is emotionally rewarding in itself; one that makes us feel good. When something is intrinsically rewarding, then the deed is, in itself, rewarding. Volunteering, helping someone in need, or donating to a charity are good adult examples of things that provide intrinsic rewards. An extrinsic reward is one in which something external to the deed provides the reward. Recognition, praise, payment, or material gains are examples of extrinsic rewards. If we mow the neighbor's lawn because she is sick and cannot do it herself, and we expect no payment, we experience an intrinsic reward. If we only mow the neighbor's lawn because we expect payment for our effort, we seek an extrinsic reward. In other words, we do certain things only because we expect some sort of external reward.

When teaching people or training animals, it is important to start with extrinsic rewards and move towards intrinsic. If someone never internalizes the idea that rewards can take the form of feelings of satisfaction, accomplishment, or confidence in completing a task, then she will continue to look for some type of external "carrot" to be dangled in front of her to do anything. Parents tell us that they feel unable to get their children to do anything unless they provide some type of payment or reward. This situation develops because the children figured out that their parents would offer incentives if they consistently did not complete a task. It is easy to fall into this pattern but it can be detrimental, especially to the child who may carry the need for extrinsic motivations with her throughout her life.

WHEN SHOULD I CHECK THE TASK LISTS?

Many times parents must constantly check to make sure all tasks are getting done. Both children and adults try to get out of doing difficult things, especially if there's something more fun to do. They will often be willing to take the consequences later in order to have fun or avoid pain in the present. While this is not logical to many parents, because they have learned that the task still needs to be done eventually, remember that children do not have the same cognitive or mental capacities that adults do, and therefore they don't think the same way. Their learning will come in time and with repeated lessons. As we have stated throughout the book, lecturing and yelling do not teach children the lessons; they need to learn them for themselves, with your support.

There are different approaches to checking up on task completion. It can be done every day, but this can become labor-intensive and can feel very frustrating. It can be done on certain days of the week, but then participants may learn to finish their tasks only on those days. Making checks on a surprise basis could cause the children to play the victim role and feel angry. You may choose to roll a dice and use that number to decide how often to check the tasks. Whether it involves dice, pulling a number out of a hat, or whatever random means is used, allowing the frequency of checking on tasks to be determined randomly reduces the odds of the child feeling victimized or conspired against.

One suggestion for checking tasks is to use an audit. If the tasks are not being followed, or are being done incompletely, then anyone has the right to call an audit. It involves having a few of the participants check up on tasks of anyone, including parents or teacher.

It is important that audits not be called too often or when someone is trying to get even with somebody else, because then it becomes a weapon, not a tool. In the event that an audit is called unfairly, an essay-writing consequence (discussed in this chapter) could be levied so the person can think through why she behaved as she did and why it was not a good idea.

To swap or not to swap

Swapping tasks such as sweeping floors, cleaning counters, vacuuming, dusting, and so on, can alleviate boredom and monotony. We recommended that task swapping occur, perhaps on a five-week basis so that each person develops a pattern of getting used to completing the task, but the tasks will be switched only once, decreasing confusion. Task swapping is a judgment call and may be reviewed as the program continues to evolve.

MINUS POINTS

At the bottom of the sample task list on page 194, you'll notice three minus points. A minus point is used when the child has been given an opportunity to follow a command with approximately five seconds to follow through, but she has chosen not to comply, thereby earning a minus point. Either mark it on her sheet at that time or write it down to mark later, so there is an immediate consequence. If she continues to not comply after another five seconds, then you mark another minus point. If you mark more than three minus points, the fourth minus point is marked on the next day. If you mark more than six minus points, the seventh minus point is marked on the day after. What the child learns is that her behaviors today may affect her tomorrow and into the future. While she may not be invested in learning this lesson at the moment of resistance, it may be something to discuss with her after the situation has died down.

It may be a good idea to put a limit on the number of minus points earned at one time, perhaps nine, because sometimes when children and adults get stuck in emotions, they are not thinking logically. Additionally, many children will try to break the program and figure out all the reasons why it's not going to work so that they can try to control the situation. If the child does not comply after the ninth minus point, then it may be a good idea to institute an essay writing consequence (discussed next). If a parent and child, or teacher and child, become embroiled in a power struggle, it is very important that the parent consider their voice tone, their actions, and their behaviors that contributed to and/or maintained the conflict.

SAMPLE TASK CHART

Tasks	M	T	W	T	F	SAT	SUN
Wake by Alarm or w/ one Notice							
Brush Teeth by 9:00 am							

Make Bed by 9:00 am							
Eat Breakfast							
Clean Breakfast Dish by 10:00 am							
Take Lunch & Books							
Clean Lunch Dish							
Homework: Math English Spelling Reading…							
Afternoon Chores… by 6:00 am							
Clean Room: Strip/Make Bed Pick-up/Sort Clothes into the sheets Clothes/ Sheets to Laundry Clean Desk Pick up Floor Dust / Vacuum Empty Trash							
Vacuuming by 6:00 pm							
Dusting by 6:00 pm							
Clear Table							
Clean Dishes							
Counters							
Sweep Kitchen Floor							
Pack Book Bag							
Pick up Clothes							
Brush Teeth							

Minus Point								
Minus Point								
Minus Point								
Day Total								

Shaded areas note days to complete those tasks.

PROGRESS CHART

	M	T	W	T	F	SAT	SUN	Performance Levels
Week 1								55% & 4/7 days
Week 2								55% & 4/7 days
Week 3								65% & 5/7 days
Week 4								65% & 5/7 days
Week 5								75% & 6/7 days
Week 6								75% & 6/7 days
Week 7								85% & 6/7 days
Week 8								85% & 6/7 days
Week 9								95% & 6/7 days
Week 10								95% & 6/7 days

THE WRITE CONSEQUENCE

In a few places throughout the book we have referred to an essay writing consequence for your children (and possibly you) to complete in the event of certain unproductive behaviors. It is not the be-all and end-all of consequences, but it can be very informative and useful to understanding your child's motives and emotions. Lying, stealing, cheating, physical aggression, and name-calling are just a few of the infractions that an essay can be used to discuss and explain some of their behaviors. So why would you want to use an essay? Primarily, it is to give your child (and/or you) some time to really think about what happened and why, without anyone evoking guilt, shame, or humiliation. You might believe that you should be the one directly delivering a lesson, but—as discussed earlier in the book—lecturing, yelling, screaming, and physical punishment often only elicit anger, resentment and defiance. The question is what other strategies do you have to teach children what is in their best interest and know that they are learning that there is a cost for their actions?

The following task is meant to be a substitute for punishments such as grounding, lectures, or physical punishments. The purpose is to help the individual think about her actions, process them on paper, and then talk about the situation and her feelings. The essay writing task is not limited to children; adults should also be willing to write essays if their behavior warrants it. The individual should be on restrictions (no TV, radio, activities…) until the essay is completed and discussed. In other words, this method incorporates grounding, but each individual determines the amount of time she is restricted, giving her a sense of power. If she is grounded for two weeks (should it take that long to write it and discuss it), then she is responsible for the duration. It is important to make the time to discuss the essay when it is finished. After the essay is processed, the situation should be resolved and the individual has her privileges returned. This technique can be used for kids and adults with at least a third grade writing level, but can be adapted to younger kids if the essay part is discussed verbally. Or the essay can be written in pictures, short sentences, or phrases.

The following scenario is an example of behaviors that would earn an essay. Johnny took one of his friend's video games, and his mother finds it hidden under his bed after he denied seeing it. Johnny's mother then tries to talk with him about what he did, and Johnny calls her names and tells her that she is a liar. Johnny's mother calls Johnny a few choice names herself. Who should write the essay?

1. Johnny should write an essay about why he took his friend's video game.

2. Johnny should also write an essay for calling his mother names.

3. Johnny's mother should write an essay for calling him a name(s).

Many adults may disagree, but an adult's willingness to write essays is a very important point, since adults are important models for children's behaviors. If you don't want Johnny calling people names, then you, as an important model to him, have to be willing to take responsibility for calling him names.

The task is for the child (or adult) to write a one and a half- to two-page essay written (one page typed in a twelve point font) about her behaviors. Restrictions stay in effect until the essay is finished and processed with the parent or other person involved in the conflict.

The essay is based on the following questions:

1. Is what I did a good idea?

2. Did it interfere with anyone or myself or harm anyone or myself.

3. Was there a different or better way to do it?

4. How was I feeling before, during, and after?

As you can see, this essay writing exercise is based on the three questions that were discussed earlier in the chapter. We hope you realize that many skills your child will learn are built from other skills and lessons. The essay should also include a section about what she was feeling before, during and after the negative behavior. Processing the underlying emotions is the most important part. Insecurity, fear, and/or jealousy are often motivating emotions. Anger is often a reaction to others' behaviors, and guilt, sadness, disrespect, shame, and failure often occur after the behavior. Emotions at each stage should be considered, as well as events that may have happened earlier that day, that week, or even that month. When a child reacts with a physical outburst, it is often in response to a seemingly small event, but is it "the straw that broke the camel's back." It is likely that many different choices could have been made that would have been different or better. In the essay, a child would create a list of options and choose the behavior they think would be in the best interest of all involved. The following is an actual essay; the names and identities have been changed.

My Essay for Today

Punching Alex was not a very good idea because I could have hurt him very badly. I also could have made his parents very upset at me. It also was not a good idea because I got suspension and I got grounded. Punching Alex hurt several people: Alex, his parents, my teachers, the principal, my parents, and me.

There are plenty of better ways to do it. I could have just told the teacher, or the principal, filled out a harassment form, or just sat there. The way I chose to do it was not a good way to handle it. I'll try to do better next time. I just overreacted way too much to a little name calling.

Before I hit him these are some of the emotions I felt: upset, angry, betrayed, confused, agitated, spit on, back-stabbed, and very hurt. When I hit him, I felt hated, dirty, rotten, stupid, hurt, confused, and betrayed. After I hit him I felt stupid, rotten, upset, angry at myself, and dirty.

All in all what I did was a stupid choice on my part. Even though what he did was wrong I guess two wrongs don't make a right. I guess I will have to ask forgiveness again. In this essay I have learned that fighting is not the solution it only makes more problems.

What happened was I sat down for lunch then Alex came in and sat down right next to me and started insulting me which made me upset. Then he started insulting my family which made me very angry. So I got up and slugged him three times in the face one for my mom one for my dad and one for me. He tried to punch me but he missed. Then I heard the teacher yell my name so I quit and walked over to her and she made me sit at another table. After that I got walked to I.S.S. (in-school suspension) where the principal talked with me and told me what I did was not a good idea. I had to sit in I.S.S. for the rest of the day. The next day I was suspended.

There also could have been legal consequences. John's parents could have sued my parents. I also could have had charges pressed against me. If I had hit John just right it could have killed him and I would be in jail forever and I would regret it for the rest of my life. I should have just told the teacher or filled out a harassment form. What I did was really stupid. I hope I will do better next time. Hopefully there won't be a next time.

If the child has difficulty writing, she can still do the exercise by drawing pictures, making a topic outline, answering the questions in words or short phrases, or sit down and talk about it when she feels ready. The key is to help the child understand the emotional motivations for her behaviors and to take responsibility for them. By having the consequences removed after the essay is complete, it gives the child the power to determine how long the consequences last, and thus increases her sense of personal power.

Sometimes your kids may engage in more significant behaviors for which a two-page essay is insufficient. We do agree that sometimes there are situations that require more significant consequences, such as: drug or alcohol use, stealing, sexual behaviors, taking the parent's car, etc. These issues might have a legal component or put people in danger. In these situations we promote a longer, more detailed essay that answers the questions and goes further. Essays such as these have even been used as part of consequences from the legal system. Judges may view this as a favorable part of a legal action, and it can be used as a tool in the probationary process. It might require a child to do research on trends in drug use, statistics on use and abuse, the legal ramifications of use, possession, or selling; she might have to interview a legal source and/or medical source for information, and it might require references. This indepth essay was used for an older teenage couple who had engaged in sexual relations. When the parents found out, they decided to limit unsupervised time until the two completed the paper together. This involved teen pregnancy data, sexually transmitted disease statistics, the concept of love, and why they felt that they needed to have sex to deepen their relationship. The process of the couple working on this together helped them see how dedicated they were to each other, and helped the parents to assess how maturely the couple was handling the issues.

This essay technique is most likely a new way to look at consequences, and as a parent or child guide, you may have many questions as you start using it as a consequence. Many of these questions may be answered once a child starts writing—parents are often surprised by what their kids write.

SUMMARY

We have given you a little insight into your child's motivations and introduced you to a few techniques that will help with not only your child's behavior, but yours. There are many variations on guiding behavior, and we encourage you to explore other techniques and perspectives. As we have discussed, there is no one right way to do things, and we all have something to offer. We will address other strategies later in the book.

We will now move our discussion to the concept of communication. Many behaviors are affected by communication, and communication comes in many different forms. This is just one more piece to the puzzle in empowered parenting.

∽ Chapter 9 ∾
Talking to the Hand: Improving Family Communication

After food and water, communication is possibly the next most important facet of human existence. We develop relationships through communication, and survival of the human race would be difficult without it. Animals communicate in various ways, from honeybees doing their dance to whales singing their songs in the sea. Through communication, we let others know our needs, feelings, attitudes, and wants. Communication sets the tone and affects the depth of our relationships. Our survival, as infants and children, depends upon communication. It follows, then, that communication between parents and children is crucial to the child's physical, emotional, spiritual, and social development. In the chapters on attachment, we discussed the importance of the quality of the communication between a parent and child; we saw how it plays a crucial role in developing a child's sense of self and worldview. Communication invariably sets the tone for many facets in a child's development in areas such as sense of safety, trust, self-esteem, and personal power.

What do you think of when someone says "communication" to you? Spoken words? Written words? Speaking, reading, and writing are probably the most obvious and conscious ways that humans communicate. However, non-verbal communication—facial expressions, voice tones, gestures, eye contact, spatial arrangements, touching, and expressive movements—influence our interactions in ways that spoken words can't. In a child's first year of life, he can't speak and can't understand much of anything we say. Parents and

200

infants find other ways to communicate by various noises, interactions, and voice tones. When the child learns to speak, however, we may believe that words substitute for all of the early communication patterns.

We can say, "I love you" in many ways. But, instead of focusing on those words, let's think about the other factors surrounding how we communicate this feeling. If we want to convey the meaning of the words "I love you," we don't say it like a monotone, emotionless robot. We don't stand stiff like a soldier, with our eyes forward, and our hands at our sides. We use voice inflections, body postures, eye contact, facial expressions, and many other non-verbal elements to convey the depth of our feelings. We can change the context of saying "I love you" by altering either the verbal or non-verbal aspects of speaking the phrase. Consider this: Dad stands over his daughter, looking at a test she brought home from school. Dad is walking away from her in exasperation, while shaking his head disapprovingly and, in an irritated voice, says, "I love you, but I'm very disappointed in you. If you keep making these stupid mistakes, you will never get anywhere in life." This scene seems conditional and hierarchical. In other words, I would love you more if you didn't make stupid mistakes.

Now, consider this same test feedback scenario, except Dad looks at the test and sits down next to his daughter. He calmly asks her how she felt about the test and whether she felt she had prepared for it. After she discusses her preparation and her possible mistakes, he says, in a compassionate tone, "I love you very much, and I want to help you to feel successful. The grade is not what's important to me; the important thing is whether you are trying your best and learning what you need to learn. Let's see how we can work together on this."

In changing from hierarchical to equity parenting styles, we can choose how to communicate with our kids. Some of these methods are verbal, and some are non-verbal. But no matter which method of communication works best for each of us, the most effective requires that we maintain a direct and respectful approach. Although we want our kids to think that we're perfect and never make mistakes, the fact is that we do. Positive and equitable parenting means owning up to our mistakes and accepting the responsibility for our actions—just as we want to teach our kids to do. Our kids learn many things from us, and setting an example for them is one of the most powerful teaching tools. Our behaviors communicate ideas and concepts to our kids, just as words do. This chapter will address some of these issues of communication, and we'll explore some strategies. We will cover more strategies related to communication in the chapter on solutions and strategies.

"FOR THE LAST TIME, I SAID NO..."

Let's start our discussion of communication with something easy. First, think about the number of times we tell our kids "no" in one day. It's worth pointing out that the third word some children learn, after "Momma" and "Dada," is "no." Children with behavioral issues hear "no's" and other negative comments, two to ten times more than other children. What kind of effect does this have? Let's try an exercise. Ask someone to say "no" to every request you may make for one hour. How do you feel at the end of that hour? Even though you set it up, there is still an emotional impact, isn't there? There's no reason to think that kids feel any differently about hearing "no" on a regular basis. When a child hears frequent no's from his parents, it can set a negative frame of reference for how the child feels about himself, toward his parents, and toward the world.

Sometimes we can find ways of avoiding these immediate "no's" but as every parent knows, sometimes it is impossible to avoid. If the kids want to know if they can jump off the roof, or are ready to put the dog into the washing machine, saying "No!" is our only option. You can then talk more after that. We can get into a habit of saying "no" without thinking about the request or seeing how we can make it work. Sometimes we may feel too busy or tired to consider many of our children's requests. One approach to avoiding the habitual "no's" involves listening closely to the child's request and trying to find ways to say "yes" or talking about other options. These are often perfect opportunities to use the three questions that we talked about in Chapter 8.

Sometimes we can't accommodate a child's wishes, but we might find alternatives to the request. For example, Billy's grades have improved and his father tells him they can go and do something together as a treat/reward. Billy asks if they can go to the mall but his dad has been having knee problems and isn't up to the walking. So, Billy's dad offers to take him to a movie, and says that maybe they can go to the mall on another day when his knee is feeling better.

In a different situation, Terrance comes into the kitchen right before dinner and asks for a cookie. His mother's initial response could be, "No, you can't have a cookie. We're almost ready to eat dinner." But with a more thoughtful approach, she might say, "Yes, you may have that cookie, as soon as you've finished all of your dinner." If Terrance hasn't done his homework and asks if he can watch TV, she may say, "Yes, you can watch TV as soon as your homework is done."

"YOU MISSED A SPOT"

Criticizing children (and many adults) often leads them to put up walls and shutdown. If we can learn to find respectful ways of confronting a child instead of criticizing him, we'll have more productive conversations. We want our talks with our kids to be productive and positive, and criticism may thwart this goal because it often feels very much like a verbal assault—in extreme cases it can be abusive. Like adults, children will naturally defend themselves if they feel assaulted.

When we speak in a way that leads a child to feel defensive, we effectively encourage him to tune us out. Criticizing a child is likely to hurt his feelings and precipitate arguments—these are wastes of time and energy and only serve to complicate the matter we want to resolve. Negative communication not only frustrates and irritates both parties, real damage can occur to the child's self-esteem and ability to feel successful.

A parent's motivation to criticize usually starts with the intention of helping the child do better; we may criticize while helping our children focus on areas that need improvement. Unfortunately, criticism usually points the child's focus toward feelings of shame, embarrassment, and inadequacy. Criticism comes in a direct tone and, at times, can be downright cruel. Comments such as, "How stupid can you be?" "What were you thinking?" and "Can't you do anything right?" are but a few of the unfortunate comments that parents make.

Backhanded, subtle criticisms or "zingers," as we call them, can feel just as painful. These indirect forms of criticism often come from parents and people who are more passive aggressive and can never be pleased. Some examples are as follows: "That's a really nice outfit, if you like that color." "You did almost as good as your brother." "Thanks for making that wonderful sweatshirt for me, but I don't wear things like that." These comments hurt because it is very difficult to know how to react to them. Zingers aimed at children may lead the child to feel as though he never gets anything quite right. Before saying one of these zingers, you should consider what motivates you. Are you feeling anger, resentment, sadness, unworthiness, or other emotions that might color your comments? At the least, you should take responsibility for your comments and make efforts to avoid them. Otherwise we can inflict damage that love can't mend.

The objective is to work toward more direct and honest feedback with our children, without being overly critical. Direct but non-critical communication often means putting the issue out in the open and saying, "This is what I feel concerned about," or "We need to talk about this thing that happened at school today." Critical comments tend to open with blaming phrases like, "You broke that window. . ." or "You never listen to a word I say. . ." or "How many times do I have to tell you. . ." and it comes across as an attack. We must separate the deed from the doer. Talk to the children about what happened, without placing blame or guilt, and try to engage them in a discussion. Instead of saying, "You did this," we can provoke them to think about the situation and tell us their thoughts, what did they think went well; and what could they have done differently, then add our feedback. Try to start with a positive. For example, suppose that this "thing" that happened at school amounted to Sharon getting into trouble for kicking her desk and making a rude comment to a teacher. When asked what she thought about the situation, Sharon said, "I wanted to hit a kid, but I didn't." Her restraint in avoiding a physical exchange with the other child is commendable. However, she should be encouraged to think about other things she could have done instead of kicking the desk or saying nasty things to the teacher. This approach sets the stage for a conversation about the events without resorting to lectures or criticism.

LOOK AT ME WHEN I AM SPEAKING TO YOU.

Consider a few things when talking with children about issues, concerns, mistakes, etc. Whether and what children learn from parent/child interactions depends upon how we use our power. Children usually feel somewhat threatened and shamed during interactions that involve problems or concerns, especially if the interaction involves trying to correct a behavior. The parent therefore is already higher in the hierarchy, and asking a child at that point to look at you when you're talking to him only humiliates him and reaffirms his inadequacy. From a power perspective, this is little more than hierarchical power trip. Why should we feel the need to prove our power to our children? Most children already think that their parents are great. Our kids need to know that we want them to learn from their mistakes and that we still love them, regardless of what they've done. Using criticism to incite feelings in a child, such as guilt, shame, humiliation, and similar emotions is not conducive to empowered parenting, it is more about the need for power. Wanting them to see your power over them does not help them to learn from their mistakes, nor does it show that we love them.

If there were a single topic in this book to lecture about, it would be the topic of lecturing. But, there's no point in lecturing about that. Why? Because like our kids, none of us will sit by and pay much attention to long-winded ranting or dissertations that involve things we don't care to hear, anyway. We tend to lecture when we want to get our point across to our children. However, when we start lecturing, we cut the child out of the communication picture; they're not listening, and we may as well be talking to the proverbial wall. Most of us remember sitting in an uncomfortable desk during a long, dull lecture and asking ourselves, "Will this guy ever shut up? Does he ever stop for a breath?" Does anyone really believe that our kids don't feel exactly the same way about us when we're harping about something? Talk a little and listen a lot, as many parents like to tell their kids. We aren't learning while we're talking.

Lecturing is a form of hierarchically showing off our status or power by demonstrating our knowledge to others. But, lecturing doesn't allow any room for the recipient of our ramblings to engage in a conversation or to feel empowered by an exchange of knowledge. And since kids tend to have short attention spans, lecturing is largely pointless anyway. Instead, we should share our feelings and thoughts and listen to theirs. It's likely that we don't have as much time for talking with our kids as we'd like. Be short, sweet, and to the point when you state the concern and help brainstorm for solutions with the kids, instead of only talking about problems. Taking too much time when pointing out problems or presenting long-winded lectures may incite feelings that are counterproductive to our goal of meaningful communication.

Let's put this in terms that adults can relate to. Suppose you are at work and your boss says, "What's your problem? You forgot to get the FedEx Pak out yesterday. You messed up, big time. There was a proposal that had a deadline on it, and you have caused a serious problem for this company. What do you have to say for yourself?" How would you respond to that, compared to a situation where the boss says, "I noticed that the proposal didn't go out yesterday. I'm not sure what happened, and I wanted to talk about this. Can we meet at 11:00? Maybe we can come up with some ways to keep this from happening again." In this example, the boss has given you some time to consider your situation and did not attack you, but set the stage to work together to prevent the issue from reoccurring. This approach lends itself to managing expectations, identifying the issue, and finding productive ways to approach the problem, incorporating the fact that some learning needs to take place in order to avoid repeating this oversight in the future.

Managing expectations sometimes involves giving others the benefit of the doubt. Your boss might say, "I know that you may have been very busy yesterday and possibly just forgot, but the proposal did not get out. I wanted to see what happened." In doing this, the boss allows you to explain the situation. Whether we're dealing with adults or children, this non-critical approach accomplishes positive results because it fosters a willingness to cooperate instead of giving rise to the feelings of inadequacy and subsequent resentment and hostility that criticism often provokes.

Even though we are dealing with children, we can't forget that we have feelings, too. When our children do something they shouldn't, we feel frustration, confusion, or anger of our own to deal with. If we are coming from an "I'm the boss," perspective, we may feel that we are supposed to know everything and be emotionless, because we should be in control. We may feel the need to hide our underlying vulnerable emotions (fear, shame, failure, doubt, helplessness, and hopelessness). Still, it is easy to direct our feelings toward the child, if we're not mindful of them.

The goal of correcting a child should be to help him learn. How do people learn? In a safe, supportive environment. Do not be afraid to use humor, and do not be afraid to use your own actions or mistakes as examples. Empower your children to teach you, and allow them to show you (and themselves) what they know.

THE FAMILY MEETING

Many families benefit from holding periodic meetings to open up channels of communication. Family meetings allow each family member to discuss things that pertain to his life, matters that pertain to the family, and/or things of general concern. Families can hold meetings as frequently or infrequently as they feel that they need them. All members of the family should attend the meeting and everyone should get equal time to speak.

At family meetings, it is especially important to remember the difference between respectful communication and criticism, as we discussed earlier. All family members need to avoid criticism and thereby avoid creating an atmosphere that feels threatening or unsafe. Parents should model respectful behavior, mediate, and dissuade children from being critical or inflammatory to other family members. Some families benefit from setting ground-rules or guidelines for these meetings before they begin and, perhaps, even developing an agenda. The participants should agree that everyone will have a turn to talk and that everyone else must allow the speakers to express themselves without interruption. A speaker may need guidance in getting to his point, and in the learning phases, parents can assist with this.

The family may choose to set the rules down in writing, so that everyone is fully aware of what the rules are. To set good examples for our kids, we should follow the same rules. In general, it is better to have rules in place, make them as specific as they need to be. If you want to divert from those rules you may want to consider making some special considerations at a separate meeting, than to wing it and veer off course. Kids benefit from structure and consistency, and the rules should stay pretty much the same from meeting to meeting.

Let's look at an example. Let's say you have a meeting to discuss a vacation destination. Everyone is able to say where he wants to go and why, and can present his pros and cons, but the family cannot agree on where. In many ways, each destination is an attractive option. The rules should provide for each person to share his perspective and get a vote. However, let's say a consensus eludes the family so the family may make a special rule to pick a vacation site from a hat. A majority vote may decide that special rule. If they cannot reach a majority vote, a parent or maybe the meeting leader may have to make a final decision, without abusing his power. If a child is making the decisions, he might need a guide through this emotional process so he can learn some life lessons.

Another example of how rules and structure help may involve setting guidelines for transportation. A rule could request that a child should arrange with his parents for transportation by the Wednesday before any Friday event. Be sure to include whether these plans involve taking and picking up friends, since that will require more of the parent's time. The family can agree upon whether Wednesday is sufficient time, or if there is another time/date that would work better. Be sure to agree on the consequence for not meeting the deadline. Each family member needs to be willing to compromise and work together on these issues, and the parents will set the tone. If we are unwilling to see where we can set firm guidelines and compromise, then our children will probably be unwilling to cooperate because they will not feel that the power structure is equitable.

How long the meeting lasts is important. Debate and discussion is healthy, especially in learning to communicate a point, but we should try to be realistic in how long we expect kids to sit and listen to everyone else. Keep meetings focused and on track and try not to cover too much ground. It is better to table an issue to discuss later than push the point and lose everyone's attention. We know our kids. We can tell when they're getting antsy and distracted. Try to gauge how long they can remain occupied by the meeting, and limit meeting times accordingly, but a half hour is probably reasonable unless there are pre-school aged children present.

Try to end these family meetings on a positive note. For this reason, it may be a good idea to save some "atta boys/girls" for the end of the meeting. Before everyone leaves the meeting, each participant should express a commitment to resolving any problems, and identify what he will do during the following week to help. In fact, providing a balance between raising issues and offering positive feedback and praise is an important part of having productive and successful family meetings. If you limit the time spent on the issues and spend more time on positive items, accomplishments, and encouragement, the children are more likely to want to attend the meetings.

Some families may even go as far as to make accomplishment certificates and award them during their family meetings. Certificates could be awarded for things like keeping bedrooms clean without being asked, straightening up around the house, feeding the animals, or maybe even just for being a great kid. At the beginning of the next meeting, start with a synopsis of how things have been going with the past concerns and recognize the efforts and family members who contribute to effecting positive changes for the family. Be careful not to make too big of a deal about what one child is doing over other kids. This can create unnecessary competition. Spend a few moments to recap before moving on to new issues and concerns. Family meetings should not consist entirely of airing grievances and resolutions. Family meetings can provide a good environment to plan outings or vacations, discuss schedules, upcoming dental or medical appointments, who will need the car on which nights, etc.

Example:

Family meeting with the Jones family consisted of setting some group rules. They were as follows.

1. We will all attend bi-monthly family meetings.

2. Meetings will consist of family goals and resolutions.

3. Meetings will last no longer than one hour.

4. We will all be respectful and take turns talking.

5. We will take turns running the meetings.

6. We will agree on assigning who is responsible for what for the next meeting.

7. A majority vote will decide upon special rules, or by the decision of the meeting leader, or parents, in that order.

Be willing to discuss and work toward compromises. For instance, Jill wants to go to Daytona for the family vacation but Tom would like to go to Orlando. They both agree that they will research places to vacation, find out what activities the family can enjoy while they're there, and present their findings at the next family meeting.

Often all the family members want to make their own plans for a particular night, like Friday. This means, often, that everyone wants to be everywhere at the same time. Therefore, families should cooperate to find equitable solutions. For instance, William often asks to go to the basketball games at school, and Mom and Dad like to have a '"date night." In this case, the family decides that by Wednesday of every week everyone needs to have set plans for where they want to be and how they intend to get there. It may be that the parents can rotate taking their children to the games, or they may have a teenaged driver that can assist. William and his parents agree that since the game starts at seven, William's friends who need a ride can come home from school with him, and Mom and Dad will drop them off at the game on their way out to dinner. One of the other kids' parents will pick them up after the game and bring William home. However, if William does not have his arrangements made by Wednesday, he risks not having transportation to the game. Taking this approach accomplishes several objectives.

Setting time limits or deadlines reinforces the importance of priorities and planning. Involving the children in finding solutions teaches them how to brainstorm for answers and gives them a say so in the things that involve them. Considering the solutions and approaches to various problems can help kids learn problem-solving skills and make them accountable for their own lives. Each of these aspects of involvement—planning, prioritization, problem resolution, and cooperation—contributes to building a sense of accomplishment when all of the pieces come together. This is why family meetings can be so important to the long-term success of children and families. Yes, they may take some time to get started, but the rewards can be priceless. This is a cornerstone to empowered parenting.

You were saying???

Having mutual respect between a parent and a child often depends upon mutual listening. As parents, we want to feel authoritative and we often try to impress our kids with the idea that they must listen to us. However, equity-based parenting and respectful communication mean that we must make a commitment to let our children talk while we listen to them as well. Effective communication with kids involves talking to them in the tone and with the same respect that you would show your best friend, co-workers, or your own parents. Children learn how to treat other people by seeing and hearing how we, their parents, treat others.

Parents should take some time to think about how they have generally spoken to their kids in the past. Have there been times or events wherein you have said or done things that weren't as positive as they could have been? Be honest. As you think about these things, instead of concentrating on the situation, or what your child did, focus on how you acted or responded to the situation.

If we want to get a feel for our habits and expectations as talkers, listeners, and observers, we have to consider what we observed when we were children.

- Did my parents listen to me when I was a child?

- Did my parents tell me to be quiet?

- What was the predominant voice tone my parents used with me?

- Did I get attention when I misbehaved?

- Did they often interrupt when I was talking?

- Did I interrupt them?

- When people talked to me, did they look me in the eyes?

- Was I easily distracted when children/people talked to me?

Now consider the present:

- Do I listen to my children?

- Am I more willing to listen to adults than children?

- What is the predominant voice tone I use with my children?

- Do my children get more attention from me when they behave, or when they misbehave?

- When was the last time I had a serious conversation with my children just to see how their lives are going, and what is important to them?

- Do I spend at least thirty minutes with each of my children, one on one, each day?

- Do I frequently look at my watch, TV, or computer screen when my children talk to me?

- When was the last time I actually got down on the floor and played with my child?

- When did I last go on vacation with my child, and what did we discuss?

- When was the last time I watched my children play, observed how they played, and listened to what they were saying?

I CAN'T TRUST YOU AS FAR AS I CAN THROW YOU

Many troubled kids feel that their parents do not trust them or lack confidence in their abilities. Sometimes even relatively small things can lead children to feel that we lack trust and confidence in them. Some common things we may do that can rattle a child's trust or confidence include finishing his sentences, or cleaning up after him when he has already tried to clean something. Most kids are not consciously aware of their feelings when these things happen, but, it may come out in conflicts or when you least expect it. Letting our kids know how much we trust them and feel confident in them is crucial to their development. Simply asking a child how he feels about himself is an easy and often effective way to discover a child's self-perceptions. To be more specific, we may ask a child what he feels confident about or which areas he feels that he needs to work on. Having a child talk about his self-perceptions often helps him build a stronger sense of self and lets him know that we're interested and listening.

Besides wanting our kids to trust and feel confident in themselves, we also want them to trust and have confidence in us and in our ability to parent them. If we do what we say and say what we do, we teach our children that we mean what we say. For example, Susie's parents told her that if she passed all her subjects and got at least three A's on her report card, they would get her a dog. Not only did she get three A's, she received all A's. When she asked her parents for a dog, they told her that a dog would mess up the house, and that they were afraid her brother might be allergic to dogs. As a sort of consolation prize, they got her a stuffed dog instead. Some parents may not see this as a big event, but after many years, Susie still felt internalized feelings of mistrust, betrayal, and anger.

Susie's parents actually set her up for disappointment. If she'd not met their challenge to make the grades to earn a dog, it is likely that she would have felt disappointed in herself, and her parents might have even heaped some shame onto her for not doing as well as they wanted her to. As it was, she made the grades, but then felt duped and upset because she still didn't get what her parents had promised her. Therefore, her parents forced her into a situation where she was going to wind up feeling disappointed and frustrated regardless of what she did or didn't do. In another, similar example, we may give a child a choice of going to the park in the morning or in the afternoon. The child picks afternoon and the parent agrees, although it may be more convenient for the parent to take the child in the morning. The parent gets busy doing something around the house and backs out of taking the child to the park at all. The child may seem okay with the broken promise at the time, but it causes mistrust and a sense of deceit between the parent and child. Children will learn the value of integrity and the importance of keeping one's word from us, or they will not likely learn it at all—we can either lead by example or fail to teach them these values altogether. We want our children to trust us, so we cannot violate their faith. If we're not willing to keep our word, then we should not give it.

We may often find ourselves showing a lack of trust or confidence in our kids. This can also damage the confidence and trust they have. Earlier we discussed the importance of not sheltering our children to the point of depriving them of learning about consequences and the growth and learning that come from experiencing disappointment or sadness. Additionally, we may sometimes feel tempted to guard the child against family or personal matters we feel he cannot handle. Sometimes this is true, but sometimes we forget that up to a certain point, children have a right to know what is happening around them.

For this example, we will consider a couple, Harold and Martha, and their kids, Jake and Shelly. In a fit of depression, sixteen-year-old Jake slashed his wrist and then immediately ran and told his parents what he'd done. His parents awakened and took him to the hospital. Shelly, who was twelve, slept through the whole incident. The doctors stitched Jake's arm and kept him for observation. The next morning, Shelly, wanted to know where her brother was. After a few awkward glances between Harold and Martha, they told her that Jake was sick and needed to stay in the hospital for a few days.

Being an intelligent and curious twelve-year-old, Shelly wanted to know what was wrong with Jake, why he was in the hospital, and when he would return home. Martha made up a story about Jake having a strange and sudden virus, but assured Shelly that they could bring Jake home in a few days. Shelly seemed to accept the answer, although it still left many questions in her mind. She wondered how Jake's illness had come on so suddenly, why they hadn't awakened her when they took him to the hospital, and whether she or another family member might catch this virus. Still, her mother had always been honest with her in the past, and she had no reason to think otherwise in this case.

Martha and Harold debated their decision to lie to their daughter, but consoled each other with the idea that they only wanted to protect Shelly; they did not want Jake to feel embarrassed about his deed, and they certainly didn't want Shelly to go to school and tell her friends about it. Initially, they felt it would be easier for all parties involved to let the matter blow over. They thought that maybe someday, when Shelly was older and could appreciate the seriousness of this event, they could tell her and not risk bringing shame or embarrassment to the family.

After a day or two, it occurred to Martha that Jake would be coming home in a couple of days with his wrists heavily bandaged and two dozen stitches beneath the bandages. She realized that Shelly would likely figure it all out, and then where would they be? Shelly would know what had happened, but she wouldn't know why. She would know that her brother had hurt himself, but she would be unable to talk to anyone about it because she wasn't supposed to know. Aside from the fear and concern she would feel, she would inevitably know that her parents told her a lie and that they apparently didn't trust her or have confidence in her.

After careful consideration, Harold and Martha agreed that Shelly should know the truth. Martha took her daughter to the park the day before Jake's return home and apologized for not telling her the truth, and explained the whole situation. When she concluded the story, she asked Shelly if she had any questions or wanted to talk about anything. Martha thought that Shelly would feel quite upset and that imparting this information would create a very uncomfortable situation for both of them. However, Martha was pleasantly surprised when Shelly simply asked, "Is Jake going to be okay? I knew something weird was going on, but I could tell that you and Dad didn't want to talk about it." That evening, Shelly helped her mother load the dishwasher without anyone asking, and she spent the evening downstairs with her parents instead of sitting in her room. Martha later said, "It was so strange, but for the first time in a long while, I felt like we were a family. We all were hurting, but we were all hurting together and, somehow, the whole situation seemed less overwhelming."

From a parenting standpoint, Harold and Martha began handling this matter hierarchically, but they resolved it equitably. Fear and shame guided Jake's parents to make their initial decisions. When they did communicate the truth to their daughter, she felt that they trusted her and more importantly, it helped her to feel like she was a part of something bigger. Granted, we should not take this approach lightly. Many kids lack the maturity to handle this sensitive information. However, if children learn, over time, to honor boundaries and maintain their integrity and the integrity of others, mishandling sensitive information will not be an issue and trust within the family can grow.

I AM SO PROUD OF YOU.

An important part of reinforcing good behavior also involves praising children for being who they are. We want our children to feel appreciated and supported when they do things we want them to do, but we don't want them to feel that they must do something in order to feel worthwhile. A healthy self-image shouldn't depend upon deeds; deeds are just that, often falsely judged as good or bad, and they are independent of the person. The person behind the deeds needs to feel accepted and valued as a person and as someone whom we love and respect. Telling a child, "I enjoy spending time with you," or "you have a very pretty smile," are simple things that remind the child that he is special to us, and that we love him for who he is, not for what he does.

While praise is important, too much is too much. Remember, equity is about balance. If we lapse into praising a child for every little thing, then it loses its value. Ultimately, we want kids to make helpful choices for themselves and others for many reasons. Mainly, we want them to consider what is in the best interest of all and to make good choices because they want to please themselves by doing things that make them feel proud, not just do things that make us feel proud.

Positive communication forms the essence of encouraging kids to cooperate, but we need to consider how we communicate with our kids. Parents often tell a child that he did a good job with cleaning his room, or that he should be proud of himself for sharing his toys, and this is a good form of parental praise. It's best to avoid praise that insinuates a basis for love. This makes the love offered to the child seem conditional. Comments like "You did a wonderful job, and I love you for that" imply that we only love him when he does a "wonderful job," or that we will love him less, or maybe not at all, if he fails to do a wonderful job in the future.

The objective is to have our children feel a sense of self-reward when they do something positive. We can reinforce this and help children understand these positive feelings by asking the child, "How do you feel about the job you did painting this picture?"

Simply ask him to tell you about his picture and have him tell you what he likes about it. Laughing, or asking "What is this?" are not positive or productive responses. We want kids to feel motivated to communicate and express themselves, so ask them about their work. Find out how they feel about what they've done and allow them to tell you about it. Focus on the colors or interesting things you may see in their artwork. These positive feelings should not be limited to situations where your child did extremely well, remember that putting forth an earnest effort, sticking with something until it is finished, and/or doing his very best at a task are also positive things that we should try to reinforce.

PRAISE EXERCISE

Families that want to bolster or renew their communication skills may play a game called "touch and talk." "Touch and Talk" is simple, and can be very meaningful. Two members of the family sit or stand close enough to touch each other in some way. They could hold hands, put their arms around each other, or just put a hand on their partner's shoulder. The object of the game is to look your partner in the eyes and tell him or her three values they have that you respect and/or admire. Things like "You have pretty hair" or "I love how white your teeth are" do not count. Appropriate comments are those that go beyond superficial appearance. You might say, "You have a fun personality and help me to laugh when I am feeling low," or "I think you are a cool person, and I respect you because you follow through with what you say you will do," or "I like the way that you like to help other people. That inspires me."

SO TELL ME HOW YOU REALLY FEEL.

Parents, often mistakenly, believe that their children don't understand emotions and can't express them. Experience shows that children as young as two years old can understand the models of power and can understand emotions. It is all in the coaching. Parents can use pictures, playing with different characters, or more simple words, but we can try to increase a child's vocabulary of emotions and enable him to tell us how he feels. Sadness, anger, guilt, fear, and failure can be easy to communicate. For example, guilt occurs when we feel as though we did something we didn't mean to, and we want to make it better. Failure is what we feel when we goofed things up and can learn from our mistakes. For a more comprehensive review of the purpose of emotions, we would encourage you to review *The Art of Managing Everyday Conflict: Understanding Emotions and Power Struggles.* Adults often have a hard time talking to children about emotions because we tend to be limited in our own attitudes and beliefs.

Here is an example. A boy we will call Barry was two-years-old when his mother took him to a psychologist because of the violent tantrums he threw at home. And Barry bit, hit, scratched, and spit on the psychologist. When Barry was in "time-outs," the psychologist spoke calmly to him about what feelings Barry might be experiencing. In response, Barry screamed, yelled, and had fits, but he finally calmed down and would then play out some similar situations using toys and characters. After the psychologist had worked through these episodes, he worked with Barry's parents to help them understand what Barry's behaviors were saying, and his behavior improved.

About one year later, the psychologist received a call from Barry's mother stating, "I hate you."

He asked, in an amused voice, "Why?"

She said, "Thanks to you, my son is more emotionally in tune than I am. He just told me that he was feeling frustrated and angry with my behavior because I was not listening to him." To this day, the psychologist is still in contact with Barry, and Barry still maintains this awareness of his emotions. This example is just one of many that typify the wisdom of children—if we believe in them and teach them to believe in themselves.

SUMMARY

We have covered a number of facets related to communication, yet it would be impossible to cover all aspects of this topic in one chapter (or, perhaps, even in a single book). We alluded to body language and its role in communication, but there are entire books devoted to this topic. Mostly we wanted to cover how we express emotions to our children and how they learn to communicate their own emotions to others. Our children will learn the ins and outs of communication of thoughts and ideas in school, in many ways. However, they seldom get a class in the expression of emotion. We need emotionally educated adults to teach our children. If that means that we need to seek out education on our own emotions, and we do so, then maybe we can rise to the occasion.

◌ Chapter 10 ◌
ALL HANDS ON DECK: GETTING KIDS TO COOPERATE

Gaining cooperation from children is often an elusive pursuit. Parents employ different approaches in an attempt to have their kids behave well. As we discussed earlier, many parents employ the parenting style that was modeled to them by their parents. Negotiation is one technique parents like to think they employ; however, this generally looks like the parent and child talking about what the parent wants, and the discussion does not end until the parent gets what she wants or the child ends up in trouble.

Sometimes it's easy to cast aside memories of how flawed this "my way or the highway" approach is. We may feel a certain amount of comfort in hearing ourselves repeating some of the same phrases our parents did ("You live in my house. I make the rules, and you will do as I say. As long as you're living under my roof, that's the way it's going to be.") and doling out the same punishments, and we'll stir up the same resentments that our parents did and cause more conflicts without even realizing our part.

Do we want our children to fear and feel overpowered by us, or do we want them to do the right things because they respect us and, therefore, choose to behave in productive ways? We need to provide positive motivation for the child's actions and not to simply make them do as we wish by any means available.

Let's consider a real-world example. One morning, Kim came downstairs and found her two-year-old son, Jason, merrily coloring the parquet floor in the kitchen with crayons. She screamed at him to stop, popped him on the butt, and gave him a long lecture about being a bad kid and how he never thinks about his actions before doing them. She sent him to his room to punish him for his wrongdoing. Jason cried and felt angry with his mother's reaction. Later that day at daycare, he pulled his playmate's hair when no adult was looking and then walked away acting innocent. Ultimately, Kim created a situation where her handling of the incident that morning led to further inappropriate behavior later that day. If Jason had gotten caught pulling his playmate's hair, Kim likely would have handled it the same way that she handled the floor coloring incident, and this probably would likely have spawned yet another episode.

How else could Kim have handled this situation? When she saw Jason scribbling on the kitchen floor, she could have asked him why he was coloring the floor. Jason may have said that he didn't like the brown floor, and that he thought it should be blue. Kim could have gotten a bucket of warm water and explained to Jason that he would have to clean the marks off of the floor, and discussed other ways that the brown floor could be changed without using crayons. Jason and Kim could probably agree that it might be a better idea to get a rug to cover the floor instead of Jason trying to do it himself, the hard way. Cleaning the floor would be a consequence for Jason, and as his arm got tired from scrubbing, he would learn how difficult it is to get crayon marks off of wood. They could have discussed the fact that when we make a choice that harms something, we have to take ownership and fix what we have done.

If we teach children to think about the consequences of their actions and show them they had other choices, two things happen. Children learn to think about what may happen if they choose to do something and why it may not be a productive thing to do. Understanding this often leads them to then consider other choices.

SETTING SAIL

Raising children is similar to sailing on the ocean; as we push harder against the waves, the harder they crash into us. For every action there is an equal and opposite reaction. As a parent creates waves by pushing in one direction, the child will attempt to push back with equal force. The parent will see and feel the impact of the waves that come back, but may not realize that she actually created these waves by her choice in dealing with a child's behavior. We want to learn how to work with the wind and the waves.

Many parents feel that if they are "in control" then their children will behave appropriately, but this hierarchical approach to parenting is what makes waves. As the parent makes waves and the child pushes back and both sides start pushing harder, the waves get bigger and bigger until both parties soon feel as though they are drowning in the conflict. Getting children to cooperate is a give and take, lifelong commitment that we, as parents, have to make to build an equity-based relationship with our children.

Using strong-arm tactics to get cooperation from kids may sometimes seem to work. Our children may comply, but at some point they will do something to retaliate against not having choices of their own. They may not verbalize it but it may come out through poor grades and/or inappropriate behavior at school, overeating, oversleeping, forgetting to do their chores, etc.

Parenting is often complicated by external pressures. Peer pressure is an often-discussed and debated influence that tends to come up when a young person's behavior is questionable or undesirable. But, parents can be influenced by peer pressure, too. Parents often observe the actions and behaviors of other people's children, and form opinions about whether the child's parents are doing a good job, whether they're being raised properly, and form conclusions about the child's home life. We may notice how other parents handle their children and compare this to our own methods. Often, if a child behaves badly in the presence of other adults, her parent feels concerned that other people will think that the child is not being raised properly.

Our parents and family influence our ideas about how to raise our children. Sometimes their presence means that we feel pressured to make a show of disciplining our child for the benefit of those who may label us "incompetent" or "complacent" in our parental duties.

WINDS OF CHANGE

If the wind changes direction, then the direction of our sailboat changes with it. Sometimes the wind blows us where it will, but we must remain at the helm and try to help things move in the right direction. Change is difficult, especially when we don't have any immediate fixes and must invest time and energy into something without seeing immediate results. If we were sailing around the world in our sailboat, and tried to measure our progress each day, the progress would seem negligible. But, with patience, guidance, and persistence, the short distances we travel each day will eventually add up to take us to our destination. Raising children is also a long journey. We put a lot of effort and time into this journey, and with patience and guidance, we meet our goals.

BLOWING IN THE WIND

Erin was a seventeen-year-old trying to find her place in the world. She was old enough to start making some decisions on her own, but not old enough to live on her own to follow through with those choices without affecting other people. She was late getting in at night, her room was a mess, she was disrespectful and never wanted to help around the house, yet she wanted to come and go as she pleased and make her own rules. Her mother and father were at their wits end and felt helpless as Erin seemed determined to do what she wanted, how she wanted, and when she wanted.

During a heated argument, Erin threatened to move out. Her mother felt tired of the constant arguing, and she told Erin that if Erin could find a family that would be willing to take her in, allow her to live with no rules or guidelines that they would arrange for her to go. Erin called a friend who got her father on the phone and after a brief conversation with Erin's mother, Erin went to stay with this family.

What do you think that Erin's mother and father were feeling? A lack of control? Fear of not having the parental role? Insecurity? All of the above? When Erin's parents wanted her to do certain things, she rebelled. When her mother forced the issue, Erin felt cornered and pressed to take action and move out. But, what went wrong?

Erin's parents could have handled the situation differently if they had used an equity-based approach. They may have engaged Erin in a conversation about her life, asked questions about what she was dealing with, and tried to find ways to work with her to make things better at home. They wouldn't have worried so much about "losing control" but would have concentrated more on Erin's welfare and looked for ways to foster respect for all. We need to forget about illusions of control and look at the whole picture. A time comes when parents can no longer physically make their kids do much of anything—the kids have to want to cooperate and the best idea is to build a desire to cooperate when they're young, and avoid forceful techniques that will not work when they are older. The wind will always blow, but we can still guide the boat.

The lesson of Erin's story is pretty simple: if we give up, or if we falsely believe we can force everything to be the way we want it to be, we can actually create an unacceptable situation for all parties involved. By talking things out, we can assist our children with problem-solving techniques.

DON'T SET SAIL IN A STORM

When we deal with our children, we want to maintain a mutual level of respect and have some boundaries and guidelines for everyone. It's unlikely that a positive journey can begin in a storm. We shouldn't approach situations with our children when we—or they—feel angry. It is best to let the waters calm before setting sail.

If a child comes home from school in a bad mood and we immediately tell her she needs to lose the attitude and clean her room up, what is likely to happen? The child is already feeling angry and weakened in some way, and we have heaped more aggravation on top of the bad feelings. In adult terms, after a bad day at work, getting stuck in a traffic jam, and dealing with a monstrous headache, the last things we want to encounter are more problems and crises when we walk in the door. Still, as parents, sometimes we may create just such a situation for our kids.

We all like for our feelings to be validated, and it is important to remember that much of our effectiveness as guides and as parents depends upon timing, and the approach we take. Let things calm down before attempting to communicate with the child, but don't miss the opportunity to communicate when the time is right. Letting things "blow over" or hoping that matters will disappear and be forgotten is not the suitable approach to fostering an equitable, empowered relationship with our children.

School teachers spend more hours a day with many children than their parents do. Some parents hear that their children are wonderful in school and that they listen and behave better than anyone else. Yet at home, the same child may be a huge disruption, pick on his siblings, break things, and refuse to behave productively. Why does a child play this Dr. Jekyll and Mr. Hyde role?

There could be many answers, but it is likely that the child is trying to tell us something without actually saying it. If the behaviors are happening only at home and not at school, it could be a sign that the child is lacking something at home. As we mentioned earlier, children need guidelines, and a consistent environment that lets them feel safe, secure, and loved. Sometimes children know that they cannot get away with inappropriate behavior at school, but can do whatever they want to at home. Sometimes a child acts out to gain the parent's attention (even if it is negative attention). Children sometimes feel hostility toward their parents and/or siblings and they act out this hostility only when in the presence of these people. But, it is our job to talk with the child and try to learn what is bothering them, and try to find ways to work through the problems and to work jointly to find solutions. Consider the following example.

Billy has been tearing up his room and refusing to clean it. He has destroyed his sister's doll by cutting its hair off and then pulling its head off. He runs in the house and often breaks things in the process. But, at school, Billy is very polite and helpful, sometimes he even stays to help the teacher tidy the classroom, and his teacher has said that he's one of the nicest, most well-behaved students she has. Why does this dichotomy exist?

Billy is getting certain things at school that he lacks in his home environment. Our time, as parents, is much better spent on trying to find out what is lacking at home instead of punishing him for his undesirable behaviors—the goal is to try to fix the problems that lead to these behaviors and not simply to stop the behaviors. Punishing behaviors is a bit like jamming chewing gum into a leaky faucet. Yes, it will stop the drip for a while, but have you fixed the problem? And in fact, punishing negative behavior doesn't teach a child to avoid the behavior, it teaches her to avoid getting caught. We haven't removed the motivation for the behavior; we've simply motivated the child to be more careful to avoid the consequences.

To find answers, we must first look at the environments for commonalities and differences. At school, there are many other children around, and only one teacher. It is likely that Billy has learned that to get positive attention at school, he must behave as expected and honor the teacher's wishes. Often, behaving well only leads to children feeling ignored because they're more likely to get our attention when they're behaving inappropriately.

The teacher praises Billy for his behavior, and he feels that she pays attention to him and likes him. His mother hustles him home from school and starts cooking dinner as soon as they arrive. Billy watches TV or plays video games until dinner is ready, he eats, and he and his mother go through their nightly argument about doing homework. When that's finished, they go through their nightly argument about taking a bath, followed by the cursory argument about going to bed. This is a normal evening at Billy's house (and in many other homes). Everything is a struggle for Billy's parents— they fight with him to clean his room, to do his homework, to do everything. What's different between Billy's home environment and that at the school? What's missing? Quality time.

Billy probably feels more motivated to behave unproductively than to cooperate. Why? Because when he does all of the things that he's supposed to do without being asked, then his parents do not interact with him at all. As it is, he's not getting any quality time with them, but at least he can get their attention several times each night by putting up a fight over every little thing.

Additionally, it may not be a simple matter of seeking attention; this situation is often compounded by a baby or a toddler who seems to sap all of the parents' time and attention. Billy destroyed his sister's doll and this may be a reflection of his feelings of resentment or jealousy toward her for getting more attention than he gets. Conversely, at school, the teacher makes Billy feel important because she makes a special point to listen to him and to share her thoughts and feelings with him. It is impossible to feel important while also feeling ignored, as he feels at home.

THERE ARE SPECIFIC REASONS KIDS DO THE THINGS THEY DO.

- They may want more attention from you.

- They may feel angry and are trying to get back at you.

- They may feel that there are no choices in their lives and that everyone is always telling them what to do.

- They may want to play the victim role and have you feel sorry for them.

We have referred to some of these earlier in the book, but if you can figure out what they want, you can usually figure out how to handle the situation to gain more cooperation. We can't change a child's behavior until we change the reaction that we have to it. For example, every time Billy's mom asked him to clean up his room, she had to focus on him. When Billy tore up his sister's doll he got in trouble, but at least his mother talked to him. Because Billy wasn't getting attention for the good things he did, he decided to get attention for negative things. At school, his teacher talked to Billy and let him help with extra projects. He got positive attention there so he didn't have to act out. Billy was simply telling his mother, in a nonverbal way, that he needed her and wanted to spend time with her. Children can't always verbalize their feelings, they just know that they don't feel right about something, and they act out how they feel. As the adults, we need to be able to put anger aside and really look at what our children are telling us. Remember too, that anger is a protective emotion and it often serves to mask other, more vulnerable feelings.

Sometimes we ask leading questions such as "Why did you do that?" which assumes guilt. Sometimes we criticize our children for "being bad" although we really mean "behaving unproductively." It seems easier to accuse first and ask questions later. We give them detailed lectures which they ignore and which we believe sound authoritative and smart, talking at them instead of fostering mutual communication by asking questions and receiving input. By asking open-ended questions, we can become more informed about the situation. Questions such as "Tell me what you were thinking" or "How do you feel about that?" work much better than "What would make you do a stupid thing like that?" When dealing with children, the old adage of giving an inch, and you give 'em a mile is rather understated. With children, if we're willing to give an inch, we're more likely to gain a yard.

WEIGHING ANCHOR

Most people these days feel overly busy and pressed to meet many demands placed upon their time, but we have to slow down and spend more time with our children. Many parents find that if they can manage to squeeze in a half an hour or so each day to spend some quality time with their children, their relationship dramatically improves. The parents feel better about themselves for making the children a priority, and the children benefit as well.

Kids like to have fun. That may sound like a silly thing to say, we all like to have fun. However, we often forget to try to make a chore seem more like fun than work. The sight of a messy house can be overwhelming, and we may not even know where to begin cleaning. When a child has a very messy room, and a parent tells her to go and clean her room, she may feel the same way. At times like these, we can step in and make a game of cleaning the room, or we can challenge the child to see how quickly she can put her toys away. Making a "train" and going around the room, picking things up and putting them away can be amusing and entertaining to small children. Use dump trucks or bulldozers to haul or push their blocks into their container. Put dolls in a car and drive them into the "garage." If you use some creativity in cleaning up, then the child doesn't mind putting things away and you can help encourage imagination and creativity.

Helping around the house should be a responsibility shared by each member of the family. Every now and then you may want to reward cooperation with some type of external reward like ice cream, a small toy, going swimming or doing something your children enjoy. You can either let them know beforehand or surprise them afterward. If only one or two of the children cooperate, then reward them and explain to the child who did not cooperate that you still love her, but the reward was for those who cooperated. Furthermore, while it is generally not a good idea to bribe a child with food, having a special family outing to the ice cream parlor is somewhat different. As mentioned earlier, however, remember that it is very important to follow through on your promises and live up to your end of the bargain, if the child lives up to hers.

As we discussed in the chapter on communication, investing effort into respectful communication is something akin to sowing the seeds of cooperation. Compromising and negotiating are two valuable tools for parents to help foster cooperation in their children. We hear some parents say that they do not discipline their kids while they feel angry. As we know, anger often clouds our judgment and can cause us to resort to excessive actions and unfairness. If a child sees us behaving in a certain way when we feel angry, we teach her to behave similarly when she is angry. If we stomp around, slam doors, and/or throw things when we feel upset, it is difficult to try to correct the child if she mimics our behavior. If we manage our behaviors effectively, even when we feel angry, we teach the child that it is inappropriate to behave violently or to scream and shout.

Even the most conscientious parents may fall into the temptation of issuing consequences while they still feel angry. What can we do then? Let us consider an example involving a man we will call Tom, and his fourteen-year-old son, Gary. Tom does not allow Gary to visit his friends when the friend's parents are not home. One day, Tom came home early from work and Gary was not home. Tom made some calls and found out that Gary had disobeyed the rule and was visiting one of his neighborhood friends although the friend's parents were not at home. Tom drove to the friend's house and knocked on the door, and his son answered. Tom told Gary to get in the car immediately, and he took Gary home.

In violation of his own policy against issuing consequences while he was angry, Tom informed Gary that he would not go anywhere other than school and that he could not use the telephone for a month. Gary went to his room and Tom calmed down. After a few hours, Gary told Tom that he felt his punishment was too harsh. Tom admitted that a month might be extreme, but did not completely back down, either. Instead, they negotiated. Tom told Gary that if Gary adhered to the imposed terms for two weeks, then it would end. If Gary violated the agreement, the consequences would revert to a month. As it turned out, Tom caught Gary sneaking to use the phone, and he extended the consequences to the full month, as he originally proposed.

Several important things happened in this example. By using this negotiation technique, Tom did not depart from his decision, and still allowed Gary to express his feelings. Tom showed willingness to compromise on the punishment, and he held Gary responsible for upholding his end of the agreement. When Gary violated the agreement, Tom responded by doing what he said he was going to do. Many of the issues that come up with adolescents represent opportunities to negotiate. Messy rooms, curfews, phone usage, dating, driving, and many other things are areas that lend themselves to compromise and negotiation. Some parents would say that Tom allowed himself to be taken advantage of when his son violated the rules of the lessened penalty. We would say that Tom gave his son the opportunity to learn a lesson, and his son chose the hard way.

We hit a major roadblock in the parent/child relationship when we behave judgmentally. There is a difference between pointing out that a child made a mistake, and speculating about her intelligence, making judgments about her character, or overly criticizing the mistake. We want the child to learn from a mistake; we do not want her to feel that we do not love her anymore, that she is a "bad" person, or that she no longer deserves our faith.

Negotiation often elicits cooperation from our children in unrelated tasks, because they see that we are willing to work with them. And cooperatively working with our children often turns a mistake into an opportunity to learn together and lessens the fear of abandonment and rejection.

Summary

A parent's ultimate goal is to work herself out of a job. As a child learns and behaves more responsibly, the less our guidance and authority is required. At different points in a child's development, we may feel painfully aware that our "baby is growing up." It is, however, easy to forget that our children learn and grow on a daily basis, not just when they take their first step, start kindergarten, or get a driver's license.

The words connected to T.E.A.C.H. and L.E.A.R.N. help to model the basic tenets of what we want you to learn to become an empowered parent.

- Talk to your children in an honest, concise way.

- Example—Lead by example and show them what you want them to do.

- Allow room for rewards and consequences.

- Consistency in dealing with children is crucial.

- Have faith in yourself and your child that together you can work out problems and grow.

- Love your children unconditionally and make sure they know that you always will.

- Earn respect and cooperation from your children by offering these things to them.

- Act out what you want to see from them.

- Respect each other as human beings.

- Notice good behavior in the child.

∞ **Chapter 11** ∞
GETTING HELP: WHO? WHY? HOW? WHAT? WHERE?

By this time in the book, you have read countless stories of children who have had challenges. We hope that you have learned a great deal about why you may have made some of the choices you have made in terms of hierarchical approaches to parenting, and that you are seeing the wisdom in more equitable, empowered approaches to parenting. This chapter will help you know when your child might benefit from professional help. Even the best parents cannot prevent all the problems and difficulties their children may encounter. Some may be resolved relatively quickly and easily while others may take more work. Physical issues, academic problems, learning disorders, medical problems, attention problems, growth issues, allergies, and many other issues often require the attention of professionals. At what point do you need to pursue finding help and what can you do when you get it? We will explore these issues in this chapter.

Far too often, parents are hesitant to get help for their children when problems are thought to be minor. They may feel afraid or embarrassed that they are overreacting. Parents tend to feel that they can handle these issues themselves, or silently hope that the problem will go away when the child outgrows a "phase" or when some unknown factor, or the passage of time, or some other element, intervenes and makes everything all better. Acknowledging that their child may have an emotional issue can mean facing their own guilt, shame, embarrassment, failure, helplessness, or other unwanted emotions. Many parents believe these emotions detract from their ability to feel like successful parents. Countless parents waited so long to get help for their children that the problems became additive. In other words, a problem that, by itself, could have been addressed easily—such as an attention deficit—was eventually compounded by other emotional issues and resulted in more challenging behaviors that required more attention.

For example, a young child may have symptoms of anxiety. This matter, in itself, may not be incredibly serious or difficult to treat. However, as years go by, the child may begin to experience feelings of frustration, inadequacy, poor self-image, and many other issues that stem from what began as a relatively simple matter. By the time we see these families, not only have those issues taken a toll on the child, but they have also taken a toll on the parents and family. All too often, the parents are feeling so distressed, frustrated, helpless, and guilty regarding their child that their ability to successfully parent has been seriously compromised. These parents are often short-tempered, controlling, demanding, and not very loving toward their "problem child." How might things have been different with many of the children discussed in this book, had their parents gotten them help sooner?

We all know that kids can have rough days and rough weeks. Developmental issues and growth changes and hormones can result in changes in mood and behavior that may last for brief or more extended periods, depending on various factors. Moving, changes in schools, the birth of a new sibling, and bad haircuts can also result in mood swings and tantrums. These are the ups and downs of life, and more often than not, kids and their families can successfully navigate them. The parents' response to these experiences will often determine how well their kids rebound. What happens when you feel you have tried everything, and nothing seems to be working? How long would you let a problem go on before you seek help? Even more, if you were getting help from a professional and nothing seemed to be changing, how long would you continue to work with that professional before asking questions or getting another opinion?

Let's look at another example. Jim was in eighth grade and had been having difficulties with his behaviors for some time. We had worked with him years before on some issues connected to ADHD and to his parents' divorce. His grades continued to fall throughout his middle school years, he had difficulty making friends, and he was often moody. When he came in to the office this time, he looked depressed. He walked almost slumped over, had poor eye contact, and his self-esteem was almost non-existent. His parents had treated his attention deficit with medication throughout the years and felt that he was just not applying himself to his schoolwork. He liked to joke around in class, often was the class clown, and ignored the teachers. He did not seem to see that the kids were laughing at him rather than with him.

When we started to look a little more deeply into his difficulties, his mother noted that he seemed to have significant behavioral changes when he ate sugar. He liked sugar and often ate sugar-coated cereals in the morning and had sugary items for lunch at school and in snacks. When asked if they had ever looked further into this, his parents replied that they had not. We discovered, after a referral to a physician, that Jim not only had problems with attention, but he also had a significant allergy to sugar. It took almost thirty days to get the sugar out of his system; without sugar in his diet, Jim's behavior was markedly different. Jim continued to sneak sugar from time to time and each time he did this it would take about thirty days to see his behavior turn fully around.

Were the attention deficit and the allergy the only problems Jim was having? No. Because the problem had not been addressed for so long, emotional consequences had taken their toll. These affected his motivation, self-esteem, anxiety level, outlook on the world, and his willingness to take risks. Resolving a physical cause for a problem does not mean that all of the secondary problem will go away. The outcome of many of these issues depends on the parents' willingness to follow through medically and therapeutically. We've seen many other cases wherein allergy issues affected the behaviors of children, but the parents did not follow up. These kids often continued to flounder in school and in their social lives. It's hard to understand why parents don't follow through on issues that could be addressed with something as easy as an allergy screening, but it is more common than you may think. Research indicates that allergies are present in about 47 percent of the ADHD population compared to only 6 percent in the general population.

This example with Jim helps to illustrate that while a problem (ADHD) was identified early, some difficulties that continued for years went unchecked. The parents probably felt that the ADHD explained his behaviors and outbursts so they did not search for another cause for his difficulties. As a result, difficulties continued and there were significant emotional consequences as a result. An incomplete solution led to more difficulties later on.

It is important to be thorough, especially when initially assessing and addressing your children's difficulties. While not as common as allergies to food or airborne allergens, chemical and electromagnetic sensitivities can also influence behavioral issues. Paints, thinners, perfumes, and cleaning products are some common chemicals children might be sensitive to, but chemicals in building products and furniture, pest control chemicals, and fertilizers are also suspect. Chemical sensitivities are thought to be influenced by a weakened or overloaded immune system. One research study reported that 13 percent of individuals surveyed stated that they had a hypersensitivity to chemicals. Of that 13 percent, 37 percent stated that they developed emotional issues after their physical symptoms emerged.

The most common sources of electromagnetic sensitivities in the past were fluorescent lights and high-tension wires. In recent years, people have reported sensitivities to cell phone tower signals. Fluorescent lighting, because of its flickering, can irritate some individuals. This effect can mimic attention-related problems. When the lights go off, it may take a little time to return to normal, but these individuals note marked differences in attention, concentration and behavior when not near fluorescent lighting. Recently, headaches and nausea that subside when people maintain a distance from cell phone antennae have been reported. Is it possible that use of cell phones themselves can cause difficulties? Some people have reported headaches and disorientation from regular cell phone use, and though these occurrences are rare, it is important to be aware of the possibilities when you are trying to pursue answers to your children's potential problems.

This next example involves a girl in high school. We will call her Joan. She has some friends, but has had a history of behaving a bit insensitively to them and had become agitated in her behavior when under stress. Some of her friendships were cut short by others' parents because she often used profanity. She had a good sense of humor, which helped her to relate to others, and she was intelligent, so she was able to do well in school. On the other hand, while her grades were good, she was known to be disruptive at times. Her teachers stated that she often yelled out in class to get attention. It was thought that she was bored and just wanted more stimulation. She also moved around a lot and talked about feeling jumpy inside. The issues did not seem significant enough to address, because she was doing well in school, and her home and social life were not very disruptive.

Difficulties arose when Joan was in her sophomore year. Classes were getting harder, and she began having more problems with peers. She experimented with drugs and alcohol. Outbursts in class were more common, and she seemed more agitated and had a nervous twitch. Her grades began to suffer, and she was much more emotional. It seemed like the stress was getting to her. As we delved into her difficulties, we noted that when she was under stress, she had more outbursts and blinked her eyes more than usual. We referred her to a neurologist, and he discovered that Joan had been experiencing a mild form of Tourette's Syndrome for some time, and it became more accentuated under stress. When her teachers were asked questions regarding her behavior and the issue of Tourette's was brought up, it seemed as if a light bulb went off with them. It made sense, and her teachers suddenly viewed Joan as something other than merely a disruptive child.

Once Joan's parents understood the underlying condition they were able to understand why she behaved as she did. She needed to understand her past and learn how to address her present and future with Tourette's. Medication management, techniques to deal with stress, and counseling to help her understand her emotions would give her some strategies to handle her difficulties. Her parents also would benefit from education.

Many times, parents are helped when they see how they have treated their children while they were unaware of or lacked understanding of the issues facing them. Letting a professional know that you need some help coping, and need information on how to deal with issues, is not a sign of weakness. It is a sign that you know your limits and know when to ask for help. We tell our children that they should never be afraid to ask for help; it follows that we should also be willing to take our own advice and admit that we need help sometimes, too.

Joan's story illustrates a situation where a child grew up with a mild problem that was only occasionally noticeable. Others assumed that it was just a behavioral issue, but it continued to take its toll on her. As the demands of life and her stress increased, she was not able to cope. This underlying issue became more obvious, but it was still not understood until a professional looked more closely at her history. It took someone who was aware of the subtleties to see something more going on than met the eye.

Often parents have a gut feeling when something is not "right" with their child. Many times it is accurate. We don't profess to have statistics, but we hear all the stories of mothers' guilt when they didn't do anything when they knew something was wrong. That intuition can be valuable when helping your child to get help. There are many stories about parents who were not satisfied with the initial conclusions and continued to search for the answer to their child's difficulties. Some ultimately found their answers and others have stopped in the wake of the judgment of others. Not every child's issues have a concrete solution. We tell parents to pursue their concerns, encourage them to do research, and suggest that they keep asking questions. The Internet is a great tool but always verify sources of information, and always get a second opinion.

MOTHER'S LITTLE HELPER

Medication can be a double-edged sword. When it comes to an illness such as strep throat or a sinus infection, it is obviously best to treat it with medication. However, emotional issues are not so cut and dry. Many medications on the market now treat symptoms of depression, anxiety, ADD/HD, and many other emotional issues. Medical models of psychological diagnoses support the fact that neurochemical imbalances contribute to emotional and behavioral reactions. Therefore, if one treats the neurochemistry, then the problem should subside. There is also evidence that many emotional issues such as anxiety, depression, and ADD/ADHD may be passed down genetically through generations. Individuals who believe in a "medical model" think that lifelong medication is necessary to keep the neurochemistry "in balance."

On the other side of the coin, there is a great deal of evidence to support environmental causes for many emotional issues. In some cases these two are interactive developmentally—early childhood trauma may alter receptor sensitivities in key areas of the brain, which leads to neurochemical imbalances. Many believe this is the process that leads to adult depression in those with Post Traumatic Stress Disorder stemming from traumatic childhood events. One example is Pre-menstrual Syndrome Dysphoria that often results from earlier experiences of sexual, physical, or even emotional abuse.

We believe that both the medical model and the environmental model are valid, however, the key is to consider each individual's case. It is also our position that parents may want to look for non-medication ways to address their child's issues first before resorting to medication. We are not physicians and are not giving medical advice, but we see so many children on medication who may be able to succeed without medication. Medication can feed a "victim mentality" and can give people an excuse to not make the most of a difficult situation. Too many times it is seen as a quick fix. Furthermore, parents may not want to make changes in their lives to better meet their kid's needs, so, when their child "is depressed" and medication can fix it, many parents are lured into the idea that the problem is solved.

What happens when the medication children have been taking is no longer working? Many times, dosages are increased and/or medications are added or changed. We have seen children as young as four years old taking three or four types medications that were not developed to treat four-year-old children. Many parents do not know that most of the medications given to children for emotional issues are not developed or tested for children, but only for adults. Nearly everyone has heard that Prozac and some other anti-depressants appeared to contribute to suicidal thought patterns in adolescents. There are very distinct differences in the way that children's and adult's brains work. More of these medications are now being tested for children, but there are still risks. Even psychiatric researchers are questioning whether or not the increases in prescribing these drugs is too much.

We do not dispute that there are cases where children benefit from medication. However, we feel concerned about those situations when a child may report feeling depressed or anxious, and they are prescribed medication from the start. Also, situations exist wherein children are prescribed medication cocktails. Any time medications are mixed, a chance exists for adverse drug interactions. While we all would like to believe that every physician or psychiatrist is considering whether the medication is truly necessary and/or has researched the possibility of drug interactions, this is not always the case. We request that you ask questions, get a second opinion, do your own research on the medication(s) that your children are prescribed, and be willing to find another physician if yours will not adequately respond to your questions or concerns.

Parents should be leery of the physician who diagnoses illness based on child's response to medication. In other words, many physicians will listen to a list of symptoms, prescribe a medication, then rely on the parent/teacher observations of the child's responses to decide if he had the correct diagnosis. If the child improved only a little, or showed no improvement at all, these physicians might first assume they had the wrong dosage, or the wrong medication(s). In this situation, the physician is conducting medical trials on your child, when in fact the problem is that the child may not have the issue he is being prescribed medication for.

At least, don't assume that because your physician has a degree, he will always know what is best for your child. This book is not intended to address medication issues, it is meant to raise your attention to issues with medication. Many excellent books, web pages, and other resources are available for further information. Be willing to do your homework before you talk to your physician about the possibility of medication, and don't feel afraid to ask questions.

THE THREE "Rs"

How many times have our kids had difficulties in a class or two in school? How do you respond? Do you yell at them, ground them, get them help? More times than not, it is an issue with motivation, sometimes a relationship issue between your child and the teacher. And it can also be a relationship issue between your child and you. Difficulties can continue for weeks, months, or even years before parents realize that there may be something more going on than they want to admit. Educational difficulties can have many causes. We have already addressed some of them.

Difficulties with learning are far from uncommon. If you think about how complex the brain is, it is easy to understand that even a minor "hard wiring" issue in the brain can translate into learning difficulties. Learning disorders, as they are called, can impact reading, writing, spelling, thinking, speaking, and mathematical calculations, among other things. Expressive language disorders affect the way people receive and communicate language through speaking, reading, listening, and writing. While you have probably learned about many of these issues here and there, there are less commonly known learning disorders called non-verbal learning disorders which result in difficulties understanding social cues, body language, and following complex directions, to name a few. Many types of learning disorders are easily addressed once accurately identified. If not treated, many individuals with these difficulties can look defiant, stupid, or frustrated, and they feel very misunderstood by others.

The challenges that come with learning disorders do not go away on their own. However, some people have learned their way around them and have developed their own strategies to deal with them. This is more the exception than the rule, though, and in many cases, unidentified learning disorders can result in a child losing faith in the education system and himself, which leads to many compounding issues.

While specific learning disorders explain many learning issues, auditory or visual processing are also issues to consider. Difficulties with processing information are involved in all learning disorders, but there can be more global difficulties in processing that aren't specific to reading, writing, math, or school subjects. Auditory and visual processing deficits can look very similar to attention deficits, but are treated totally differently. We have seen many instances where children diagnosed with an attention deficit because children having difficulties with processing information can give the impression that they are not paying attention. Processing has to do with the way we interpret and digest information. Attention has to do with what we can focus on when information comes to us. Also, there are differences in auditory and visual skills associated with processing and attention. Processing deficits are not treated with medication; they are addressed through remediation, similar to other learning disabilities.

Kirsten came to the office due to difficulties with behavior and a poor attitude in her freshman year of high school. In talking with her parents, I learned that she'd had problems for a number of years. In class, she was often at a loss for words, and on written tests her grades often suffered. We talked about a number of issues in therapy, and we asked her father to write an essay regarding his own behavior toward his daughter. After two weeks he produced only a page of text. When asked why he had written only one page, he stated that he always had problems writing, just like his daughter, and his performance in school was not much different than hers. As tears rolled down his cheeks, he said that he never wanted his kids to go through what he had experienced. He felt extremely guilty, and felt that it was his fault that she had these problems. He had never admitted to her that he had such difficulties because of his own feelings of shame, failure, and guilt.

Because of his own difficulties, he never pushed to get her help. When he was in school, no one ever talked about the possibilities of learning disorders, let alone disorders of written expression. Her father just thought he was dumb; therefore, he thought his daughter was dumb and didn't know how to help her. The biggest issue was that he couldn't face the fact that a problem existed until it was almost too late. The sooner that you can identify the possibility that your child may be having a significant problem, the sooner he can get the needed support, and the sooner he can succeed.

SECOND SIGHT

Charlotte was a fourth grader being home-schooled. She had had difficulties with reading and spelling from the very beginning, and her teachers in public school did not want to take the time to help her. She had been teased often and would not read aloud in class. She was very difficult to deal with, behaviorally, because she cried easily and then stopped trying. Her teachers and parents felt frustrated, sometimes making negative comments to her. They often accused her of not trying, and after a few years of this treatment, she did stop trying and shut down. No matter where she turned, she felt that she would let everyone down. Her reading scores quickly fell behind and those around her believed that she was just not applying herself because there were no obvious signs of a learning disorder. Her parents, at times, were very impatient with her, but they also knew that the school was not helping.

She was brought in for therapy to work on self-esteem and motivation issues. I noticed, however, that sometimes in the afternoon, her eyes looked out of alignment, slightly crossed. Other times, at mid-day appointments, her eye alignment looked normal. I pointed this out to her parents, and they continued to keep track of this for a few weeks. She was referred to an optometrist who performed a typical eye exam and assessed her for occulo-motor dysfunctions. This occurs when the eyes are not in alignment and do not converge on the same visual field. The actual occurrence of this condition can be debated, and the diagnosis has been considered to be somewhat controversial, though treatments have shown some success. Charlotte did, in fact, experience difficulties with visual coordination, and interventions successfully helped her to improve her reading scores over time. However, the emotional implications of her years of repeated failure took some time to address, therapeutically.

When difficult-to-identify issues are accurately diagnosed and people receive proper treatment, their lives are changed forever. What can seem like such a simple issue can make a drastic difference in the lives of these children and even in the lives of some adults.

CLASS... CLASS... SHUT UP!!! THANK YOU.

This classic line above from the old days of Cheech and Chong comedy comes from a parody of a high school classroom. Although this is intended as humor, it is far too commonly based on reality. We would all like to think that the teachers responsible for the proper education of our children would also take responsibility for our children's emotional and moral education, as well as their own. However, we have heard and seen teachers and administrators treat children with incredible disrespect and humiliation. Yelling, screaming, name-calling and bizarre punishments occur every day in our schools. But what happens when kids report them?

George was a third grader who had problems with behavior. He made noise while the teacher was talking, failed to do his class work, and made comments about the teacher. George often told his parents about things that happened at school, and he always had a reason for his behavior in school. He said that the teachers were mean to him and told him to "shut up." He said that one time, in front of the entire class, his teacher told him that there was something wrong with him. The teacher denied these events, and to most, it was felt that George was lying. He was sent to the principal's office numerous times through the school year, and was ultimately placed in a classroom for kids classified with emotional and behavioral disorders, (E.B.D.).

In an E.B.D. classroom, children with behavioral issues are placed with a teacher who is trained to deal with these issues and help guide these children toward success. Unfortunately, these class-rooms can become "holding pens," and the teachers can become burned out and overwhelmed.

In this classroom, George's behaviors did not change. If any-thing, they got worse. He had more frequent power struggles with his teacher, and he also felt that the administration did not like him.

He said that the assistant principal sometimes forcibly grabbed him by the arm and pulled him around. George's parents had a hard time believing his stories and usually they punished him at home for things that happened at school. George started coming home from school and saying that he was being locked in a room during the day. He described the room as a furnace room with equipment and boxes in it. He said his teacher put a chair in the room and told him to sit in the chair and not to move. George said that some days he spent half the day in there. His parents felt that this was such an outlandish story that they did not believe it. He began having bouts with an upset stomach often, had a hard time sleeping, and seemed depressed. His symptoms were obviously worse on school days. One day, George came home in tears, and he begged his parents to not make him go to school. When they asked him why, he said that he just could not sit in that room one more day.

Finally, his parents decided to go to school to see just what was going on. When they went into the classroom, they saw a door in the back of the room. The room behind the door contained heating ducts, boxes, and a chair, just as George had described. They sank inside when they saw this. They asked the teacher if he put their son in this room, and the teacher hemmed and hawed and stated only for short periods of time. When they talked to the administrators about this, the administrators minimized it and implied that their son must have done something to deserve this behavior.

Situations like these have a serious impact on a child's education, and life. They affect a child's ability to trust any adult, let alone an educator. The problem was further compounded by the fact that George was telling his parents the truth and they did not believe him. Furthermore, they sometimes punished him when he was guilty of nothing more than telling them the truth. A situation such as this can create countless issues in many ways and in many areas of a person's life.

Situations like this happen to children at all levels of education. Many times parents are not equipped to handle the events. In situations like George's, parents feel helpless and afraid to push the issues. If parents make too much noise, their kids often suffer.

If it takes a legal route, the schools often take the victim role and paint the parents as aggressive and unreasonable. The teachers and administrators who emotionally scar and physically harm our kids rarely experience consequences or have to go through any education or therapy, and it is not just one child that this happens to. This is often part of a pattern.

On the other hand, children often take on the victim role when talking about school events, and parents believe the worst. At parent-teacher conferences, however, parents often learn that their child has either not told the whole story or told a totally different one. When parents go to the school to defend their child only to find that their child has manipulated them, they feel betrayed, embarrassed, humiliated, and shamed. Why do children make up these stories? Because they still want to look good in front of their parents. Who is going to pay the price for their child's need to be seen in a good light? Both the parents and the child. The parents have a hard time trusting their child, and the child often feels his own shame and guilt, as well as experiencing punishment. Trust is affected on both sides, and this can last a long time.

Far too often, a "boy who cried wolf" mentality develops, and when things do happen, the parents don't believe it. The guilt that follows when the parents find out that their child was telling the truth can cut to the heart. Understand that your child is going to want you to come to his rescue, and does not want to look bad in your eyes. Get all of the information you can about what happened at school. Let your child know that you are going to talk with the faculty to find out what they feel happened. Be a fact finder. Understand that the faculty want to look as though they are good and right also.

Document everything you may find out, and talk to parents of other students to find out if their children have reported anything. Also understand that many other parents feel afraid to shake things up that might have an impact on their child. The more documentation you have, the better off you are. If you should need to consider legal action, your documentation will help support your position. If you have the support of other parents, take advantage of it.

Educators who treat children disrespectfully and abusively do not deserve to influence our children. In some cases, children have been psychologically harmed because of the school personnel's ignorance about how to recognize and work with the child's diagnostic issues, as well as over-utilizing the school's "zero tolerance" guidelines. Legal action should be one of your last resorts unless your child has been physically harmed. If you do consider this course, contact a lawyer who has experiences with schools to see what your rights are. You may also consider consulting with a psychologist to discuss the issues and possibly even ask the psychologist to come to school meetings with you so that you have an objective third party. We have often found that when this happens, the parents are able to keep their cool better, and the school faculty takes the matter more seriously.

How you handle situations with the schools that impact your child will greatly affect your relationship with him. If he feels that you are more interested in taking everybody else's side, he will not feel able to look to you for help when it is needed. If you go into the school with guns blazing, your child is going to learn how to deflect the attention off of himself and on to other people, not taking responsibility for his own actions. Both of these outcomes are detrimental to you and your child.

A BULLY BY ANY OTHER NAME . . .

Eric was a third grader who always wanted to do his best. He tried hard in school and felt stupid and embarrassed when his grades were less than perfect. He didn't let on much to others about that. It had been a tough year for Eric. He had a family tragedy early in the year and was having a difficult time adjusting. He tried to act like it didn't bother him. He occasionally had issues getting along with other kids, but it was more because his sense of humor was a little off. He did not like to fight.

Eric was in gym class one day, and a teacher came in to take him out of gym class. As soon as they left, she then twisted his arm behind his back and pushed him into her classroom. Inside the classroom, she pulled his arm up further behind his back to the point that he thought it might tear out of the joint. She then stated, "You look at each of these children in this classroom. If I hear that you have touched another kid in my class, next time I will break your arm." She then pulled harder at his arm again. Most of the kids in the class looked on with fear, except for two kids in the back of the room who were smiling and quietly laughing.

After this incident, it was discovered that one of the boys who was silently laughing had his mother call the school and claim that Eric was beating up other kids in his class. He then told the kids in the class to say that Eric was beating them up. Many of them went along with his prompting.

So many things went wrong in this example. Keep in mind that Eric was an ordinary kid, not a troublemaker, a good student, but he had a power struggle with the child who made up a wild story. The teacher tried to verify information but did not count on the classroom manipulation, or on the dysfunctionality of the boy in her class and his mother. The teacher should have talked with the administration, but instead, took matters into her own hands. Eric had no chance to give his side of the story and was assumed guilty. His parents were not made aware of the situation before action was taken, and after this experience, they were infuriated but felt that they may make more problems if they said anything. Though Eric's parents did believe him because he had no history of telling lies or stories, Eric felt that the matter was just supposed to go away, and that he was more responsible for how his parents felt than how he felt. He also thought that he must have done something wrong.

This issue was dropped and not talked about for some time. The teacher did not return the next year, but nothing was ever discussed with Eric or his parents. Being able to get closure to experiences like these is very important for children, and would have been for Eric. While things like this do happen, many wonderful teachers love what they do and want the best for children.

Use these examples as guides, and know that if you develop trusting, open communications with your kids and their teachers, these situations should never happen to you.

So, When Do I Get Some Help?

Up to this point in the chapter we have introduced a number of issues that may require your attention. If you see anything that seems to ring true, we would encourage you to continue your research. The Internet and various books in your library or bookstore can help. More importantly, we believe that it is always a good idea to talk to a professional when you have a concern. If your car was stalling or your television screen kept going blank, chances are you would take it to someone to get it repaired without a second thought. Furthermore, if your child had a fever or a sprain, you would probably take him to a doctor. Why, then, don't we think the same way about our kids when they have a difficult time with their emotions or at school? Our kids are more valuable to us than any material object, and their trust in us is priceless. Many professionals are trained to help you work through these issues. The most important thing you can do is model to your child that there is a mature way to handle these situations, and that he is an important part of the solution.

The Couch Trip

When you realize that your child is having difficulties, you should consider where the problems are. If there are primarily emotional or relationship difficulties, you may want to consult a psychologist for therapy. When looking for a therapist, see if you know others who have been happy with a particular one. Word of mouth can be a great referral. In today's society of managed care, you will probably have to look at your plan or call member relations and see who they have on your list in your area. However, also know that just because a therapist is on your plan, it doesn't mean that he or she will work well with your child or family, or specialize in the types of problems your child may have. Ideally, you want to find a therapist that will be able to be almost a case manager. In other words, he or she would be knowledgeable enough to quickly evaluate your situation and make referrals for evaluations, therapies, and schools, and/or other interventions while helping your child/family.

We suggest interviewing the therapist before you take your child in for an appointment. If a child has a negative experience with a therapist, he may not want to go back to another. We also feel that a therapist who enjoys his work will take the time to talk with you on the phone for a short time; ten minutes is ideal. If you meet in person, you can get more time to know him, but be willing to pay for that time.

Whether you have a phone conversation or meet with the therapist in person, ask about his experience with your specific issues and with similar matters. You may also ask about his attitudes regarding discipline with children and whether he feels comfortable working with the whole family if necessary. Ask if there is a certain theory that he approaches cases with. You are looking for someone who will take the time to talk with you, is open when answering questions, is not too harsh or rigid, is flexible but has professional boundaries, and has a sound model he or she approaches therapy from. You want someone who can look at the issues from many angles and who feels comfortable handling the issues as a family, one who is not just looking to change your child.

There are also many wonderful therapists with Masters Degrees. We have found that the degree a person has does not always equate to better therapy. Therapy is a skill that often cannot be taught. Sometimes professionals have incredible book knowledge, but don't know how to connect to people. If your child has an issue with a professional, talk with the professional about it and encourage your child to talk with him as well, even with your help. If it doesn't work out, don't give up. Sometimes your kid will find something wrong with everyone, because he doesn't want to talk or feels that something has to be really wrong if he is talking to a therapist.

Sometimes a few sessions of therapy can make a huge difference with your child and your family. Someone who is willing to provide usable strategies can help with quick results; however, you also have to be willing to be patient and realize that the issues did not start yesterday and won't be solved tomorrow. Don't see the need for counseling as a sign of failure. We all need help at some time, and it takes more courage to admit that we need help than it does to hide from our fears. Be open to feedback and realize that the more you change, the more your child has room to change. Look at the patterns in your family—not just your immediate family but the patterns that often occur over generations. If you recognize that you have had similar difficulties, let them be known up front. If you feel you need to disclose these to the therapist before you meet as a family or before your child meets with him, then let the therapist know this in advance. Observe your child's need for confidentiality and don't pump him for information after sessions. Know that your child's therapist has limitations as to what you can be told; if you find a therapist wants to share everything your child says, there may be boundary issues with that therapist. Give your child a safe place to share their feelings and trust the process.

When would your child and your family benefit from therapy? Many parents stress over this for months and even years. Here are some questions to ask yourself. What is your attitude about therapy? Do you think that therapy is a bad thing, that it is a sign of failure or weakness? Do you think that your child would feel like a loser if you took him to therapy? How would you feel if your parents, family, friends, or neighbors knew you were taking your child or your whole family to a therapist? In the past, stigmas abounded about getting help for problems. Many families feel that they should take care of problems in the family. They don't want others to know that there is anything bad, wrong, or weak about their family. This is an issue of shame and arrogance, not about wanting what may be truly in the best interest of your children.

Taking your child (or family) to a therapist does not mean it will continue throughout childhood. Many therapists are solution-focused. They want to help you find answers and meaningful solutions to your issues quickly. You must have a positive attitude toward the process or it can undermine the therapist's efforts. If you are not willing to cooperate with the process, it can prolong therapy much longer than may have been necessary and even make problems worse.

We feel that most families would benefit from a few sessions with a good therapist when conflicts or problems persist over a period of more than a few months. There are often power dynamics that can easily be assessed and addressed to get your family back on track. Chronic problems with school should always be addressed, and often these can involve problems with staff members. Also, kids can have difficulties getting along with peers; not getting along with one or two kids is one thing, but not getting along with kids year after year is more than just a passing phase.

Being teased, bullied, picked on, or being the bully, teaser, or picking on others are all important issues to address—they all spell problems with self-esteem. If your child avoids other kids, is shy, stutters, has a chronic bed-wetting issue, is unwilling to stay at a friend's house overnight after school age, then the child may be presenting issues to address. Toddlers who engage in biting, kicking, scratching, punching, and/or talking back need to be addressed. Many times parents' approaches to solving these problems can compound the issues. In many of these situations, kids are trying to communicate something that is not being heard. Therapists can often take a look and help put a parent at ease. Remember that you don't have to have all the answers.

Other more serious issues should always be assessed by a professional. They involve: possible molestation (either being molested by or molesting other children); possible or probable physical or sexual abuse by an adult; suicide attempts, gestures, or comments; self mutilation; multiple fights with others; stealing; lying; threatening others with bodily harm; panic attacks; depression, hearing voices or feeling like others want to harm them; and chronic nightmares. It is surprising how often parents do not get their children help for these issues.

Borderline issues that you might want to consider are name-calling, perfectionist behavior, sleeping problems, performance anxiety, bouts of crying, anger outbursts and tantrums, and similar behaviors. A good rule of thumb is, if you wonder whether or not you could use help, get it. Don't rely on friends or family to tell you if you need help. Sometimes they can give great advice, but not always. They may have the same blind spots that you do. Additionally, you may do well to remember, when seeking advice from friends or family, that an alarming number of people in our society believe that stricter rules, increased punishment, and harsher treatment of children is the answer to every behavioral problem. Such advice is quite incorrect and often harmful to all involved.

Family therapy may be necessary when issues involve conflicts between your kids and/or you. There can be so many dynamics between family members that it takes someone from the outside to get a better look at what is going on. Even when your child is working with an individual therapist, the therapist may feel that it might be beneficial for the family to meet together or seek another professional to help. Use of verbal and body language, attitudes of parents and kids, discipline patterns, boundaries, and limits are just a few of the issues often addressed. All the advice books in the world cannot substitute for good advice from a live person with the experience and wisdom to look at the challenges affecting your family.

Throughout this book, we have spent a great deal of time helping you to look at yourself. As you have probably figured out by now, this is sometimes the best way to help your child. Numerous examples have been provided to help you understand where and how you may be contributing to your child's issues. Individual and couples work can be beneficial for parents to help them understand themselves and their issues related to their children. Remember that children can be barometers for many parents' problems. Much of this book has been about the effects your modeling behaviors have on your children. What better modeling could you provide than to demonstrate that you are willing to face your issues and make a positive difference in your life and the lives of those you love?

EVALUATION AND DIAGNOSIS

We hope that by reading this chapter, you realize that what looks like a simple problem may be more complex. Whether it looks like an attention deficit, a learning problem, or allergies, you don't want to take a risk with your child's future.

If your child's issues go deeper than mild emotional or relationship problems, and involve school-related issues, you may want to consider the need for a professional evaluation. If you are seeing a therapist or wish to start with therapy to see if the problems improve, your therapist may make this recommendation, However, we also feel that if want to make sure that you are correctly addressing issues from the start, you may want to begin the process with a comprehensive psychological evaluation. The schools may do evaluations in certain circumstances, but they have limitations. Furthermore, even if the school does perform an evaluation, you may want supporting evidence and/or take what they have done and add to it, allowing for another interpretation from another professional.

A comprehensive evaluation can be costly, over $1000.00. Many parents look at this as prohibitive, and many insurance companies exclude coverage for them because they view them as unnecessary. They feel that the schools should evaluate for educational difficulties. It's no secret that many insurance companies will not pay for "well visits" or preventative medicine, and it would seem that psychological evaluations are viewed with the same apathy as a check-up at the doctor's office.

What is the impact of doing nothing? How can you measure the emotional toll, the intellectual toll, and the financial toll? If you consider that your child may not be accurately assessed with the school evaluations, and therefore feels that he cannot live up to expectations or is just plain dumb, how is that going to affect the rest of his education, his relationships, and his occupational choices? If you then consider that your child is placed in classes where he does not belong that are either too hard or too easy, how does that impact his learning? He might resent his education to the point of not going on to college. The financial implications can run into the millions.

Can you afford not to make this investment? Would you spend $2000 on a television, a sound system, a pool table? Would you spend an extra $3000 for a more expensive car than one that easily gets you from point A to point B? Would you pay tens of thousands of dollars for your child to go to college? If your answer is "yes" to any of these questions, then why wouldn't you make what could be the best investment of your and your child's future and one that could alter the course of his life?

We have presented this argument to many parents over the years, and when it is put in these terms, parents often warm up to the idea. We expect that our insurance plans should pay for our healthcare needs. If they don't pay, many people will just forego what they may need. We recognize that these can be expensive procedures, and many other necessities may need to come before you can consider an evaluation. Credit cards and other forms of payment are often an option. Talk to the evaluator about what options they have. Don't say "no" before you consider all of your options.

SO WHO DO I TALK TO?

In the past twenty years, the information collected and how it is collected has improved our ability to accurately identify what is going on inside people's heads. As a psychologist, I was trained to perform evaluations primarily for emotional and academic issues. While I felt competent in these areas, I realized that there were gaps in what I was able to identify. I could often say what a problem was or wasn't, but I knew that there was still more to look for. The more evaluations I performed, the more I felt that there were things I missed. This is where a neuropsychologist is appropriate.

Neuropsychology is a specific specialty of psychology. The neuropsychologist is trained to look for more complex difficulties in the brain related to head injuries, attention deficits, learning problems, processing problems, etc. This helps prevent serious errors in the identification of problems, and additional loss of money and time if an incorrect referral for follow-up services is made.

If your child is having mostly emotional issues, a psychologist would be appropriate. Not all neuropsychologists are trained or interested in providing emotional testing, just as not all psychologists are trained or interested in neuropsychological testing. There are, however, neuropsychologists who are very well trained in both types of testing. As suggested above, interview these professionals and ask them about their experience. Ask them how many evaluations they have done, and what kind of issues they have experience with. Ask if they will help you communicate this information to the schools, and if they will go to the school to meet with them if necessary to help your child with placement issues. Does the neuropsychologist make referrals to other professionals such as occupational therapists, speech therapists, neurologists, ophthalmologists, or learning specialists? You want to make sure that the person doing the testing can help you follow up, if it becomes necessary.

WHO SHOULD GET TESTED?

We feel that every child would benefit from a professionally administered IQ test, at least, especially in the first three years of their education. This test will help you get a better idea of where they should be placed educationally by more clearly identifying their strengths and weaknesses. You want to be sure that your child is placed in classes appropriate to his abilities. Professionally administered IQ tests also look at specific strengths and weaknesses, and various aspects of intelligence that can make huge differences in how your child should be taught. You may also be able to see where he may have troubles and where he should perform well.

We believe that kids who have emotional problems at school and around homework issues at home should be considered for testing. Kids who are having difficulties in a single subject for a period of time, or with reading words, comprehension of written language, continuous spelling problems, challenges with speaking in class, and other chronic difficulties are also candidates for testing. The earlier that you can identify the problems, if there are any, the sooner you can help get your child on track. Many times parents feel that they will have wasted their money if the testing shows that there is nothing "wrong" with their child. Instead, this finding should give you peace of mind. You can then address the other possible emotional issues that are likely the bigger influence in their behavior.

WHAT DO I WANT TO LOOK FOR IN AN EVALUATION?

We want to discuss the different areas you may want to consider in an evaluation and why. These can help identify attention deficits; they also contribute to other diagnostic issues. All will likely not be appropriate for your child, but they will let you know what may need to be considered. The following are the list of sources that you may consider.

- background information and family data
- behavioral observations
- intellectual strengths and weaknesses
- auditory and visual distractibility
- auditory and visual processing
- visual and auditory memory
- motor coordination
- learning abilities/ disabilities
- possible writing samples
- vision and auditory screening
- emotional issues
- neurological trends

This list covers many issues we would want considered, but may not be exhaustive. Reviewing this information may involve a team of professionals including a psychologist/ neuropsychologist, pediatrician, neurologist, school counselor, teacher and/or other professional(s). Teachers and parents are also integral to the process of an accurate diagnosis. Since many of these difficulties can be multifaceted psycho-physiological disorders, each individual will present a somewhat different profile of difficulties, strengths, challenges, and gifts, and they need to be explored thoroughly. We will address a few of these issues here.

BACKGROUND INFORMATION AND FAMILY DATA

Background information is important to review. Medical history, educational histories, past behavioral trends, living environment, socioeconomic status and other historical events may provide helpful information. Because some diagnoses such as ADD/HD are linked to genetics, it is often crucial to collect information about both the immediate and extended family. This can help in corroboration of results of other data. Allergies, chemical sensitivities, aversions, sleep patterns, developmental milestones, and vision and auditory data also need to be considered. Background information can often be the most important data, so being thorough and accurate is crucial. If your child is adopted, do whatever you can, within reason, to find this information out.

BEHAVIORAL OBSERVATIONS

Behavioral observations may be collected in the office during intake, testing, and/or therapy, but it is most helpful to observe the client in school, at home, with friends, or at work if he is older. It is also advantageous to collect behavioral information from teachers, daycare providers, and even babysitters and the parents of the child's friends, or others who have had opportunities to observe your children. Psychologists will typically request to have such individuals' complete questionnaires. The behavioral data is important because often the person doing the testing will not see the behaviors in question. It is important to take multiple settings into account to see if the problem behaviors are setting-specific, and the younger the child, the more the need to do observations in natural settings because how he behaves in the office may vary significantly from how he behaves in school or at home. If allergies are a concern, behavior and observations in the settings that trigger the allergies will want to be considered. Some allergies can result in rapid behavior changes.

INTELLECTUAL STRENGTHS AND WEAKNESSES

Intellectual testing will obtain a baseline of the client's abilities to perform in educational and vocational settings. Intelligence tests assess a variety of skills, including acquired knowledge, vocabulary, mathematical abilities, visual motor skills, visual organization skills, and other abilities. Results of testing address strengths and weaknesses, which offer hypotheses and clues as to whether attention difficulties or other learning problems may be present. Although some people do not like the label of an IQ score and feel that it could become limiting for some or place high expectations on others, the benefits outweigh the detriments. You, as a parent, want to make sure that the information is used carefully.

As mentioned earlier, for educational purposes it is important to know a chid's intellectual abilities. As your children progress through their schooling, you may want to reassess them to see if there have been changes in their scores. IQ should stay relatively stable over time. In the event of any type of head injury, previous results can be helpful in assessing possible damage to the brain.

In considering learning disorders, IQ scores are compared to scores on achievement tests. When considering ADD/HD, the different subtests are often compared to find weaknesses on certain subtests relative to others.

AUDITORY AND VISUAL ATTENTION/DISTRACTIBILITY VERSUS PROCESSING SKILLS

Earlier in the text, we mentioned the discrimination between auditory and visual distractibility, and auditory and visual processing. In order to make reliable recommendations for school, job, and home, appropriate assessment of these modalities is important. Many times, we find that previously evaluated individuals were not assessed reliably on measures of distractibility or processing, and/or no discrimination was made between visual and auditory strengths and weaknesses. To assess attention and distraction, computerized tasks help assess auditory and visual attention and the differences between them. The participant's task is to identify certain targets from the information presented, either visually or aurally. Through this technique we are able to assess the differences in focus, impulsivity, hesitance, processing speed, and sustained attention, with reasonable accuracy. However, other possible intervening variables exist which could produce similar output. It is very important to examine the manner in which individuals process and perceive information coming through auditory and visual senses, as well as how information is translated between vision and motor coordination skills (writing, hitting, kicking, etc.). These areas of assessment are often overlooked and, if not at least screened for in the evaluation, may look very similar to attention difficulties. Questionnaires and checklists are commonly used to screen for attention deficits. They are a good source of supporting evidence, but never use only questionnaires to diagnose. They are unable to identify auditory vs. visual weaknesses, and can also provide inconclusive results.

To assess processing, there are other tests that have been developed to see how someone visually and aurally processes what they see and hear. There are distinct differences between processing skills and attention skills, but the output can look similar to the untrained person. Processing has to do with how the information is received by the brain and what is done with the information. Attention skills have to do with the person's ability to focus on the information presented, regardless of the brain's ability to optimally process it.

In an inaccurate or incomplete diagnosis, medication aimed, for example, at improving attention may help a problem in attention, but will not improve a processing deficit, learning deficit, or many other cognitive problems. Be aware of these issues. You might want to ask the professional testing your child whether consideration is given to the differences between visual and auditory issues, as well as attention versus processing. If the evaluator doesn't know what you are talking about, you should probably look elsewhere.

MEMORY

Memory problems are less likely to be associated with children than older adults, but what we remember can be affected by attention and processing. If the information is not being attended to, it doesn't get into memory, and if the information is not processed, it will not be remembered. On its own, memory problems need to be assessed, especially when it comes to differences between auditory and visual memory.

NEUROLOGICAL TRENDS

Some diagnoses are easily observed through the examination of brainwave patterns and brain functioning. These include Tic Disorders and Tourette's Disorder, brain injuries, and ADD/HD and Learning Disorders. Brainwaves are produced by the firing of neurons or nerve cells in the brain. How the neurons fire results in the production of brainwaves patterns which aid in some cognitive processes but hinder others. Brainwaves cause minute levels of electrical output, and they can be measured. A fully functioning brain is thought to be able to produce up to ten watts of electricity.

Here are the four common brainwaves and the functions they are most often related to.

Beta waves occur most commonly when people are focusing or paying attention. For the sake of our discussion, they have been noted as the fastest brainwaves. As you can imagine we use beta waves when we are reading, listening in class or in conversation, learning new material, or working on a problem.

Alpha waves are the next fastest wave form. They occur when we are reflecting, lightly daydreaming, relaxing, creating, or at least predisposed to creating—essentially when the brain is in a resting state, i.e., after our work is done, when we are going for a walk, or when we meditate.

Theta waves are the next fastest wave form after Alpha waves. They are more commonly observed in a deeper daydream, the ones where you are at the beach sitting in the sun and you barely hear the person next to you asking you a question. We are less in touch with "reality" when we are in a theta state. This can also occur when we are watching a TV show and got lost in time or when driving on highway roads and later wonder how we got to our destination without crashing. In a theta state, tasks become automatic. We do them without thinking.

Delta waves are the slowest waves and occur most commonly in a sleeping state, but sometimes in deep states of meditation. They are part of the dream cycle. Theta and alpha also occur in sleep.

In Attention Deficits, different brainwave patterns commonly arise. Additionally, the different brainwave profiles respond better to different medications and to different non-medication treatments. Not all Attention Deficits should be treated the same way, which is why you may want to consider looking at these neurological trends. In fact, treating some "subtypes" of ADD with stimulant medications such as Ritalin, Concerta, or Adderall can actually make the problem worse. A skilled, experienced clinician should know this.

Tic Disorders, Tourette's Disorder, and Seizure Disorders are not caused by a brainwave pattern; they in fact contribute to the disruption of brainwave patterns, an electrical spike in the brain, or other forms of misfiring of neurons. Electrical spikes in the brain are often a reflection of a seizure disorder; they are like electrical surges on a computer. You don't necessarily lose what is stored on the hard drive, but you will lose what was on your screen.. Kids with seizure disorders can look like they have attention deficits, because it looks like they are having a hard time paying attention, but what might actually be happening is that they are paying attention just fine, but when they have an electrical spike, everything they were paying attention to is lost and they have to "reboot" and start all over again. Seizure disorders can have a huge impact on a child's performance and behavior in school. It can feel extremely frustrating to have these difficulties, and the children often go undiagnosed for some time. Many of these kids may look like they space out or "just don't get it." Stimulant medication is typically not used to treat this disorder. In some cases, this class of medications can make the problem worse. With seizure and tic disorders, the goal is to stabilize brain activity, not increase stimulation.

Electroencephalograms, or EEGs, measure the regularity of electrical (brainwave) activity in the brain. They can involve placing an electrode cap on the head that looks like a swimming cap with a bunch of wires coming out that connect to the instrument that measures the output. The output can be displayed on a computer screen or on paper. If there is abnormal electrical activity, EEGs will show this. Spikes may occur in any area of the brain, so it is important to take a look at the entire brain. Also, the location of the electrical activity will impact different skills, behaviors, and abilities. EEGs are commonly used to aid in the diagnosis of Tic Disorders, Tourette's and Seizure Disorders.

Neurometrics, Brain Mapping, Quantitative Electroencephalogram (QEEG), or BEAM Studies, as they may be called interchangeably, are used to aid in the diagnosis of Attention Deficits, Learning Disorders, brain injuries and some other cognitive issues. While these terms have been used interchangeably, each technique makes some specific references to certain databases or variations on the same general technique. The Quantitative EEG (QEEG) uses the computer to collect and digitize the information, and permit a more detailed analysis of the brain activity than conventional EEGs. It provides objective evidence of brain dysfunctions that underlie attention difficulties and other behavioral and cognitive disturbances. (The QEEG does not provide a diagnosis but is one of the tools to help confirm one.)

Other brain functional tools often used in conjunction with the QEEG are the Auditory and Visual Evoked Potentials. These tests measure the brain's specific response to a specific sensory or cognitive challenge, and they help to identify variability in auditory and visual sensory/perceptual processing that can impact attention.

The QEEG has proven to be a useful aid in the diagnostic process, in that it helps to diagnose the presence or absence of brain functional difficulties. The brainwave patterns of these individuals may be compared to brainwave patterns of other individuals with known diagnoses, and it has been found that different types of profiles appear to respond better to different medications and/or medication combinations. Many individuals and families have had positive results with the QEEG after having had numerous difficulties and perceived failures with medication. Many have found that the QEEG has provided them with insights into some of the difficulties that have had, and a more successful regimen of medication may be suggested from test results.

EMOTIONAL DATA

With all of the background data, IQ testing, and other cognitive testing collected, you may feel that you and your child have been through the gamut. While you may have set out with the goal to figure out why your child was not performing at school, emotional issues can be more significant than the cognitive difficulties they may have. Evaluators may ask your child to perform a sentence completion test, to draw a person, tree or house, to fill out a personality inventory, answer questionnaires, have him tell some stories based on pictures, or complete the Rorschach Inkblot Test. These are some of the sources of data that help psychologists and neuropsychologists get better insight into what is going on emotionally and with their personality.

Minimal evaluations omit the personality inventories, story telling, or Rorschach. However, these can provide the most helpful information, especially the stories and the Rorschach. Many people do not like to be open with their issues or challenges, and both children and adults try to fool the tests. They are not honest, or they try to minimize their problems because they want to feel normal. Therefore, the projective tests, such as the story telling and the Rorschach, can give the most astute insight.

Some psychologists have reservations about giving projective tests. Many feel skeptical that a person's description of an inkblot, or a story he makes up about a picture, can really tell a lot about an individual. Another reservation is that these tests take training to administer and time to score. If a clinician can save time in the scoring and write up, or by not administering a labor-intensive test, he will often do that to keep costs down. Many professionals in the field question the validity of projective tests, but our experience has been that in the hands of someone who is experienced and skilled, they add a great deal of insight and value that can be difficult to obtain from other sources.

In fact, we believe that projective tests are absolutely invaluable in many situations. They get below the surface to see what kids are often trying to hide and/or do not have the words to explain. We have seen that these tests also help to refine the approaches people take toward life. They can help us see what is going on at the moment and what their behavior may be predisposed to over time. They are also helpful in understanding relationships with others and why there may be problems with those relationships. If you find a clinician who feels that they are a waste of time, he probably does not understand the underlying value of these instruments.

Whether your child has an identifiable reason for having difficulties in school, there is almost always an emotional influence. Motivation, anxiety, poor self-esteem, depression, relationship problems, and fears of success and failure are just a few of the issues that may be influencing their performance. Sometimes this can be discovered with more certainty through the emotional data. Countless times children with cognitive diagnoses such as Attention Deficits, Learning Disorders, and/or others, have significant emotional consequences as a result of feeling misunderstood, feeling different from others, being teased, not understanding situations or questions, and being told—or treated as if—they are stupid. Often the cognitive diagnoses are just the beginning of identifying the entire picture. A child's attention deficit or learning problem may be treated with medication or remediation, but that will not change the way he sees the world. For that, he will need help and guidance.

The emotional consequences of many cognitive difficulties can feel overwhelming. Kids who have ADD/HD often have a difficult time mastering the art of building relationships because they may not pay attention to the subtle cues. They are also corrected a great deal for their behaviors and therefore feel more failure, shame, and guilt. Do they want to admit to these? No. That is where the emotional component of the evaluation can help set the course for treatment of the child, family, and school staff. Non-verbal learning problems also come with difficulties because kids do not realize the impact of their behaviors and do not receive feedback in a manner they can understand. The way these kids are treated by others greatly influences the way they view the world, especially without a deeper understanding of what makes them tick.

ANALYSIS OF DATA AND THE REPORT

Once all the relevant data has been collected, it is necessary to make sense of it. This is when a neuropsychologist is worth his weight in gold. Information collected needs to be scored. Once the data is scored, the scores are compared to other people's performance through the use of normative data. This can help evaluate how your child did and should perform in academic and vocational settings. Another step in the analysis is to evaluate your child's range of test scores to see where he scored high and low, not only compared to his peers but also within his own skill areas. This analysis is important in consideration of ADD, processing deficits, learning disabilities, and cognitive deficits. We call this "subtest scatter," and a lot of "scatter" or big differences between scores of certain tests and subtests helps identify what may be going on.

Often data collected from mood and personality inventories can help us understand intellectual functioning, attention and concentration, and learning problems. The converse is also true. Sometimes, minor differences on certain tests can make a big difference in the diagnosis or lack thereof. The interpretation and analysis is not something to be minimized or rushed through. Many mistakes can be made at this stage, which can render all the testing and data collection just about useless. As we stated earlier, even the results of the emotional data can be critical to a diagnosis of ADD/HD and other issues.

Once the analysis of data is complete, it is put into a report form and often presented to the parents, teachers, and other pertinent individuals or professionals. You want to have a report you can understand, not something that can only be understood by another doctor or expert. If you can't understand it, chances are that the teachers can't either. Don't feel afraid to let the clinician know that you would like the data put in a more user-friendly style or touched up a bit to more clearly explain the issues. This is another reason to have the psychologist attend school SST or IEP meetings.

Slightly different report formats may be required by each profession. Some people recommend removing the background information and emotional results from reports that may go to the school, for confidentiality purposes. The recommendations section is one of the most important pieces of the report. It should be designed specifically for the individual and should point to how strengths can be used to reduce the affect of apparent weaknesses and what interventions are suggested to ameliorate weaker areas of performance. Due to the complexity of many of the cases, it is often helpful for the clinician to become personally involved with the physician, the school, and other professionals, to make sure that recommendations are being followed and are workable in the environment that the individual inhabits. Psychologists are often trained to help others adapt environments to meet the needs of individuals. Many other professionals specialize in this to help kids with special needs to succeed.

Summary

We hope that we have helped put your mind at ease as to when and how to get help for your children and your family. There is only so much that you can do to help your child with academic, emotional, and/or social issues. Being aware of your own issues and attitudes is important because they can't help but impact your child. Make sure you look deeply within yourself and realize that you have a responsibility to get help for your child and/or your family, and have the courage and wisdom to get it.

The old saying, "where there's smoke, there's fire," is not always true—just most of the time. If you believe that your child has a problem, then he or she probably does. This is where having a commitment to doing research, asking questions, and making the effort to really understand your child come into play. Getting input from other people who regularly interact with your child can sometimes help you in knowing where the most effective form of help may be found. Sometimes, we are too close to our kids or too close to the problem to objectively see the bigger picture.

We are not suggesting that if a child has a temper tantrum or wets his bed that he should immediately be whisked off for an extensive psychological evaluation. Sometimes children do go through phases and sometimes problems do go away. However, we also believe in erring on the side of caution. If you honestly believe that something isn't right or that your child is not functioning as he should be, it never hurts to discuss the matter with a qualified expert. Many of the difficulties and problems your child(ren) has don't simply go away, nor will kids outgrow them.

Waiting is not always the best policy.

An evaluation to assess your child's needs is an investment, and it is often worth it for your child's academic, emotional, and financial future.

᪣ **Chapter 12** ᪣
Solutions and Strategies for a Lifetime of Empowered Parenting

This has been some journey we've taken. We hope that the book has illustrated some of the ins and outs of what works and what doesn't in our approaches to parenting, and how to help your child grow into a more confident and insightful adult. Our goal throughout has been to make all of your lives easier, empowered, and more peaceful.

Our journey began by discussing where the state of parenting and the family is, to date, and why we have run into the challenges we have, given the manner in which we look at power. We also discussed the roles that people may play in the family, such as victim, persecutor, rescuer, and instigator, and how these roles contribute to conflict and power struggles. Our next stop was intended to help you see another view of power from the standpoint of equity, and see the wisdom in giving power to get power. Through understanding power and the different ways we use it, you can see how it influences emotions and the way that you and your children may use them. You cannot remove emotions from parenting, so we hope to have provided you with the ability to use them wisely and decrease the chance that they will be used to harm your children and your relationship with them. Remember, your job is to prepare your child for the rest of her life by providing the tools for her to succeed.

Developing strategies and solutions involves having a model to refer back to in order to put the pieces together. As we stated in the beginning, most parents' strategies are developed from the models given to them by their parents, most centered in the hierarchical model of power. Changing the models we brought from childhood takes time, patience, and perseverance, and mistakes will occur. We hope that you will begin to transition to a model based in equity that will provide empowerment for all. Realize that in this transition, you will make mistakes; each mistake is an opportunity to learn. The models provided will work not only with your children, they can also apply to any aspect of your life. This chapter is meant to summarize what we've covered and to help you piece together the information in developing the strategies to succeed as a family.

We know that it is impossible to provide answers for every possible scenario that could happen with your children. Nor can you provide your child with every answer to everything that could happen in her life. We have intended to give you a set of tools, and rules to use, to develop strategies and pass them down to your children.

REMEMBER YOUR HUMAN FLAWS

According to the hierarchical, control-based models you may have been raised with, you are not supposed to show your weakness or flaws to your children. Because of our fear of being seeing as weak or vulnerable by our kids, we have a hard time admitting when we make a mistake. We have discussed the pitfalls of this throughout the book. The more you share your humanness with your children (equity-based), the more likely they are to share theirs with you. This does not mean pouring your heart out about your fears and failures, but it does involve acknowledging mistakes you make with parenting, being willing to correct them, and sharing some of your past experiences with your children that may be appropriate to their life experiences. The results are often a deeper trust and respect for all.

EMPOWER YOUR CHILDREN TO SOLVE THEIR ISSUES

In developing your strategies and building solutions, you'll want to follow some basic rules in addressing issues and problems that occur. If your child tells you that her friend took her toy, consider whether or not the dispute involves hurting or damaging anything. You may be anxious to engage yourself in the matter (hierarchical, control-based), but your best courses of action—if possible—involves allowing the children to work out their own methods of addressing the situation through providing them with strategies to work through their issues (equity-empowered-based). Sometimes you may have to step in when they are not making the best choices.

If your children want equity, they will want to make equitable choices. You are still, in part, responsible for their actions—redirecting or halting fighting, name-calling, or any use of violence is important. But children can surprise us with their ability to work out ways of sharing and cooperating with each other when they have the tools. There is some judgment involved in evaluating the situation, but try to allow your child(ren) to work some things out on their own, when the situation permits.

Having children commit to finding a solution is important. If they are not motivated to find a solution, then the problem often persists. It is also important to remember that we should not sell kids short. Children have a greater capacity to solve problems than we sometimes realize.

TEACH AND PROMOTE COOPERATION

When children have conflicts, whether personal or over some mutually desired toy, often our best approach is to let them exercise their powers of cooperation. One such approach involves using "thinking chairs." When children aren't playing nicely or are having trouble getting along, put the children in chairs, close enough that they can talk, but far enough that they cannot hit or kick each other, and tell them that they have the power to think about how to solve this problem. Tell the kids that they must sit in their thinking chairs until they have decided on a way to work things out, for up to thirty minutes. When they have figured out a solution, they need to tell you what their plan is before they can go back to playing. Give them some ideas on solutions, and let them know that they can come up with their own. If they can't figure it out in thirty minutes, you will come up with a solution for them.

BE FLEXIBLE WHEN UNDERSTANDING YOUR CHILD'S NEEDS AND EMOTIONS

We can often save ourselves some grief if we recognize when our child is having a bad day, isn't feeling well, or is tired. If we drag a tired or irritable child along with us to the grocery store, for example, we may set ourselves up for a difficult shopping experience. Certainly, we can't always juggle our schedule to accommodate a child's mood or energy level, but sometimes we can. On those occasions when we must shop or run errands and our child is cranky or tired, we can do many things to help her remain occupied and stimulated. Depending upon her age, different approaches are appropriate.

Small children can help you find something blue on the shelves, or find things of a certain shape. Older children also enjoy helping with the shopping. You may give them their own little shopping cart and shopping list, and let them gather some items. A good way to avoid tantrums about a wanted item is to tell the child ahead of time, before entering a store, that you can only buy items on the shopping list. You may also tell her that you may come back another day and buy some goodies or special things. In many cases, this reduces the chances of the child asking for items you don't want her to have. Even in the cases where children still ask for treats and goodies, they tend to handle your refusal much better than they would if they hadn't been forewarned. Just remember to be firm, consistent, and fair. If your children want junk food, let them know that they can spend their own money on it, if they wish. When you get home, make sure their food is identified and that others observe their boundaries, and set limits on when and how much junk food they are permitted to eat.

To help kids remain entertained when shopping or on other adult-oriented tasks (concerts, church, weddings, parties), make up a small "surprise" bag with little toys in it, and allow children to pull a toy out and play with it as you do your shopping. Some parents find that taking a few picture books or a small toy that the child really enjoys can ease the strain of trying to cope with a fussy child. Always keep in mind that your children do not have experience in understanding or dealing with emotions, and they require your guidance to learn how to handle them. If you do not feel confident knowing how to handle their emotions, get some help.

TEACH ACCOUNTABILITY AND RESPONSIBILITY

An important aspect of empowered parenting involves building a relationship with a child that can help us seek solutions, address issues, and overcome behavioral problems. We have discussed the need to hold your children accountable for their actions, and use choices and consequences that allow them to know that they have the ability to manage their life. Set clearly defined guidelines that the child understands, and consistently enforce and reinforce them. As you parent from an equity model, your child will develop the skills to help you and make your job as a parent easier.

Let's do a little review and extension of House Rules. As we discussed in Chapter 9, you can use the family meeting to help set up the rules, and all members of the house should agree upon the house rules. There should be an incentive and a consequence for each rule. For example, if the child's bedtime is 9 p.m., the child knows that if she does not go to bed on time, she must go to bed fifteen minutes early on the following night. However, if she goes to bed on time at least five nights out of the week, she can stay up until 10 p.m. on Friday or Saturday night.

Remember to write the rules in a positive way—this means writing the rule to state what we expect. If the rule addresses running in the house, it might say, "Please remember to walk inside. Outside is a better place to run." Writing rules in this manner makes your expectations clear and defines where or when it is alright to run, play, yell or scream. While creating this list of rules, it is important to discuss why each rule is necessary and what the purpose of each one is. By explaining rules clearly, you are helping your child improve their problem solving skills. How much does your child learn from "Because I said so"? It may also be productive to state a rule and then ask the children if they can think of reasons why this is a good rule and how it makes life better for the whole family. Children, like adults, are more apt to follow rules if they understand the purpose for them.

Remember, from Chapter 2, that the "Do as I say" (hierarchical, control-based) approaches only contribute to more conflict. It is the "Do unto others" (equity, empowered-based) approach you want to model. Leading by positive example teaches a child a mutual, love-based respect, rather than a fear-based respect (do it or else). For example, it can be effective to say, "I am going to go and clean my room. How about if you clean your room also? Let's see if we can finish cleaning our rooms at the same time." By demonstrating that we are willing to do the same thing we are asking our child to do, we are modeling the behavior we want her to exhibit and that we are "practicing what we preach." We are also teaching that cleaning is not merely a punishment and in fact is something that every family member must do. Another option is to say, "I will help you to clean your room if you will help me clean mine." All too often, we think of work as just that—work—or we use it as punishment, making it even less attractive.

We often give little thought to trying to make tasks more interesting or fun, and we tend to struggle through them because we know that we have to uphold our responsibilities. It is difficult for a child to feel motivated to do something that has no reward and is not fun, or if it is something she is sometimes made to do as punishment. However, if suggestions involve intrinsic motivations, children will feel good about the outcome and be more likely to do it again. When using extrinsic rewards, remember not to continually bribe children with gifts, toys, or money. However, as mentioned earlier, it may be necessary to start with these extrinsic rewards to get them going and work toward intrinsic rewards. The term "reward" can take on many forms. A child may feel rewarded by getting an extra bedtime story, by having a parent tell her what a great job she did, or by being allowed to do something she enjoys. Sometimes the game of doing a task is enough of a reward.

LEAD BY EXAMPLE

Remember that setting a positive example means living by your own rules, not just enforcing them with your kids. If you expect your kids to let you know where they are and when they plan to return home, then you should do the same. If you tell them that they cannot eat or have snacks in the living room, you should not eat in the living room. Or you may let them know that when they have demonstrated the proper skills, i.e., not spilling anything on the kitchen table for one month, or cleaning up after themselves, then you will allow them to eat in the living room. To maintain the privilege, they must continue to follow the rules. Double standards for children and adults cause resentment and lead children to believe they are not being treated fairly. Like adults, kids respond more readily to your requests if they believe that you are willing to do whatever you ask them to do.

BE AWARE OF YOUR VOICE TONES AND BODY LANGUAGE

In your strategies with your children, remember to monitor how you communicate even when you are feeling emotional. There is no doubt that we will sometimes feel upset or angry about something our children do. It is important to avoid holding grudges. If a child misbehaves and you enforce consequences, the matter should end with the consequences. No one enjoys repeatedly hearing about mistakes or misjudgments in the past, and this is especially true with children. Also, no one likes to feel scorned or humiliated by having a misdeed recounted to people outside the home. When a child feels shameful about misbehaving, it's bad enough that the parents express displeasure; it's worse if the neighbors and family friends also sit in judgment of the misdeed. Keep in mind that your child may not be making the same mistake on purpose. Sometimes they may make it to avoid responsibility or to mess with your power. Many times parents take it personally, feel disrespected, and respond with anger. The more you keep your cool and follow through, the less likely it is that your child will involve more emotion in her response, and also, the less need the child will feel to mess with your power.

When we find ourselves angry with our child's actions, it seems almost instinctive to shout or raise our voice. It would be more productive to say, "I'm feeling angry with your actions, right now, so I apologize in advance if my tone is a little harsh. I'm also feeling disrespected and betrayed by your choices and want you to learn from this. Think about why you made the choices you made and I will take some time to cool down so we can talk about it." Remember that children tune us out when we shout. Children who grow up with parents who shout, learn to shout to be heard.

KEEP YOUR COOL

When you feel that you need a quick reaction to your children's behavior, would you believe that whispering tends to get a child's attention whereas screaming often fails? By lowering your voice and communicating with your child in a hushed, yet firm tone, you can often make yourself heard far more effectively than you do when you shout. Using a quiet voice to talk to a child encourages the child to calm down and listen to your words.

BE PURPOSEFUL IN YOUR CONSEQUENCES

Many of us grew up with punishments imposed on us that taught us little or nothing, and did not provide us with any meaningful experience. Teachers who forced us to write, "I will not chew gum in class" five hundred times did little more than waste our time. We only avoided punishable behavior out of fear, or we learned to hide our behavior. This did not teach respect, it taught avoidance. This was often true when we were spanked, sent to our room for the day, or swatted on the hand. Find ways to stop punishing and start teaching. Instead of having a child write "I will not chew gum in class" five hundred times, a more creative teacher might have the child write a paper explaining why she should not chew gum in school and why it is important to follow the rules. Or instead of making a child sit alone in her room for an hour or two, you may do the opposite—sit down and talk to the child about what happened and why she misbehaved.

There's no way to enumerate all the ways and behaviors that constitute breaking the rules. Some common misbehaviors and logical, positive consequences follow. A child rides her bike in the street despite the fact that this is breaking a guideline. Your first inclination might be to spank, ground, or send her to her room for the evening. However, wouldn't it make more sense to take the bike away until she can recite the rules of riding her bike that you all came up with as a family? How about if she was only allowed to ride her bike in your presence for a probationary period? If a child is supposed to pick up all of her toys before going to bed, and she chooses not to do so, remove the toys she did not clean up, put them away for a day, and reinforce the message that there are consequences that come with failing to follow guidelines. Alternatively, you can wake her up before you go to bed and have her clean up her toys. You could also increase the time the toys are removed for each additional infraction.

Response cost is another technique to teach lessons; it may feel more difficult or painful to your children. For example, if a child steals another child's toy, have her pick one of her favorite toys and donate it to charity. Your children will learn that if she takes something of someone else's, the cost of that response will be the loss of something she values. Always try to make sure that your children know the possible consequences beforehand so they know what to expect. Approaches like these can work with many violations of household rules, and violations of the rights and space of others. This consequence may be viewed as hierarchical and control-based, but remember, we have said that if they play the hierarchical games, they may suffer the hierarchical consequences.

Depending upon your child's age, she may spend too much time on the phone, watching TV, playing video games, or visit off-limit places on the Internet. Revoking the privilege to use these things until she has demonstrated the wisdom in understanding how she broke the rules can be an effective way of teaching the child to make good choices and adhere to the rules, or suffer the consequences. So how do you know when your child has demonstrated the ability to understand the error of her ways? This is when the essay writing consequence that we discussed in Chapter 9 comes into play.

Removing or restricting privileges serves several purposes in this approach to empowered parenting. Perhaps the most important lessons the child learns are that there are reasons for rules, and there are consequences if we fail to follow them. It is likely that the child will feel angry when the parent removes or restricts a privilege, but your interest is having your child recognize that she made the choice that caused the consequence. Therefore, the child realizes that she had a choice to make, did not make a good choice, and has created a situation she does not like. Along with these other lessons, consistently enforcing the house rules teaches the child that the parents mean what they say and the child can trust that the parents have boundaries, and they will enforce them.

The point of consequences and rewards is to reinforce the concept of responsibility. Consider this point in your strategies and solutions. Children often receive an allowance for upholding their responsibilities. However, if we give them money but allow them to shirk their responsibilities, then we have undermined one of the most important principles we want to teach them—that they can neglect their duties and still be rewarded. Rewarding their misdeeds or misbehavior removes incentive for following the rules and may teach children that they can get away with negligence. On the other hand, we also don't want them coming to us with an outstretched hand, expecting money or treats each and every time they do something productive. When children violate rules, there should always be consequences. But, as stated earlier, behaving well and meeting responsibilities should not automatically prompt money, treats, or other tangible rewards.

If one of your parenting strategies is to increase the chance that your child will see the value in following through on her responsibilities, see the wisdom in compensating them fairly for completing the tasks, and remember that praise, an extra fifteen minutes of TV time, or allowing her an extra bedtime story also count as compensation. This generalizes to the rest of her life in the work world and other arenas. Allowances can work within the guidelines of a task chart. By having to complete predetermined tasks, your child earns an allowance and does not come to expect money from the parent each week for doing nothing. If the child fails to do her chores, money may be docked from her allowance. Furthermore, she can see that properly completing the listed tasks merits a full allowance payment, similar to what will happen when she has a job one day.

While withholding a portion of the child's allowance is appropriate for teaching responsibility, other instances may require a different approach. Response costs may be appropriate here too. Let's say, for example, that a house rule states that Jimmy is not to run in the house. Jimmy does run in the house, and he breaks a lamp in the process. Instead of offering some arbitrary consequence, we may find it more productive to take Jimmy with us as we shop for another lamp, and let him see how much the new lamp costs. We may decide to make Jimmy pay for the new lamp or pay some portion of the cost. Again, the point is to teach your children responsibility and accountability for the things they do, preparing them for life.

Have Fun and Grow... Together

When dealing with our kids, we have many powerful tools at our disposal, but we tend to forget about them. We have a sense of humor that we can use to diffuse situations or to correct bad behavior, but often, we forget to have fun with our kids. How often do we go for a walk or toss a ball with them? When was the last time your family went on a picnic? Small kids love to play games, sing songs, or create art with a parent. The interaction involved in these activities is the most important aspect. The object is to bond with the child through involvement, and it takes two people to form a bond. Modern day parents tend to look for ways to occupy the child's time without requiring much, if any, effort on their own part. Children often have stacks of videos, CD's, electronic games, and other electronic gizmos, all of which are wonderful—as long as they do not act as substitutes for personal interaction and quality time with the rest of the family. Children do not learn social skills or personal interaction from machines, even those designed to be educational, and we need to ensure that our children get plenty of attention and personal involvement from the family.

Besides enjoying our kids and thinking of creative ways to address problems and reward good behavior, we need to remember that our children should feel as though they can approach us and talk about anything. Kids need to know that you may not always agree with or like what they say, but you will always listen and always love them. Children need the reassurance of knowing that we love and are there for them, even when we feel unhappy about something that they did or said.

We hope that you have enjoyed our journey together and that it has better prepared you for yours. Keep in mind that there are no perfect parents. We are all here to grow and learn together, and our journey with our children is the most important one we will ever take.

∽ Recommended Reading ∽

Brazelton, T. B. 1992. *Touchpoints: Your Child's Emotional and Behavioral Development, Birth to 3.* New York: Perseus Books.

Brazelton, T. B., and J. D. Sparrow, 2003. *Discipline: The Brazelton Way.* New York: Perseus Books.

Brazelton, T. B., and S. I. Greenspan. 2000. *The Irreducible Needs of Children: What Every Child Must Have to Grow, Learn, and Flourish.* New York: Perseus Publishing.

Chopra, D. 2006. *The Seven Spiritual Laws for Parents: Guiding Your Children to Success and Fulfillment.* Reprint edition. New York: Three Rivers Press.

Chopra, D., and M. Chopra. 2005. 100 *Promises to My Baby.* New York: Rodale Books.

Dinkmeyer Jr., D. D. Dinkmeyer Sr. J. S. Dinkmeyer, G. D. McKay and J. McKay. 1989. *Parenting Young Children: Systematic Training for Effective Parenting (Step) of Children Under Six.* New York: Random House.

Faber, A., and E. Mazlish. 1987. *Siblings Without Rivalry: How to Help Your Children Live Together So You Can Live Too.* New York: W. W. Norton & Company, Inc.

Faber, A., and E. Mazlish. 1980. *How to Talk so Kids Will Listen and Listen so Kids Will Talk.* New York: Avon Books, Inc.

Fisher, E. A. and Sharp, S. W. 2004. *The Art of Managing Everyday Conflict: Understanding Emotions and Power Struggles.* Westport, Connecticut: Praeger Publishers.

Holt, P., and G. Ketterman. 1997. *Don't Give In, Give Choices; Winning Your Child's Cooperation.* Wheaton: Harold Shaw Publishers.

Keck, G. C., and R. M. Kupecky. 1998. *Adopting the Hurt Child: Hope for Families with Special-Needs Kids: A Guide for Parents and Professionals.* Colorado Springs: Navpress Publishing Group.

Keck, G. C., and R. M. Kupecky. 2002. *Parenting the Hurt Child: Helping Adoptive Families Heal and Grow.* Colorado Springs: Pinon Press.

Moorman, C. 2003. *Parent Talk: How to Talk to Your Children in Language That Builds Self-Esteem and Encourages Responsibility.* New York: Fireside.

Moorman, C., and T. Haller. 2004. *The 10 Commitments: Parenting with Purpose.* Merrill: Personal Power Press.

Pelzer, D. 1995. *A Child Called "It": One Child's Courage to Survive.* Deerfield Beach: Health Communications, Inc.

Pelzer, D. 1997. *The Lost Boy: A Foster Child's Search for the Love of a Family.* Deerfield Beach, FL: Health Communications, Inc.

Pelzer, D. 2000. *A Man Named Dave: A Story of Triumph and Forgiveness.* New York: Plume.

Pelzer, D. 2001. *Help Yourself: Finding Hope, Courage, and Happiness.* New York: Plume.

Pelzer, D. 2002. *Life's Lessons: From a Man Who Knows.* New York: HarperCollins.

Pelzer, D. 2004. *My Story*. London: Orion.

Pelzer, D. 2004. *The Privilege of Youth: A Teenager's Story of Longing for Acceptance and Friendship*. New York: Penguin Group.

Pelzer, D. 2005. *Help Yourself for Teens: Real-Life Advice for Real-Life Challenges*. New York: Penguin Group.

Pelzer, R. 2005. *A Brother's Journey: Surviving a Childhood of Abuse*. New York: Warner Books.

Phelan, T. W. 1996. *Self-Esteem Revolutions in Children: Understanding and Managing the Critical Transitions in Your Child's Life*. Glen Ellyn: Parentmagic, Inc.

Phelan, T. W. 1998. *Surviving Your Adolescents: How to Manage-and Let Go of-Your 13-18 Year Olds*. Second edition. Glen Ellyn: Parentmagic, Inc.

Phelan, T. W. 2000. *All About Attention Deficit Disorder: Symptoms, Diagnosis, and Treatment: Children and Adults*. Second edition. Glen Ellyn: Parentmagic, Inc.

Phelan, T. W. 2001. *I Never Get Anything! How to Keep Your Kids from Running Your Life*. Glen Ellyn: Parentmagic, Inc.

Phelan, T. W. 2003. *1-2-3 Magic: Effective Discipline for Children 2-12*. Third edition. Glen Ellyn: Parentmagic, Inc.

Tieger, P., and B. Barron-Tieger. 1997. *Nurture by Nature: Understand Your Child's Personality Type-And Become a Better Parent*. New York: Little, Brown Book Group.

Turecki, S., and L. Tonner. 2000. *The Difficult Child: Expanded and Revised Edition*. New York: Bantam Books.

Turecki, S., and S. Wernick. 1994. *Normal Children Have Problems, Too: How Parents Can Understand and Help.* New York: Bantam Books.

Wallerstein, J. S., J.M. Lewis, and S. Blakeslee. 2000. *The Unexpected Legacy of Divorce.* New York: Hyperion.

Welch, M., and M.E. Mark. 1998. *Holding Time: The Breakthrough Program for Happy Mothers and Loving, Self-Confident Children without Tantrums, Tugs-of-War, or Sibling Rivalry.* New York: Simon & Schuster.

Wyckoff, J., and B. Unell. 1991. *Discipline without Shouting Or Spanking: Practical Solutions to the Most Common Preschool Behavior Problems.* New York: Simon & Schuster.

❧ BIBLIOGRAPHY ❧

Andersson, H. W. (1999). Infant temperamental factors as predictors of problem behavior and IQ at age 5 years: Interactional effects of biological and social risk factors. *Child Study Journal,* 29 (3): 207-226. Academic Search Premier Database, EBSCOhost (30 AUG 2006).

Arseneault, L., Moffitt, T. E., Caspi, A., Taylor, A., Rijsdijk, F. V., Jaffee, S. R., et al. (2003). Strong genetic effects on cross-situational antisocial behaviour among 5-year-old children according to mothers, teachers, examiner-observers, and twins' self-reports. *Journal of Child Psychology & Psychiatry & Allied Disciplines,* 44 (6): 832-848. Academic Search Premier Database, EBSCOhost (30 AUG 2006).

Atella, L. D., DiPietro, J. A., Smith, B. A., & St. James-Roberts, I. (2003). More than meets the eye: Parental and infant contributors to maternal and paternal reports of early infant difficultness. *Parenting: Science & Practice,* 3 (4): 265-284. Academic Search Premier Database, EBSCOhost (30 AUG 2006).

Bagley, C., & Mallick, K. (2000). Spiralling up and spiralling down: Implications of a long-term study of temperament and conduct disorder for social work with children. *Child & Family Social Work,* 5 (4): 291-301. Academic Search Premier Database, EBSCOhost (30 AUG 2006).

Barnow, S., Lucht, M., & Freyberger, H.-J. (2005). Correlates of aggressive and delinquent conduct problems in adolescence.

Aggressive Behavior, 31 (1): 24-39. Academic Search Premier Database, EBSCOhost (30 AUG 2006).

Baumgartner, N. A. *Knowing a Spirited Child's Temperament Can Help Parents Cope.* University of Wisconsin-Extension. 24 NOV 2002. http://www.uwex.edu/news/2002/11 (accessed 01 SEP 2006).

Behavioral-Developmental Initiatives. *Clinical Practice and Temperament.* http://www.temperament.com/clinical.html (accessed 01 SEP 2006).

Bor, W., McGee, T. R., & Fagan, A. A. (2004). Early risk factors for adolescent antisocial behaviour: An Australian longitudinal study. *Australian & New Zealand Journal of Psychiatry*, 38 (5): 365-372. Academic Search Premier Database, EBSCOhost (30 AUG 2006).

Brody, G. H., & Stoneman, Z. (1996). Parent-child relationships, family problem-solving behavior, and sibling relationship quality: The moderating role of sibling temperaments. *Child Development*, 67 (3): 1289-1300. Academic Search Premier Database, EBSCOhost (30 AUG 2006).

Bussing, R., Lehninger, F., & Eyberg, S. (2006). Difficult child temperament and Attention-Deficit/Hyperactivity Disorder in preschool children. *Infants & Young Children: An Interdisciplinary Journal of Special Care Practices*, 19 (2): 123-131. Academic Search Premier Database, EBSCOhost (30 AUG 2006).

Caci, H., Robert, P., & Boyer, P. (2004). Novelty seekers and impulsive subjects are low in morningness. *European Psychiatry*, 19 (2): 79-84. Academic Search Premier Database, EBSCOhost (30 AUG 2006).

Carlson, E. A. (1998). A prospective longitudinal study of attachment disorganization / disorientation. *Child Development*, 69 (4): 1107-1128.

Côté, S., Tremblay, R. E., Nagin, D., Zoccolillo, M., & Vitaro, F. (2002). The development of impulsivity, fearfulness, and helpfulness during childhood: Patterns of consistency and change in the trajectories of boys and girls. *Journal of Child Psychology & Psychiatry & Allied Disciplines*, 43 (5): 609-618. Academic Search Premier Database, EBSCOhost (30 AUG 2006).

Davé, S., Nazareth, I., Sherr, L., & Senior, R. (2005). The association of paternal mood and infant temperament: A pilot study. *British Journal of Developmental Psychology*, 23 (4): 609-621. Academic Search Premier Database, EBSCOhost (30 AUG 2006).

Deater-Deckard, K. (2001). Nonshared environmental processes in social-emotional development: An observational study of identical twin differences in the preschool period. *Developmental Science*, 4 (2): 1-6. Academic Search Premier Database, EBSCOhost (30 AUG 2006).

Drug Enforcement Administration. *Hearing before the Subcommittee on Crime of the Committee on the Judiciary House of Representatives*, 106 Congress, 1st session, 29 JUL 1999. http://commdocs.house.gov/committees/judiciary/hju63855.000/hju63855_0f.htm (accessed 01 SEP 2006).

Egeland, B., & Carlson, E. A. (in press). Attachment and Psychopathology. In L. Atkinson (Eds.) *Clinical Applications of Attachment*. Mahwah, NJ: Lawrence Erlbaum & Associates.

Emde, R. N., & Plomin, R. (1992). Temperament, emotion, and cognition at fourteen months: The MacArthur longitudinal twin study. *Child Development*, 63 (6): 1437-1455. Academic Search Premier Database, EBSCOhost (30 AUG 2006).

Entwisle, D. R., Alexander, K. L., & Olson, L. S. (2005). First grade and educational attainment by age 22: A new story. *American Journal of Sociology,* 110 (5): 1458-1502. Academic Search Premier Database, EBSCOhost (30 AUG 2006).

Eun Young Mun, J. L., Fitzgerald, H. E., von Eye, A., Puttler, L. I., & Zucker, R. A. (2001). Temperamental characteristics as predictors of externalizing and internalizing child behavior problems in the contexts of high and low parental psychopathology. *Infant Mental Health Journal,* 22 (3): 393-415. Academic Search Premier Database, EBSCOhost (30 AUG 2006).

Fackelmann, K. "Teen Drug Use on Decline." *USA Today,* 16 DEC 2002. http://www.usatoday.com/news/nation/2002-12-16-teens-drugs_x.htm (accessed 01 SEP 2006).

Facts in Action, Associated Early Care & Education. (2002). In brief: Majority of Kids Under Five in Child Care. http://www.factsinaction.org/brief/brjun022.htm (accessed 23 NOV 2003).

Facts in Action, Associated Early Care & Education. (2003). In brief: Child care in the first year may improve mother-infant attachment. http://www.factsinaction.org/brief/brapr033.htm (accessed 23 NOV 2003).

Facts in Action, Associated Early Care & Education. (2003). In brief: New study stirs debate over the effects of child care. http://www.factsinaction.org/brief/brjul034.htm (accessed 23 NOV 2003).

Facts in Action, Associated Early Care & Education. (2003). Quick facts to clip and quote: Number of family child care providers grows. http://www.factsinaction.org/quickfacts/qfsep03.htm (accessed 23 NOV 2003).

Fisher, E. A. and Sharp, S. W. 2004. *The Art of Managing Everyday*

Conflict: Understanding Emotions and Power Struggles. Westport, Connecticut: Praeger Publishers.

Fox, N. A., Henderson, H. A., Marshall, P. J., Nichols, K. E., & Ghera, M. M. (2005). Behavioral inhibition: Linking biology and behavior within a developmental framework. *Annual Review of Psychology,* 56 (1): 235-262. Academic Search Premier Database, EBSCOhost (30 AUG 2006).

Gallagher, M. Day careless. (cover story) *National Review,* 26 JAN 1998, 37-43. Academic Search Premier Database, EBSCOhost (30 AUG 2006).

Gardner, F., Ward, S., Burton, J., & Wilson, C. (2003). The role of mother–child joint play in the early development of children's conduct problems: A longitudinal observational study. *Social Development,* 12 (3): 361-378. Academic Search Premier Database, EBSCOhost (30 AUG 2006).

Garner, P. W., & Spears, F. M. (2000). Emotion regulation in low-income preschoolers. *Social Development,* 9 (2): 246-264. Academic Search Premier Database, EBSCOhost (30 AUG 2006).

Goodman, R. F. *Childcare Dilemma: Are Children at Risk?* 25 APR 2001. http://www.aboutourkids.org/aboutour/articles/childcare.html (accessed 01 SEP 2006).

Gosche, M. *Divorce Adjustment Influenced by Child's Temperament and Mother's Parenting Style.* 26 SEP 2005. http://missourifamilies.org/FEATURES/divorcearticles/divorcefeature32.htm (accessed 01 SEP 2006).

Hazel, C. (2005). Building positive behavior support systems in schools: Functional behavioral assessment. *Psychology in the Schools,* 42 (2): 217-218. Academic Search Premier Database, EBSCOhost (30 AUG 2006).

Hernandez, D. J. (1995). Changing Demographics: Past and Future Demands for Early Childhood Programs. In R. E. Behrman (Ed.) *The Future of Children: Long-Term Outcomes of Early Childhood Programs.* http://www.futureofchildren.org/information2826/information_show.htm?doc_id=77711 (accessed 01 SEP 2006).

In Defense of Animals. CU Medical Center tortures helpless monkeys in useless Maternal Deprivation Experiments. http://www.vivisectioninfo.org/deprivation/ (accessed 20 NOV 2003).

Intelegen Inc. *What is the function of the various brainwaves?* http://www.web-us.com/brainwavesfunction.htm (accessed 01 SEP 2006).

Jenkins, J., Simpson, A., Dunn, J., Rasbash, J., & O'Connor, T. G. (2005). Mutual influence of marital conflict and children's behavior problems: Shared and nonshared family risks. *Child Development,* 76 (1): 24-39. Academic Search Premier Database, EBSCOhost (30 AUG 2006).

Keck, G. C. Holding Therapy. Attachment and Bonding Center of Ohio. Cleveland, OH. http://abcofohio.net/holding.htm (accessed 11 NOV 2003).

Kemp, D., & Center, D. (2000). Troubled children grown-up: Antisocial Behavior in young adult criminals. *Education & Treatment of Children,* 23 (3): 223-238. Academic Search Premier Database, EBSCOhost (30 AUG 2006).

Kim-Cohen, J., Moffitt, T. E., Caspi, A., & Taylor, A. (2004). Genetic and environmental processes in young children's resilience and vulnerability to socioeconomic deprivation. *Child Development,* 75 (3): 651-668. Academic Search Premier Database, EBSCOhost (30 AUG 2006).

Kovacs, M., & Devlin, B. (1998). Internalizing disorders in childhood. *Journal of Child Psychology & Psychiatry & Allied Disciplines,* 39 (1), 47-63. Academic Search Premier Database, EBSCOhost (30 AUG 2006).

Lee, M., Vernon-Feagans, L., Vazquez, A., & Kolak, A. (2003). The influence of family environment and child temperament on work/family role strain for mothers and fathers. *Infant & Child Development,* 12 (5): 421-439. Academic Search Premier Database, EBSCOhost (30 AUG 2006).

Legrand, L. N., McGue, M., & Iacono, W. G. (1999). Searching for interactive effects in the etiology of early-onset substance use. *Behavior Genetics,* 29 (6): 433-444. Academic Search Premier Database, EBSCOhost (30 AUG 2006).

Lemery, K. S., & Goldsmith, H. H. (2001). Genetic and environmental influences on preschool sibling cooperation and conflict: Associations with difficult temperament and parenting style. *Marriage & Family Review,* 33 (1): 77-99. Academic Search Premier Database, EBSCOhost (30 AUG 2006).

Martin, G. C., & Wertheim, E. H. (2000). A longitudinal study of the role of childhood temperament in the later development of eating concerns. *International Journal of Eating Disorders,* 27 (2): 150-162. Academic Search Premier Database, EBSCOhost (30 AUG 2006).

McClowry, S., & Galehouse, P. (2002). Planning a temperament-based parenting program for inner-city families. *Journal of Child & Adolescent Psychiatric Nursing,* 15 (3): 97-105. Academic Search Premier Database, EBSCOhost (30 AUG 2006).

McClowry, S. G. (1998). The science and art of using temperament as the basis for intervention. *School Psychology Re-*

view, 27 (4): 551-563. Academic Search Premier Database, EBSCOhost (30 AUG 2006).

McGuire, S., Manke, B., Eftekhari, A., Dunn, J. (2000). Children's perceptions of sibling conflict during middle childhood: Issues and sibling (dis)similarity. *Social Development*, 9 (2): 173-190. Academic Search Premier Database, EBSCOhost (30 AUG 2006).

Meredith, D. "The Nine-to-Five Dilemma." *Psychology Today*, FEB 1986. http://www.findarticles.com/p/articles/mi_m1175/is_v20/ai_4116539 (accessed 01 SEP 2006).

Mylod, D. E., Whitman, T. L., & Borkowski, J. G. (1997). Predicting adolescent mothers' transition to adulthood. *Journal of Research on Adolescence*, 7 (4): 457-478. Academic Search Premier Database, EBSCOhost (30 AUG 2006).

Nair, H., & Murray, A. D. (2005). Predictors of attachment security in preschool children from intact and divorced families. *Journal of Genetic Psychology*, 166 (3): 245-263. Academic Search Premier Database, EBSCOhost (30 AUG 2006).

National Center for Education Statistics (NCES). (2004). Estimates of resident population, by age group: 1970 to 2003. In Digest of Education Statistics, 2004. http://www.nces.ed.gov/programs/digest/d04/tables/dt04_015.asp (accessed 01 SEP 2006).

National Center for Education Statistics (NCES). (2004). Percent of the population 3 to 34 years old enrolled in school, by age group: Selected years, 1940 to 2003. In Digest of Education Statistics, 2004. http://www.nces.ed.gov/programs/digest/d04/tables/dt04_007.asp (accessed 01 SEP 2006).

National Center for Education Statistics (NCES). (2004). Percent of the population 3 to 34 years old enrolled in school, by race/ethnicity, sex, and age: Selected years, 1980 to 2003. In *Digest of Education Statistics, 2004.* http://www.nces.ed.gov/programs/digest/d04/tables/dt04_006.asp (accessed 01 SEP 2006).

National Institute of Mental Health (NIMH). *Treatment of Children with Mental Disorders.* 2004. http://www.nimh.nih.gov/publicat/childqa.cfm (accessed 01 SEP 2006)

NICHD Early Child Care Research Network. (1997). The effects of infant child care on infant-mother attachment security: Results of the NICHD Study of Early Child Care. Abstract. *Child Development,* 68: 860-879. http://secc.rti.org/abstracts.cfm?abstract=9 (accessed 14 NOV 2003).

NICHD Early Child Care Research Network. (1998). Early child care and self-control, compliance and problem behavior at twenty-four and thirty-six months. Abstract. Child Development, 69: 1145-1170. http://secc.rti.org/abstracts.cfm?abstract=11 (accessed 01 SEP 2006).

NICHD Early Child Care Research Network. (2001). Child care and children's peer interaction at 24 and 36 months: The NICHD Study of Early Child Care. Abstract. *Child Development,* 72: 1478-1500. http://secc.rti.org/abstracts.cfm?abstract=24 (accessed 14 NOV 2003).

NICHD Early Child Care Research Network. (2002). The interaction of child care and family risk in relation to child development at 24 and 36 months. Abstract. *Applied Developmental Science,* 6: 144-156. http://secc.rti.org/abstracts.cfm?abstract=28 (accessed 14 NOV 2003).

NICHD Early Child Care Research Network. (2002). Early child care and children's development prior to school entry: Results from the NICHD Study of Early Child Care. Abstract. *Ameri-*

can Educational Research Journal, 39: 133-164. http://secc.rti. org/abstracts.cfm?abstract=30 (accessed 14 NOV 2003).

Niolon, R. *Child Temperament from Psychpage.* DEC 1999. http:// www.psychpage.com/family/library/temperm.html (accessed 01 SEP 2006).

Oberklaid, F., Sewell, J., Sanson, A., & Prior, M. (1991). Temperament and behavior of preterm infants: A six-year follow-up. *Pediatrics,* 87 (6): 854-861. Academic Search Premier Database, EBSCOhost (30 AUG 2006).

O'Connor, M. J. (2001). Prenatal alcohol exposure and infant negative affect as precursors of depressive features in children. *Infant Mental Health Journal,* 22 (3): 291-299. Academic Search Premier Database, EBSCOhost (30 AUG 2006).

Oesterreich, L. (1995). Ages & stages - Newborn to 1 year. In L. Oesterreich, B. Holt, & S. Karas (Eds.) *Iowa Family Child Care Handbook,* 192-196. Ames, IA: Iowa State University Extension. http://www.nncc.org/Child.Dev/ages.stages.new.one.html (accessed 26 OCT 2003).

Oliver, K. (2002). Understanding your child's temperament. *Family Life Month Packet 2002.* Family and Consumer Sciences, Ohio State University Extension, The Ohio State University. http:// ohioline.osu.edu/flm02/FS05.html (accessed 01 SEP 2006).

O'Neil, D. *Personality Development.* 20 JUN 2006. http://anthro. palomar.edu/social/soc_3.htm (accessed 01 Spetember 2006).

Ono, Y., Ando, J., Yoshimura, K., Momose, T., Hirano, M., & Kanba, S. (2002). Dimensions of temperament as vulnerability factors in depression. *Molecular Psychiatry,* 7 (9): 948-953. Academic Search Premier Database, EBSCOhost (30 AUG 2006).

Paterson, G., & Sanson, A. (1999). The association of behavioural adjustment to temperament, parenting and family characteristics among 5-year-old children. *Social Development*, 8 (3): 293-309. Academic Search Premier Database, EBSCOhost (30 AUG 2006).

Peck, S. D. (2003). Measuring sensitivity moment-by-moment: A microanalytic look at the transmission of attachment. *Attachment & Human Development*, 5 (1): 38-63. Academic Search Premier Database, EBSCOhost (30 AUG 2006).

Peeking at twins. *Economist*, 03 NOV 1990, p99-100. Academic Search Premier Database, EBSCOhost (30 AUG 2006).

Pierce, R. P. NIH Press Release - *The NICHD Study of Early Child Care*. Reported at Society for Research in Child Development Meeting, 04 APR 1997. http://www.nih.gov/pr/apr97/nichd-03.htm (accessed 20 NOV 2003).

Pierce, R. P. *The NICHD Study of Early Child Care*. Bethesda, Maryland: NICHD, 1998. http://www.childresearch.net/resource/data/survey/nichd/index.htm (accessed 12 NOV 2003).

Preventive Ounce, The. *About Temperament*. http://www.preventiveoz.org/aboutemp.html (accessed 01 SEP 2006).

Raffaelli, M., & Crockett, L. J. (2003). Sexual risk taking in adolescence: The role of self-regulation and attraction to risk. *Developmental Psychology*, 39 (6): 1036-1046. Academic Search Premier Database, EBSCOhost (30 AUG 2006).

Ransom-Wiley, J. *38% of Americans own video game consoles*. 02 AUG 2005. http://www.joystiq.com/2005/08/02/38-of-americans-own-video-game-consoles/ (accessed 01 SEP 2006).

Reed-Victor, E. (2004). Individual differences and early school adjustment: Teacher appraisals of young children with special needs. *Early Child Development & Care,* 174 (1): 59-79. Academic Search Premier Database, EBSCOhost (30 AUG 2006).

Rosack, J. (2003). Prescription data on youth raise important questions. *Psychiatric News,* 38 (3). http://pn.psychiatryonline.org/cgi/content/full/38/3/1 (accessed 01 SEP 2006).

Rubin, K. H., Nelson, L. J., Hastings, P., & Asendorpf, J. (1999). The transaction between parents' perceptions of their children's shyness and their parenting styles. *International Journal of Behavioral Development,* 23 (4): 937-957. Academic Search Premier Database, EBSCOhost (30 AUG 2006).

Sanson, A., Hemphill, S. A., & Smart, D. (2004). Connections between temperament and social development: A review. *Social Development,* 13 (1): 142-170. Academic Search Premier Database, EBSCOhost (30 AUG 2006).

Scher, A., Tirosh, E., & Lavie, P. (1998). The relationship between sleep and temperament revisited: Evidence for 12-month-olds: A research note. *Journal of Child Psychology & Psychiatry & Allied Disciplines,* 39 (5): 785-788. Academic Search Premier Database, EBSCOhost (30 AUG 2006).

Schmitz, S., & Saudino, K. J. (1996). Genetic and environmental influences on temperament in middle childhood: Analyses of teacher and tester ratings. *Child Development,* 67 (2): 409-422. Academic Search Premier Database, EBSCOhost (30 AUG 2006).

Schultz, D., & Shaw, D. S. (2003). Boys' maladaptive social information processing, family emotional climate, and pathways to early conduct problems. *Social Development,* 12 (3), 440-460. Academic Search Premier Database, EBSCOhost (30 AUG 2006).

Schwebel, D. C., & Plumert, J. M. (1999). Longitudinal and concurrent relations among temperament, ability estimation, and injury proneness. *Child Development*, 70 (3): 700-712. Academic Search Premier Database, EBSCOhost (30 AUG 2006).

Shah, C. S. "Personality Development." *International Forum for Neo Vedantins*. http://www.geocities.com/neovedanta/acxxii.html (accessed 01 SEP 2006).

Sheeber, L. B., & Johnson, J. H. (1994). Evaluation of a temperament-focused, parent-training program. *Journal of Clinical Child Psychology*, 23 (3): 249-259. Academic Search Premier Database, EBSCOhost (30 AUG 2006).

Shiner, R., & Caspi, A. (2003). Personality differences in childhood and adolescence: Measurement, development, and consequences. *Journal of Child Psychology & Psychiatry & Allied Disciplines*, 44 (1): 2-32. Academic Search Premier Database, EBSCOhost (30 AUG 2006).

Spere, K. A., Schmidt, L. A., Theall-Honey, L. A., & Martin-Chang, S. (2004). Expressive and receptive language skills of temperamentally shy preschoolers. *Infant & Child Development*, 13 (2): 123-133. Academic Search Premier Database, EBSCOhost (30 AUG 2006).

Sroufe, L. A. (in press). From infant attachment to promotion of adolescent autonomy: Prospective, longitudinal data on the role of parents in development. In Brokowski, J., Ramey, S., & Bristol-Power, M. (Eds.) *Parenting and Your Child's World*. Mahwah, NJ: Lawrence Erlbaum & Associates.

Sroufe, L. A., Carlson, E. A., Levy, A. K., & Egeland, B. (1999). Implications of attachment theory for developmental psychopathology. *Development and Psychopathology*, 11: 1-13. Cambridge, Cambridge University Press.

Steele, H., & Steele, M. (1996). Associations among attachment classifications of mothers, fathers, and their infants. *Child Development*, 67 (2): 541-555. Academic Search Premier Database, EBSCOhost (30 AUG 2006).

Thinkquest Team C004361. *That's Me: A Guide to Personality.* http://library.thinkquest.org/C004361/index1.html (accessed 01 SEP 2006).

Vassallo, S., Smart, D., Sanson, A., & Dussuyer, I. At risk but not antisocial. Family Matters, Winter 2004, no. 68: 13-20. Academic Search Premier Database, EBSCOhost (30 AUG 2006).

Wade, T. D., & Kendler, S. (2001). Parent, child, and social correlates of parental discipline style: A retrospective, multi-informant investigation with female twins. *Social Psychiatry & Psychiatric Epidemiology*, 36 (4): 177-185. Academic Search Premier Database, EBSCOhost (30 AUG 2006).

Walker, S., Berthelsen, D., & Irving, K. (2001). Temperament and peer acceptance in early childhood: Sex and social status differences. *Child Study Journal*, 31 (3): 177-192. Academic Search Premier Database, EBSCOhost (30 AUG 2006).

Warner, L. A., Pottick, K. J., & Mukherjee, A. (2004). Brief reports: Use of psychotropic medications by youths with psychiatric diagnoses in the U.S. Mental Health System. *Psychiatric Services*, 55:309-311. http://psychservices.psychiatryonline.org/cgi/content/full/55/3/309 (accessed 01 SEP 2006).

Warren, S. A., Huston, L., Egeland, B., & Sroufe, L. A. (1997). Child and adolescent anxiety disorders and early attachment. *Journal of American Academy of Child Adolescent Psychiatry*, 36 (5): 637-644.

Weinfield, N. S., Sroufe, L. A., Egeland, B., & Carlson, E. (1999). The nature of individual differences in infant-caregiver attachment. In J. Cassidy & P. Shaver (Eds.), Handbook of Attachment: *Theory, Research, and Clinical Applications*, 73-95. New York: Guilford Press.

Weisman, J. "Tax Burden Shifts to the Middle: New Report Could Roil Presidential Campaign. *The Washington Post*, 13 AUG 2004. http://msnbc.msn.com/id/5689001/ (accessed 01 SEP 2006).

Wells, J. C. K., Stanley, M., Laidlaw, A. S., Day, J. M. E., Stafford, M., & Davies, P. S. W. (1997). Investigation of the relationship between infant temperament and later body composition. *International Journal of Obesity*, 21 (5): 400-406. Academic Search Premier Database, EBSCOhost (30 AUG 2006).

West, A. E., & Newman, D. L. (2003). Worried and blue: Mild parental anxiety and depression in relation to the development of young children's temperament and behavior problems. *Parenting: Science & Practice*, 3 (2): 133-154. Academic Search Premier Database, EBSCOhost (30 AUG 2006).

Wills, T. A., & Dishion, T. J. (2004). Temperament and adolescent substance use: A transactional analysis of emerging self-control. *Journal of Clinical Child & Adolescent Psychology*, 33 (1): 69-81. Academic Search Premier Database, EBSCOhost (30 AUG 2006).

Wong, I. C. K., Murray, M. L., Camilleri-Novak, D., & Stephens, P. (2004). Increased Prescribing trends of paediatric psychotropic medications. *Archives of Disease in Childhood* 89:1131-1132. http://adc.bmjjournals.com/cgi/content/full/89/12/1131 (accessed 01 SEP 2006).

Yoshikawa. H. (1995). Long-Term Effects of Early Childhood Programs on Social Outcomes and Delinquency. In R. E. Behrman (Ed.) *The Future of Children: Long-Term Outcomes of Early Childhood Programs*. http://www.futureofchildren.org/information2826/information_show.htm?doc_id=77669 (accessed 01 SEP 2006).

⌾ ABOUT THE AUTHORS ⌾

Dr. Erik Fisher is a husband, father, psychologist, author, and media consultant working in the Atlanta area. His unique approach to working with children and families has resulted in positive outcomes for even the most challenging cases. His work has been featured on CNN, and he has been interviewed for NBC, CBS, FOX, and regional and syndicated radio stations, newspapers and magazines throughout the United States and Canada. His mission is to help individuals and families evolve in the way that they see the world as a place for growth and opportunity when they find their personal power within. His first book with Steven Sharp, *The Art of Managing Everyday Conflict*, explores the relationship between power and emotion in conflict.

Steven Wayne Sharp has been a freelance, technical, and commercial writer for over twenty years. Steven is highly interested in topics pertaining to quality of life, and he feels quite motivated to provide readers with life-enhancing, easy-to-understand information in the areas of health, psychology, and environmental issues. A native and lifelong resident of Huntsville, Alabama, Steven and his wife, Samantha, enjoy traveling, spending time together, and tending to their house full of cats and dogs.

Diane Fivaz Wichman is a wife, mother and co-founder of CHOICES for Growth, Inc, a company dedicated to contracting with local departments of family and children's services as in-home parent educators and child advocates. They work hand-in-hand with families to establish respectful and empowering family situations. Her goal in her work is to enable parents to not only teach their children but also to learn from them as she has done with her own children and grandchild. Diane encourages parents to remember to have fun and live a life full of love and laughter.